T0330181

A Legal Theory of Economic Power

NEW HORIZONS IN COMPETITION LAW AND ECONOMICS

Series Editors: Steven D. Anderman, *Department of Law, University of Essex, UK* and Rudolph J.R. Peritz, *New York Law School, USA*

This series has been created to provide research based analysis and discussion of the appropriate role for economic thinking in the formulation of competition law and policy. The books in the series will move beyond studies of the traditional role of economics – that of helping to define markets and assess market power – to explore the extent to which economic thinking can play a role in the formulation of legal norms, such as abuse of a dominant position, restriction of competition and substantial impediments to or lessening of competition. This in many ways is the *new horizon* of competition law policy.

US antitrust policy, influenced in its formative years by the Chicago School, has already experienced an expansion of the role of economic thinking in its competition rules. Now the EU is committed to a greater role for economic thinking in its Block Exemption Regulations and Modernisation package as well as possibly in its reform of Article 102. Yet these developments still raise the issue of the *extent* to which economics should be adopted in defining the public interest in competition policy and what role economists should play in legal argument. The series will provide a forum for research perspectives that are critical of an unduly-expanded role for economics as well as those that support its greater use.

Titles in the series include:

A Legal Theory of Economic Power

Implications for Social and Economic Development

Calixto Salomão Filho

Professor of Law, University of São Paulo Law School, Brazil and the Institut d'études Politiques (Sciences Po), Paris, France

NEW HORIZONS IN COMPETITION LAW AND ECONOMICS

Edward Elgar
Cheltenham, UK • Northampton, MA, USA

© Calixto Salomão Filho 2011

All rights reserved. No part of this publication may be reproduced, stored in a retrieval system or transmitted in any form or by any means, electronic, mechanical or photocopying, recording, or otherwise without the prior permission of the publisher.

Published by
Edward Elgar Publishing Limited
The Lypiatts
15 Lansdown Road
Cheltenham
Glos GL50 2JA
UK

Edward Elgar Publishing, Inc.
William Pratt House
9 Dewey Court
Northampton
Massachusetts 01060
USA

A catalogue record for this book
is available from the British Library

Library of Congress Control Number: 2011931007

MIX
Paper from
responsible sources
FSC® C018575

ISBN 978 0 85793 186 3

Printed and bound by MPG Books Group, UK

Contents

Preface

A book about forgotten realities. This is perhaps the best description of this work.

Its title, *A Legal Theory of Economic Power*, is very revealing in this sense. The old times of antitrust law, centered on market rationality, are gone. Economic power is pervasive in society and cannot be treated as a mere economic phenomenon, based on market rationality paradigms. There are many and very important 'forgotten realities' that stayed out of this treatment.

Therefore, a theory of economic power must be treated as such, as a general theory. The reference to antitrust law must nowadays be historical. This does not mean that, when treating power created in the market, the theoretical tools should not include classical 'antitrust' discussions, though in a revised and critical version. That is what this book tries to do.

Power with legal roots and social roots is also treated, however, with different theoretical paradigms. Through them, some of the 'forgotten realities' are included and treated. Through them, the reader can also understand another fundamental aspect of the concentration of economic power: its influence on social and economic development patterns.

An intended general theory of economic power. That is what the title says and that is what the book intends to be. Too pretentious? That is an answer to be given by a critical reader after reading the book, as long as he/she remains impartial, i.e., allows himself/herself to read the book free from the 'shadows of the past', the past of the old 'market rationality-based' antitrust law.

Calixto Salomão Filho
June 2011

Acknowledgements

The author wishes to thank Mr Carlos Portugal Gouvea, Mr Jose Antônio de Moura Ziebarth and Mrs Daniella Omoto, who in different but important degrees all collaborated in the final revision of the book. Many thanks are also due to Mr Rubens Heredia, whose collaboration was fundamental in the language revision of the manuscript.

1. A neo-structural legal perspective to economic power analysis

1. INTRODUCTION: THE INSUFFICIENCY OF THE ANTITRUST CONCEPTS AND INSTRUMENTS

For decades, antitrust theory has been moribund and read like an obituary. New ideas have been few and far between, and what little has come on the scene takes pride in having mere practical application, all foundational theories and justifications for antitrust having long since had their day.

In fact, the strong tendency toward simplification and doctrinal negativism has a double origin. In the first instance, it is based upon a superficial analysis of the economic landscape that leads to the belief that the effects of private economic power in society are limited to the manufacturer–consumer relationship.

Economic history, both in developing and developed countries, shows that the effects of monopoly power are much more pervasive than just the consumer–producer relationship, affecting development patterns and even distribution patterns in society.

In the second instance, there is a powerful and again simplistic faith in the ability of economic theory to predict results and, consequently, in our ability to identify the most efficient result in the consumer–manufacturer relationship.

This efficient result is, in its turn, the product of a rationality-based analysis of the market functioning. Therefore law and antitrust law in particular have been oriented to correct imperfections in the market functioning. Market power structures, in this (neoclassical)[1] view, are nothing more than the product of an imperfect functioning of the market.

Adding these two simplifications together leads to a belief in the possibility of identifying one unique theoretical objective in antitrust law, which consists of obtaining a certain economic result based on principles of rational functioning of the market. This analysis is, as will be demonstrated, too simplistic for various reasons.

---

[1]   The word neoclassical has many different meanings in economic history and economic science. When used in the book, it is equivalent to the Chicago School microeconomic theory as applied to Antitrust Law.

First of all, because economic power cannot be considered a mere market phenomenon. As will be demonstrated, not all structures with economic power are created in the market, even if they have effects on it. Many of them are created by the law or by social relations. Their analysis in terms of market rationality is therefore impossible.

But this is not all. The exclusive (or predominant) market rationality paradigm can be criticized not only based on the source of economic power but also on its effects. The effects of economic power structures are not limited to the market. They are much broader, involving, as will be seen in the next sections, negative wealth distribution effects and negative social effects. Consequently, all structures, even those created in the market, are neither well perceived nor analyzed by market rationality paradigms.

If all this is true and economic power has not only market but also legal and sometimes social roots and on the other hand produces effects far beyond the market, economic rationality cannot be predominantly a market rationality but instead a rationality of power and power exercise. Evidently such a broad reality cannot be well perceived by traditional antitrust law.

2. ECONOMIC POWER AND ITS MULTIPLE EFFECTS ON THE SOCIAL AND ECONOMIC SPHERES: MONOPOLIES AND UNDERDEVELOPMENT

If this is true, then an analysis of the relationships and effects generated by economic power should originate not in mathematical assumptions about economic results but in the study of the economic history of countries in which this power is more structured and deeply rooted in social and economic structures. The reason is simple. It is first of all in these regions that these broader effects of economic power are easier to identify. As in all theoretical analyses, using examples with more pronounced characteristics helps to identify tendencies and demonstrate propositions. This does not mean that such results are invalid for countries in which economic power is less disseminated and less profound. It only means that the results obtained will likely be less intense.

The countries in which economic power is historically most concentrated and consolidated are former European colonies in South America and Asia. In those countries, economic power is a phenomenon that is historically part of society and, therefore, much easier to identify. This statement is not new, but its consequences for the economics and internal legal systems in place in developing countries were disregarded in the past and are still belittled.

There is no doubt that in the former colonies, as contrasted with today's developed countries, economic power was made up of economic relationships that were relevant factors even for the formation of the national states. The histories of most, if not all, of these countries are tightly intertwined with European colonization. This is an important element to be noted. The status of 'colony', far beyond external dependence, created internal power structures that marked and still influences many aspects of development (or underdevelopment) in these societies.

This is why it appears possible to revisit their development processes, starting from the structures of economic power and the structure of income distribution that follow them. The bonds of colonial dependence that motivated underdevelopment, even if the root cause, are not its ultimate cause. The explanation is simple, but must be well understood. The internal economic structures are what permit or inhibit, in the necessary moments, the breakthrough from dependency. As we all know, this rarely took place in the history of developing countries. Apart from rare and exceptional situations, in these countries the bonds of dependency are rarely counter-attacked and even less frequently broken. This is owing to internal power structures and income distribution that benefits, even if indirectly, from these bonds.

It is therefore on these structures that the analysis should be focused. In addition, the relationship between economic power and income distribution must be addressed in the light of historic evidence. This relationship is intense.

Traditional analysis tends to identify only certain superficial relationships between a monopolistic company and the consumer, to wit, essentially identifying it as the value of the monopolist's extraordinary profit, which is extracted from consumers through the imposition of monopolistic prices. As has been shown in empirical studies, this value may not be dismissed and accounts for a relevant portion of income concentration.

The fact is that this relationship between economic concentration and income distribution is much deeper and more extensive. This is especially true of structurally concentrated economies such as the former colonies. On the one hand, the relationship is much more extensive in the product market, affecting industrial organization itself. As well as the imbalance in relations between consumers and manufacturers, with the consequent inefficiencies in allocation and distribution, it leads to an absolute disproportion amongst economic sectors. The dynamic sector of the economy since colonial times is generally concentrated in primary products or low technology manufactured goods for export and in the durable consumer goods to be consumed internally by the high income segment of the population. These two sectors, monopolized or oligopolized, concentrate inversions and productivity gains. They therefore drain resources from the economic system either directly, through monopolistic profits obtained from suppliers, or indirectly, via the siphoning of investments that would otherwise be invested in other sectors (hereafter called peripheral economic sectors).

The effects are also deeper. As well as the consumer market and peripheral economic sectors, there is also strong interference in the labor market. Thus, in many, if not most, of these countries, income concentration ends up becoming a fundamental condition for economic growth. This is precisely because, based on the production of primary products and simple raw materials, be it for the domestic or foreign market, productivity gains in these economies cannot be obtained only through technological improvements (which are at times insufficient in such low technology sectors). Gains in productivity that are fundamental for economic growth should be based on an increase in workforce productivity, which can be achieved through reducing real salaries or through an effective reduction in the workforce (source of the first so-called economies of scale achieved with economic concentration). This movement is only made possible, however, via a high level of monopolization in the economy, which also creates great monopolistic conglomerates in the labor market. As previously mentioned, this state of affairs is explained not only by the fact that competitors in the relevant sector are scarce and hardly relevant, but also because, in such economies, the colonial monopolistic standard ensures that there is a lack of competition among economic sectors. Sectors with real economic dynamism, capable of accumulating capital and absorbing the labor force, are few and concentrated.

Only through such an absolutely concentrated growth standard is it possible to have capital accumulation and therefore productive investment that leads to growth. That said, such a growth standard requires, for its own existence, inverse income redistribution, with impoverishment (relative for employed workers and absolute for those who lose their jobs) of lower income groups and relative impoverishment of peripheral economic sectors.

Placing the spotlight on structures also implies that predominant sociological-individualistic explanations for underdevelopment are not accepted. These justifications are frequently incorporated into neo-institutional reasoning to explain underdevelopment and suggested solutions. Hence, according to these theories, with the individual motivation of colonizers of Latin America and Asia, colonial exploitation, different from that of immigrants to North America and Oceania, was reflected in the entire institutional structure of society. This kind of statement errs in being an under and overstatement at the same time. On the one hand, it exaggerates the differences in the individual spirit of colonizers. Interesting studies demonstrate that the colonial experience is richer than this distinction appears to suggest. Within the same colonies, there coexisted regions of mere exploitation with regions where colonizers considered settling and remaining. Both situations happened in colonized countries in Latin America, Asia and even Africa (South Africa, for example). In these countries, be they Argentina, Australia or India, the capitalist colonial spirit was similar.[2]

On the other hand, what these sociologic-individualistic theories fail to consider is precisely the study of economic structures created by exploitive colonization. These structures, and not individual motivation, are the main factors that lead to differences between economies based on exploitive monopoly and societies in which these structures do not prevail. They end up determining economic cycles and influencing the whole of a society's socio-economic system, prevailing over the similarities or differences that regions that experienced the definitive settling of populations, as opposed to those where populations were merely exploited, could have from the point of view of the motivations of explorers. Thus, regions of similar colonial spirit like Buenos Aires in Argentina and Sydney in Australia result in countries and regions of social and economic development levels that are absolutely different.

Structural concentration of economic power therefore produces effects on the entire system, concentrating income between industrial sectors and between social strata. This concentration of power and income also causes economic growth patterns to change substantially. The increase is strongly based, among other factors, in productivity gains resulting from the inverse redistribution of income from workers (both employed and surplus) to the great conglomerates (and their small number of shareholders).[3]

It is important to observe as of now that this hypothesis, once explained, can help solve two apparent paradoxes of contemporary economic history, which are, in fact, directly correlated.

The first consists of reproducing underdevelopment (with absolute or at least relative deterioration of the main social and income distribution indicators) even in countries that have had important economic growth rates. The hypothesis presented here can help explain this apparent paradox. If the hypothesis for concentration of economic power as a generator of inverse income distribution in the consumer, work and inter-industrial markets in the developing countries is admitted, it is possible to understand the reason for economic growth with deterioration of social indicators. This happens precisely because of inverse income distribution, in other words, owing to the fact that gains in productivity result from a loss in real salaries or more

---

[2]   See D. Denoon, *Settler Capitalism: The Dynamics of Dependent Development in the Southern Hemisphere*, 1983, p. 18, *et seq.*

[3]   For an econometric analysis of the relationship between market concentration (monopolies) and poverty in Brazil during colonial times see C. Salomão Filho, B. Ferrão and I. C. Ribeiro, *Concentração, estruturas e desigualdade – as origens coloniais da pobreza e da má distribuição de renda*, 2009.

recently from an increase in the exclusionary process created by unemployment.[4] The final result is the existence of constantly underdeveloped economies, in which the more economic power structures grow, the more poverty and social inequalities are produced.

The second apparent paradox is in the convergence of relative prices between developed and developing countries identified in empirical studies.[5] According to this research, it is possible to show a positive correlation between international convergence in prices of commodities and convergence of relative prices of production factors (principally wages and land prices, the wage–rental ratio). This convergence is followed, and thus the apparent paradox, by an increase in differences in living standards in the developed and developing worlds. Obviously it is not sufficient, as is done in these studies (see note 4), to identify technology gains to explain these results. The approximation of prices of commodities followed by an approximation in wage–rental ratios should also lead to smaller and not greater differences in living standards, even with various technologies. After all, commodity and

---

[4] Whereas in colonial and early industrial time productivity gains were obtained from real salary reduction, in modern times productivity or 'efficiency' gains are obtained from cost reduction in concentration processes, specially through lay-offs. The problem is that the 'economic exclusion' created by this lay-off process is much more serious than just unemployment. Unemployment, when coupled with an environment where other people are included in the economic process, completely marginalizes the individual. Since he is incapable of paying any kind of prices or any kinds of goods (from food to real estate) that the non-marginalized pay, he is constrained normally into a parallel economic environment, of the excluded. Poverty, violence, gang formation and drug addiction create a vicious circle parallel to the economic process out of which it is difficult to take the individual. Although many developing countries like Brazil, experimented in latter times relevant growth rates coupled with improvement in many social indicators, this is due mainly to governmental anti poverty and inclusionary programs (as Bolsa Família in Brazil). Even in those countries, however, the above stated influence of economic structures in exclusion is an important reason why probably urban poverty has proved so much more difficult to eradicate than rural poverty through anti-poverty programs (*Bolsa Família* in Brazil, for example). For instance, see 'Brazil's Bolsa Família' in *the Economist*, 31 July 2010, p. 19. For recent data and analysis, see 'Gastos com a Política Social: alavanca para o crescimento com distribuição de renda', Comunicado no. 75, Comunicados do IPEA, February 2011, available in Portuguese at *www.ipea.gov.br*. The Institute for Applied Economic Research (IPEA) is a federal public foundation linked to the Strategic Affairs Secretariat of the Presidency of the Republic. It provides technical and institutional support to government for the formulation and reformulation of public policies and development programs in Brazil.

[5] See J. Williamson, 'Land, Labor and Globalization in the Third World, 1870–1940', in *The Journal of Economic History*, 62(1), March 2002, p. 55 (68); see also previous work by the same author, 'Globalization, Convergence and History', in *The Journal of Economic History*, 56(2), June 1996, p. 277, *et seq.*

land prices account for much of what is required to improve social and economic indicators of a region. Even with other important factors influencing these indicators, the full discrepancy can show only that there is a particular segment of the population taking advantage of the best wage–rental ratios.

In relation to different and successive economic phases typical of developing countries in which the primary products and raw materials industries are substituted for a rural economy, these results are in reality indicators of economic concentration and inverse redistribution of income and not improvements in quality of living. In these economies, in this particular historic moment of industrialization, the reduction of land prices is more than proportional to the reduction in real wages that, however, still exists. This is because the demand for land drops more in periods of industrialization than the demand for workers and also because, during this period, union organization begins in most developing countries, avoiding an even greater deterioration of real wages levels. What is actually happening is a concentration of wealth in the top segments of society, which can accumulate even more capital through the purchase of land. In addition to the association of better wage–rental ratios and worse social indicators, this also explains another peculiar characteristic of developing economies. It is a fact that 50 years after the start of the industrialization process in the majority of the developing countries, we are witnessing a re-concentration of agricultural property in the hands of large landowners and the marginalization of farm workers in such countries. The accumulation of capital, having happened in an unbalanced manner, is such that only the top layers of society can take advantage of reductions in land prices. For the working classes, employed or even unemployed, there is no access to agrarian property. This explains the prevalence and endemic character of the agrarian conflicts in these economies, in spite of the relative abundance of land.

What we are saying, in fact, is that the opposing positions of the classic theory of comparative advantages and the structural theory (in the initial version by Prebish) should be revised. Even with an approximation between the values of the production factors (in a certain period of time),[6] this approximation is not relevant for the economic development of these regions. This is because the central problem of colonialism is not in the structures of international commerce, but in the domestic structures of economic power (related or not to foreign economic and trade issues) whose establishment and implementation were very much favored by colonialism.

---

[6]   Approximation not completely shown. There is relevant data in the opposite sense – see on this issue J. Love, 'Economic Ideas and Ideologies in Latin America since 1930', in *Cambridge History of Latin America*, vol. VI, 1, 1994, p. 393 (p. 423, especially note 91).

Furthermore, as mentioned above, the history of colonialism and the monopolistic structures deriving from it impacts the societies of the Southern Hemisphere profoundly, to the point of constituting social and economic structures that will affect the entire future economic development of such societies. It is for this reason that this book begins with a recapitulation of the economic history of developing countries.

Mention of social and economic structures is intentional. It is not correct to start from a unilateral predefinition of human behavior, to wit, that people are moved exclusively by economic rationality as defined by G. Becker,[7] or by predominantly social motives, as was so passionately and effectively defended by K. Polanyi.[8] The definition between these two tendencies when studying development (underdevelopment) is therefore unnecessary.

In fact, colonization deeply affects not only economic structures but also social structures. Attachment to the cultures and living standards of developed countries and a certain contempt nurtured by the upper and even middle classes for their own civilization is a common characteristic in most developing countries. More importantly, the monopoly of economic knowledge introduced by the colonial monopolies roots itself in social structures, creating tension amongst the classes and worsening cooperation. These beliefs and structures create great impediments to development.

In the economic field, the effect of such structures is even greater. It affects, as seen above, the accumulation of capital and the distribution of its gains. Analysis of the means of addressing such serious economic structural problems should be more detailed. It demands analysis of the structures and economic behavior present in the economic order of developing countries resulting from monopolistic structures, as well as a legal proposition capable of offering a way out of the vicious circle of underdevelopment caused by them.

A last and very important point must be made. The central importance to underdevelopment of the monopolistic structure created in the colonies does not imply that it is always the opposite of what we are looking for, that is, the generalized existence of decentralized economic structures in the economy. It is a common and perhaps intentional mistake among neoclassic theoreticians: opposing the great monopolies with an economic structure of (inefficient, according to them) small and medium-sized enterprises.

Not even from the logical point of view are there only two alternatives. In fact, the real alternative to concentrated economic power is a balanced economic structure (in terms of information and bargaining capacity) between

---

[7]   See G. Becker, *The Economic Approach to Human Behavior*, 1976.
[8]   K. Polanyi, *The Great Transformation*, 1957, esp. p. 46.

supply and demand. To address the correct organization of supply and demand and not only the best configuration of the industrial structure is the real objective of an economic system and the laws that aim to protect it.

This also does not imply that fighting monopolies is enough, on its own, for economic development. In particular, it should be emphasized that economic structures affect structural characteristics in society and not quantitative data. Therefore, singling out monopolies is not a very effective way to explain why, amongst the developing countries, there are differing degrees of relative growth. For this, there are other decisive factors such as population growth, the importance and relative value that each country's main product has in the international market,[9] and also varied institutional configurations.

3.   THE ECONOMIC HISTORY OF MONOPOLISTIC COLONIAL SYSTEMS AND ITS EFFECT ON THE DEVELOPMENT PROCESS

The relationship between monopolies and underdevelopment is, however, not best seen through theoretical arguments. Its best demonstration lies in history.[10]

To achieve the objective of stressing the effect of monopolistic colonialism on underdevelopment, some examples of the operation of monopolistic structures in Latin America, Africa and Asia must be analyzed during three different historical periods: (a) the colonial period; (b) the industrialization period; and (c) the most recent economic internationalization period.

Colonial Monopolistic Systems

The colonial period is a long and particularly effervescent one in the history of capitalism. From the economic standpoint, it lasts four centuries, from the beginning of the sixteenth to the end of the nineteenth century. Throughout these many centuries, a constant economic pattern was maintained as a result of the connection with the metropolises: the monoculture, or the agriculture of

---

[9]   On this subject, see the interesting description of the many levels of growth obtained by Latin American countries in the nineteenth century owing to *commodity lottery* – V. B. Thomas, *The Economic History of Latin America since Independence*, 1994, esp. p. 43, *et seq.*

[10]   Since it is not the primary objective of this study the historical description is in fact shortened. For a deeper description and analysis of the historical relationship between monopolies and underdevelopment see C. Salomão Filho, *Histoire critique des monopoles – une perpective juridique et economique*, 2010.

a single product over a very large area, usually covering whole countries, and the exploitation of a single natural resource, in both cases focused on exports. In conjunction with the monopolistic system, this economic structure provided the extraction of the highest possible economic value of the colony, because the focus on one single product reduced costs of export goods, while preventing the colonies from creating a domestic market, which would also guarantee high profits on imports from the metropolis.

This leads not only to say that such economic structures impacted the contemporary social organization of underdeveloped countries. It leads also to understand how the monopolistic colonial system managed to have such a diffuse and long-lasting influence over the economic and social systems of the colonies. This is best seen through the description and comparison of the two different modes of colonization implemented in what are now called underdeveloped countries: the public and the private monopolistic colonial systems.

The public monopoly regime may be described generally as the mode of colonization used by Portugal and Spain during the colonization of Latin America. It may be described as an absolute monopoly controlled by the metropolis of imported and exported products by the colony. The literature often disregards the effect of such tight control of the metropolises over the economic activities of the colonies when studying the contemporary levels of economic development of the countries that were subject to such colonial mechanisms. Some colonies were actually formally prohibited from having industrial activities.

For the purposes of their metropolises, they had to produce only agricultural goods, and import all industrialized products from Europe, always through the channels provided by the metropolis. Such structures actually produced a triple draining effect over the economy that prevented any kind of endogenous development. The purchase of basic consumer goods was subject to monopoly by the metropolis, therefore a monopolistic surplus was charged there; the labor market was subject to the same monopoly structure and dependent entirely on the product of the cycle of the moment, that is, workforce and labor was completely drained by the existing structures.

Finally, and that is the third draining, there were no dynamic sectors in the economy other than the monopolized sectors. Therefore sectors were economically drained into the monopolized ones (that varied according to the varying interests of the metropolis in exporting products such as sugar, gold, coffee, etc.) and the economy gained no autonomy or self determination.

The private monopoly regime implemented in Asia was somewhat different from the public monopoly in Latin America. It was a colonization system driven mainly by commercial interests, not really interested in controlling the whole economy of the regions (whose population was, by the way, significantly larger and much better organized from the economic point of view). As a result, colonization was limited to the products that their colonizers were interested in buying and selling.

After the seventeenth century, the newly-established system of royal privileges provided that only companies holding privileges granted by the metropolis, such as the East India Company, were allowed to trade certain specific goods. However, this was only a relative monopoly, because other companies could still trade products not controlled by the East India Company. There was also tolerance regarding local agricultural production. The interregional commerce of products that were not considered as priorities by the British were tolerated, and even stimulated, as means of generating income to local communities.

Considering such differences, it is easy to understand why there was less hurry in the decolonization of Asia than of Latin America. The industrial powers controlling Asian economies used to stimulate a local consumer market, based on endogenous economic growth. In contrast, in Latin America the colonial system was structured to protect products and markets for the metropolises, mostly Portugal and Spain, which, since the mid seventeenth century were not part of the dynamic center of the capitalist system. Hence the pressure coming from the great industrial powers of the nineteenth and early twentieth centuries for decolonization of Latin American countries, in order to allow the creation of new consumer markets, open to the big industrial powers and independent from the metropolises.

The comparison between Latin America and Asia in the colonial period reveals very different approaches to the export economy. In Latin America, the export economy is strictly monopolized. The absolute export monopoly is actually the main element of the colonization process. Under its shadows, nothing blossoms; neither the consumer market, nor any complementary economic sector, which remain continuously centered on subsistence activities and dependent on the great exporting entrepreneurship. Also the workforce (slaves) is not paid a salary and therefore there is no creation of rent inside the colonies. The slave or semi-slave work used in Latin America during colonial times guaranteed that no endogenous demand power could be created internally in the colonies.

In Asia, the landscape was significantly different. Colonization was driven by large commercial enterprises, in which concern with the exploitation of local resources was followed by interest in developing a local consumer market. As a result, small agricultural enterprise was stimulated and interregional commerce was tolerated. Autonomous economic dynamism was tolerated from the beginning.

Such economic characteristics, inherited from the colonial period, help to partially explain why certain Asian economies performed better in terms of economic growth based on exports than Latin American countries toward the end of the twentieth and beginning of the twenty-first centuries.

In contrast, this loose colonization system that prevailed in Asia also led to much higher rates of rural poverty if compared to Latin America. The devastating famines of the twentieth century in Asia, so well described and analyzed by Sen as a consequence of the absence of entitlements,[11] are actually a byproduct of this pattern of colonization that focused only on valuable export products and 'forgot' completely a part of the population that was not devoted to their production.

In Latin America, on the other hand, poverty closely followed the main economic activities. While the production was mainly agricultural, poverty remained mainly a rural phenomenon. When the dynamics shifted to the industrial sector in the second half of the twentieth century, poverty changed rapidly to be an urban phenomenon.[12] This close link between social and economic structure is certainly deeply influenced by the economic structures created during colonial times that, as observed earlier, created a great dependence of the whole economy and of the workforce on its activities.

The Industrialization Period

The industrialization of most of the former colonies is related to the process of decolonization. In Latin America this process happened more clearly, with most countries becoming independent toward the end of the nineteenth century, and industrialization following some decades thereafter. In Asia, the process of industrialization happened in different periods, as countries maintained varying degrees of political dependence from the major economic powers throughout the nineteenth and twentieth centuries. However, the bulk of the decolonization process followed the end of World War II.

Despite such significant differences, it is possible to identify certain common elements. For most countries, the decolonization process was carefully tailored in order to avoid any rupture in the balance of economic forces that supported the old colonial order. For most countries it was an independence process in the political sphere, but not a process of economic transformation. Despite some conflicts among the economic elite, the most powerful economic group would be one related to the most relevant export products, as it was in the colonial period.

---

[11]   See A. Sen, *Poverty and Famines: An Essay on Entitlement and Deprivation*, 1982.

[12]   See C. Salomão Filho, B. Ferrão and I. C. Ribeiro, *Concentração, estruturas e desigualdade – as origens coloniais da pobreza e da má distribuição de renda*, cit., where the relationship between economic structures and poverty in Brazil during the colonial times is econometrically analyzed.

If, beforehand, this economic elite maintained its power because of its close connection with the metropolis, after independence it is the connection with the government that maintains the concentration of economic power. This symbiotic relationship between private monopolies and political power is a natural consequence of the relationships that created such nation states from former colonies. In the independent states, the bureaucratic apparatus is developed to serve an already established monopolistic structure, which ranges from local private agents (major colonial companies or landlords holding concessions to exploit natural resources) to the trade monopoly by the metropolis (or, in the Asian case, the colonial companies with trade privileges granted by the metropolis). Political leaders of the colonies had to ask for support from its internally powerful economic groups, and, in exchange for their support, they were assured the maintenance of their privileges.

As a result, the process of independence is also the process by which the economically powerful groups also gained independence, and learned to shape the economic and political structure to their benefit, no longer connected to the metropolis and no longer dependent on it for decision making. This is why it is possible to speak about a linkage between decolonization and industrialization. Although not simultaneous and not directly connected, it is only after independence that internal dominating economic structures can decide exclusively based on their best interest and choose, when necessary, to invest their capital and energies in the industrialization process.

In Latin America, the export monopolies simply changed from agricultural to industrialized products, maintaining other economic sectors and even the government under their total control. As such, export sectors were dependent on commodities prices; there were no virtuous circles of income and investment generation. Even when it happened, its isolated effects on the export sectors did not create relevant income in other sectors owing to the intersectoral draining effect of the existing monopolies explained in the previous section. As a consequence, there was very little stimulus to the formation of a consumer market as a result of industrialization.

In Asia, the decolonization process generally took longer to occur. Yet the greater economic freedom of economic sectors not directly connected to the export monopolies and the comparatively lesser importance of monopolies to the internal economic process created a better structure for economic development. Also, the great agricultural companies that were established in the region during the nineteenth century were not regarded as connected to the national interests that motivated the independence process. As a result, after independence, Asian governments were freer than Latin American ones from control by the economic elite and had more leeway to influence industrial organization and land distribution. Governments took time to exercise such freedom, as it is expected, considering the weight of colonial heritage, particularly because of mechanisms implemented by the colonial powers to gain control over these countries, such as reinforcing social stratifications and stimulating internal rivalries. Poverty rates were, however, always higher in Asia owing to the great portion of neglected rural population, a byproduct of the private monopoly system of Asian colonization. This is still a substantial barrier to the full development of countries such as India and China.

Internationalization of Monopolistic Structures

It is not possible to fully comprehend the movement of economic internationalization (or globalization) without the understanding of the progression of monopolistic structures. The recent history of capitalism demonstrates that, from the point of view of companies engaged in the production of goods and services, geographic expansion is a natural progression. Profits tend to decrease with time in regions with higher industrial and technological development, as a result of the great competition among companies. As a result, they need to look for new markets where competition is not as fierce and monopolistic profits may still be extracted. This global expansion based on the creation of new monopolies in developing countries has four dreadful effects: (i) increasing levels of unemployment and higher economic inequality; (ii) disruption of the safety net of public services; (iii) exhaustion of natural resources; and (iv) increasing technological dominance and the power of monopolistic structures that control such technologies. What is new is that those effects are produced throughout the world, both in developing and developed countries, there is, therefore, not only economic globalization, but also a globalization of social problems.

The expansion of companies to new markets is partially justified by the lower labor cost in developing countries. This creates unemployment in developed countries. This process is accompanied by a broad mergers and acquisitions movement that creates unemployment, even in the developing countries to which production was transferred, and increases the market power of monopolies. Therefore, it is easier to drain resources from the labor market, not anymore by lowering salaries (as happened during the early industrial era) but by means of unemployment created by the great mergers or delocalization of enterprises.

The expansion of monopolistic structures from developed countries to developing ones also led to the substitution of many public services for private ones. The concept of natural monopolies is then broadened, justifying the process of privatization of public services traditionally managed by governments. As a result, the inter-industrial concentration, one of the other elements of the triple draining effect, is expanded and sophisticated in this new international phase, if compared to the prior colonial and industrial periods. The monopolistic structures expand to the so-called new dynamic sectors. The inter-industrial draining is no longer a result of the draining of resources from other economic sectors, but also and mainly from the expansion of monopolistic power to new sectors, such as public services previously provided by the government. The social safety net of public services such as health care, sanitation, energy and water distribution, disappears and the effects of economic imbalances in underdeveloped economies are multiplied.

The same reasons that led to the internationalization of monopolies led also to the predatory use of the environment. The search for cost savings that already drove companies to developing countries in search for cheap labor also led such companies to use the lower protection to the environment in poor countries as a source of savings. This predatory exploitation of natural resources was initially understood by developing nations as means to allow fast economic growth and gain access to global markets. The costs of such predatory use of natural resources, however, do not have such immediate effects. Such predatory practices take longer to show their full strength, and they will certainly take much longer to disappear. It took only a few years for many developing nations to notice that the costs are much higher than the benefits and that the environmental costs will remain while many companies will move again.

Finally, the internationalization of monopolies deepens their overall domination of technology and information, particularly considering the global network effect that became possible with the new information technologies, creating material conditions for global monopolies that previously could not even be imagined. Such a process has in its turn two important effects. First, it becomes more difficult to discipline or regulate the behavior of such structures. Their international character and the changing character of technologies (that can completely shift in a few years) make their existence more liquid[13] and difficult to control. Second, their technological domination allows consumption patterns to be further determined. Technological domination allows companies dominating them to create tastes and uses for their new products and technologies. As a result, the last element of the triple draining effect, the extraction of abnormal profits from consumption, is expanded.

It is important to observe that, as a result of the process of internationalization, the negative effects of monopolistic structures (the triple draining effects) also reach the so-called developed world. Unemployment, domination of public services by private monopolies, and consumerism are common features

---

[13]   The term liquid as applied to modern societies and their components had its most influential use by Z. Bauman, *Liquid Modernity*, 2000. The author mentions among the characteristics of such modernity exactly the 'liquid' character of modern companies and technologies.

throughout the world. Predatory use of the environment is a common problem. Structural solutions are therefore no longer required only in respect to under-developed countries, but also to the capitalist system as a whole.

4.   ECONOMIC RESULTS VS LEGAL VALUES

Economic Results as Legal Guidelines

Criticism of the current simplified rationale for antitrust law is not and cannot be solely internal and empirical (historical). Not only the understatement of the importance of economic structures for society as a whole should be criti-cized (demonstrated through various examples in the previous section), but also the search for economic results itself must be regarded with reservations.

The problem is not in the search for these results, but in the belief that these results may be correctly anticipated. At this juncture, it is helpful to revisit the classic discussion on the possibility (or not) of theorizing economic knowl-edge. The initial step for this discussion is given by Hayekian studies on economics and information. For him, many of the neoclassic constructions on equilibrium are, in effect, tautologies, that is, mere results of the presupposi-tions from which one started.[14]

Market equilibrium (and not only individual balance) would exist only where individuals' expectations corresponded to real data. This correspon-dence, however, would exist only where information is transmitted between market agents. Note that this statement implies a denial of something Hayek himself would come to say years later. Price cannot be the factor in the trans-mission of this information because it is a product of the information and not its creator.[15] In other words, stating that price is the instrument for solving the information problem means a return to the tautology. In fact, price is only considered an information transmitter in a market in equilibrium or tending to equilibrium (in which price, therefore, cannot be necessary to reach it).

The same can be said in different words. In order for price to be a perfect information transmitter, everyone's evaluations (evaluations that make up the

---

[14]   The best stated theoretical construction of the criticism is in the original arti-cle by F. Hayek on 'Economics and Knowledge', in *Economica – New Series*, 4(13), February 1937, p. 33, *et seq.*

[15]   This statement will be made by Hayek in a later article, better known, however theoretically less consistent, as 'The Use of Knowledge in Society', in *American Economic Review*, xxxv(4), September 1945, p. 519, *et seq.* In this last arti-cle Hayek is already influenced by the ideological premises that will influence the rest of his academic life and are responsible for its decay in quality.

price) on use, relative value and usefulness of the products would have to converge and adhere to reality. The fact is that, in this situation, equilibrium would already have been achieved. The correct transmission of information through price is, therefore, a consequence and not the cause of equilibrium.

More recently, these statements have come to be confirmed by research undertaken by theoreticians in economics and information. These models show that information is intrinsically poorly distributed in the majority of markets, which, in many of them, purely and simply renders its functioning impossible.[16]

Being so, the great difficulty is found in the means for transmitting information. The search for answers, here brought to light by the conclusions of information economics, should be more realistic: the issue is not believing or searching for a perfect manner of information distribution, but, rather, it is about doing exactly the opposite, specifically, to ascertain that information is imperfectly distributed and that information, however unequally, is distributed and diffused among individuals.

There is not and cannot be, therefore, perfect correspondence between subjective expectations and objective data. There is not and cannot be, therefore, equilibrium. What can and does exist is a constant state of friction and contrast between expectations and reality that leads to an also constant change in expectations.

Evidently, what is set out for discovery here is what can be found that is constant and not relative. What is meant is that there must be something on which individuals base their decisions. This something, which helps them make forecasts of possible behavior patterns, is the existing economic structures, which are the only elements indicating how the market works from which it is possible to reach conclusions.

There is a rather simple reason for this. There is today a theoretical consensus around the fact that it is possible to predict behavior patterns in certain economic structures. Monopolistic or oligopolistic rationality is well known and does not arise necessarily from predefinitions of equilibrium situations. It simply comes from the fact that there is no economic power that is not exercised – as this would imply denying the situation of power itself.

With equilibrium being unobtainable and information rare and badly distributed, it is not to be supposed that any regulation or legal discipline focused on results is to be trusted. In this sense, its use as a parameter for applying antitrust law, or any other branch of economic law, cannot have a

---

[16]   The most influential article and point of departure of the modern information economics is G. Akerloff, 'The Market for Lemons: Quality Uncertainty and the Market Mechanism', in *Quarterly Journal of Economics*, 89, 1970, p. 488.

technical justification, as it is an economic policy decision among many possible others.

The Legal Approach: Economic Law as an Economic Procedure Model

The considerations above lead to an interesting conclusion. On the one hand, economic structures, that is, the centers of economic power, are relevant data for understanding and correcting the functioning of the economy, since they account for important characteristics in the underdevelopment process. On the other hand, these structures allow agents and regulators to make some presumptions about the probable behavior of economic agents.

There is a rather simple reason for this. There is today a theoretical consensus around the fact that it is possible to predict behavior patterns in certain economic structures. Monopolistic or oligopolistic rationality is well known and does not arise necessarily from predefinitions of equilibrium situations. It simply comes from the fact that there is no economic power that is not exercised – since this would, as mentioned just above, imply denying the situation of power itself.

What has yet to be defined is the kind of legal instruments that can be used to correct the orientation and behavior of these structures. As we have seen, the economic instruments are worth little as they do not supply concrete economic results that are susceptible to empirical verification. Standing in the way of the use of legal instruments, however, is the apparent difficulty in applying social policy directives to the economic sphere. For many years, the decisions that have affected the economic order have been left primarily to economic theories to which the discussion of values is unfamiliar. It is time, therefore, for a legal theory of economic behavior.

Legal scholars view knowledge in a different way from social scientists. While knowledge in the social sciences is something that is eminently empirical, whether theoretical as perceived by dogmatic Marxists and neoclassical scholars, or practical as viewed by Hayek, knowledge for law scholars is something that is eminently constructed around values.[17]

The moment for addressing values, if well understood and used, is precisely what gives the law its distinctive character and capacity for social change. According to the concept as defined here, political-institutional change is only possible through a profound political discussion of norm-protected values. The

---

[17]   See on this issue E. J. Mestmäcker, 'Markt, Recht, Wirtschafts-verfassung', in *Zeitschrift für das gesamte Handelsrecht und Wirtschaftsrecht*, 137, 1973, p. 101.

transformative and propelling force of the law is found in the fact that, more than a form of defining values, it can itself be an instrument of knowledge for society. To postulate that knowledge is value-related is nothing more than stating that the values of a certain society may influence – and they do – in a determinative manner the knowledge we have of it.

This relationship of values/knowledge in a society is relatively clear in the economic field. Protecting competition and allowing choice, for instance, leads to the discovery of the real utility of products and better choices for the consumer. The value of competition, therefore, influences reality, allowing every individual to know it.

Once generalized, this statement on the cognitive force of the law implies a transformation in economic law itself. It is a necessary transformation, as the law has an important cognitive role. A legal system, before disciplining the functioning of society, must allow this society to know itself.

In a legal system so conceived, legal rules in the economic field necessarily change their nature. It is no longer possible to admit that there are only, on the one hand, rules protective of individual economic rights and, on the other, only aims-oriented norms, defining aims and objectives of the economic process. An example of the first, property law (as it is typically known in a capitalistic state), is insufficient to meet the needs of society as a whole as it currently exists. The latter, strongly being dependent upon a mediation of interests that are at times ideologically opposed (as is the case, for example, with the principles of free initiative and social justice), frequently lack practical application.

There is an urge, therefore, to acknowledge norms that incorporate values allowing individuals and society to acquire knowledge about society and the objectives and fundamental values of economic norms, as seen above. This can only be done through norms that guarantee equilibrium in economic interactions, since, as seen, it is in these interactions (and not before them) that individuals can supply each other with information about their specific needs and uses.

It shall, therefore, not be a surprise that this kind of norm is also instrumental for the proper functioning of the economic and social system. When the equilibrium of economic interaction is guaranteed, individuals or social groups will 'discover' their economic preferences. Therefore, these rules have to assume a clear procedural character, of real *due process* in the economic sphere.[18]

---

18   Here an analogy may be made to the reasoning of the more progressive lines of thinking in judicial realism, which, when faced with the problem of the foundation of the judicial norm, suggest a procedural rule that would lead to a fair judicial solution and not a material rule that would not escape political and ideological discussions.

Rules defined by these parameters contain values that are democratically established and debated. On the other hand, they do not predefine the most convenient solution. At the same time that they give the system stability and the citizens assurances, they allow for social and institutional experimentalism. The law thus established leads 'to' and does not derive 'from' the fairest solution. It is a safer system and a more flexible one, as it allows for its own improvement.

It is important to observe that such a rule has a very specific character. It is not enough to ensure the correction of procedures. It is fundamental to ensure balance between the interacting parties not only in legal processes, but also in economic ones.

Thus understood, the rule of due process in economics is the basis of explicit redistributive principles in the regulatory sense, such as, for example, the universalization of services for the public interest. For the principle to be truly effective, it is necessary to include a multitude of citizens who have been jettisoned from the economic process. As is well defined by the theory of the legal process itself, the rule for the right legal process implies ample participation in the process. This idea may and should be extended to economic relations and procedures.

Note that, in the realistic line, the procedural thinking is so accentuated that it is taken for granted, where the discussion is about the best institutions in which to apply it. This is what happens with the two main lines – the Yale School and the Harvard School. The former sees in the activity of the judiciary system a political evaluation of opposing interests, and takes up again, therefore, former ideas of the interests of case law (see H. Sasswell and M. Mc Dougal, 'Legal Education and Public Policy: Professional Training in the Public Interest', in *Yale Law Journal*, 52, 1943; see also B. Ackerman, *Reconstructing American Law*, 1984). The Harvard School, which is more original, centers the discussion of law on the issue of which institution is more apt to apply it (see H. Hart and A. Sacks, *The Legal Process*, 1958). More recently, the progressive realism school questions, in a way that joins the Yale and Harvard concepts set forth above, how judicial decisions may influence the public and private spheres that hold power, improving them (see O. Fiss, 'The Social and Political Foundations of Adjudication', in *Law and Human Behaviour*, 6, 1982, p. 121, *et seq.*). This procedural method approaches also the reasoning developed by J. Habermas in the political field, which places a minimum procedure ('prozeduralistisches Minimum') at the centre of democracy, without which it could not exist. In this minimum procedure, evidently influenced by the individualist liberalism that features the most recent phase of his scientific work, is included the principle of the egalitarian and ample participation of all citizens (*Faktizität und Geltung- Beiträge zur Diskurstheorie des Rechts und des demokratischen Rechtsstaats*, 1998, p. 368). Note that proceduralism in the economic field is very different from that of the political field, since while equal participation could be just a formal element in the latter, any procedural idea in the former depends, to maintain a minimum level of effectiveness, on a real re-equilibrium of forces, i.e., of effective redistributive measures.

Effective choice and access to information by all are, therefore, the center of the economic law. In its application, the state should act energetically so as to ensure the existence of choice.[19]

Confronted with such a definition of law, with all its direct implications to fields like antitrust and regulatory law, it is not surprising that this theory opposes the neoclassical approach. The neoclassical model assumes that it is possible to know the utility for each consumer of every product before that product is used, that is, that a product is purchased because it has use rather than a product has use because it is purchased.

According to the theory here defined, this last statement – and not the first – is correct. It seems rather obvious, and that is exactly what the economic process means as a discovery process, that the more product alternatives the consumer can examine and discard, the more his choice will be full of information relative to his preferences.

Thus, if there is no alternative to the choice of a product, it is not possible to know how much utility the non-chosen alternative would bring to the consumer. And even if the alternative exists, it is only possible to know the level of utility for the consumer when this alternative is chosen.[20]

This theoretical premise is accepted by the new institutional economics itself (which does not represent a total rupture with the neoclassic tradition). The limited rationality and opportunistic conduct only make the utility become more uncertain and dependent upon empirical verification.[21]

---

[19]   This interventionist competition position, as it is institutional and procedural, may even be considered super-ideological. The historic experience corroborates this point of view. Much of the consensus around the immediate post-war German model of social capitalism is attributed to the political-ideological consensus formed around the ordoliberal ideas on competition and state interventionism achieved through antitrust law. It is in the fight against monopolies that the German democratic socialists identified the social element in antitrust law (see J. Gotthold, 'Neuere Entwicklungen der Wettbewerbstheorie – kritische Bemerkungen zur neo-liberalen Theorie der Wettbewerbspolitik', in *ZHR*, 145, 1981, p. 286.

[20]   See F. Denozza, who, confronted with this issue, uncovers a flaw in the neoclassical thesis and concludes: 'In un impostazione che pone al centro i desideri del singolo individuo e l'utilità (o i dollari) che il singolo guadagnerà in conseguenza di certe decisioni, il valore delle cose non può essere stabilito *a priori* (è ben noto che esistono impostazioni diverse, le teorie c.d. oggetive del valore, come la marxiana teoria del valore lavoro, ma è altretanto noto che essi conducono verso lidi assai lontani da quelli prediletti della scuola di pensiero in esame)' – 'Chicago, l'efficienza e il diritto antitruste', in *Giurisprudenza Commerciale* I, 1988, p. 23.

[21]   The more progressive representatives of the new economic institutionalism school already accept the difficulty and even impossibility of establishing values from economic rules, admitting that cultural and moral values have great enough influence over economic behavior and institutions to stop this kind of presumption. This tendency is particularly emphasized in the Nordic School of the new institutional

Being so, the only instrument capable of fulfilling the consumer's need for information is the existence of alternatives. Only an economic system based upon alternatives is sensitive to variations in consumer tastes and can transform itself in response to these changes. Only the existence of access to choice and alternatives is capable of fulfilling the great information vacuum caused by the market.

The possibility of choice has a social value that cannot be denied and must necessarily be acknowledged by the law. The market, on the other hand, does not necessarily lead to this result. That is where the state should interfere, ensuring the former and not the latter.

5. AN ALTERNATIVE: LEGAL STRUCTURALISM AND SOCIAL ORGANIZATION

This procedural concept of the functioning of the economic sphere demands a redefinition not only of antitrust law, regulatory law and economic law, but of the notion of law itself. It is this notion from now on that will be referred to as the 'neo-structural concept of law'.

Antitrust, regulatory patent law and even property law itself, in its neo-structural concept, do not impose a result or economic result, but ensure that the relationship between parties is fair and that alternatives exist effectively, not being substituted for the ruling of the powerful (economic structures) that is typical of free markets. In this way, they aim to ensure that economic agents discover the best options, and discipline economic relations in the fairest and most balanced way possible.

The final effect of such a theory is that economic power must be substituted as the most relevant element for the organization of economic relations. Law aimed at providing choice and access to information shall substitute power as this organizing element.

This is not an easy task. Economic power is not only deeply rooted in existing economic structures but also in existing economic relations. Relations are defined and organized based on power exercise.

The law must rise to the challenge of regaining control of social relations. To do so, legal analysis should free itself from legal positivism and be able to propose a structural approach to economic relations.

---

economics (see T. Eggertsson, 'The Economics of Control and the Costs of Property Rights', in *Rights to Nature – Ecological, Economic, Cultural and Political Principles of Institutions for the Environment*, p. 157 (167); A. Sen, 'Rational Fools: A Critique of the Behavioral Foundations of Economic Theory', in *Choice, Welfare and Measurement*, cit., pp. 84–106).

It is no longer possible to rely only on compensatory measures to groups damaged by the economic activities of monopolistic groups. Legal institutions with a compensatory characteristic, such as labor law or consumer law, are useful tools, but clearly insufficient to discipline the effects of monopolies and prevent what is described here as the 'triple draining' of the consumer, labor and inter-industrial markets. In monopolized societies, compensatory mechanisms became almost useless because of two reasons: (i) it is not possible to implement public policies through legal mechanisms, since compensatory measures are enforced by means of individual judicial decisions, which lack coordination and coherence; and (ii) it is difficult to achieve economic transformation because ad hoc compensation will always be insufficient to overcome inequalities continuously created by concentrated economic structures.

Solutions grounded on legal structuralism focusing on a profound revision of the operations of the economic system also require that certain basic legal concepts, such as property rights, intellectual property, and regulation, be revisited in a creative way. Developments in the theory of common goods, creative thinking about patents of socially essential goods and their mandatory licensing in the public interest, and new regulation of capital markets leading to the existence of fewer markets (only those where the flow and understanding of information are possible) are just some examples of how structural solutions could look.

What meaning of law is being suggested? What structures and which discipline of economic relations allow access to individual and social choice? It is time to sum up what has been said until now legal structuralism.

Evidently the answer can be correctly arrived at only when the subject of law and its interpretation are properly analyzed. For the time being, two characteristics and two consequences of these characteristics can be mentioned.

On the one hand, it must be clear that legal structuralism, contrary to economic structuralism, does not trust the production of certain predefined economic results. Consequently, it is not feasible to set forth, as intended by the Harvard structuralist line of thinking in the 1960s, a structure-conduct-performance model. The study of structures does not aim to ensure results, but rather the access of all to information and choice. Consequently, the structural study of economic power will focus on ensuring choices and inclusion of people (that is, access to economic knowledge) and not on predetermined models of business dimension or economic dilution.

From here derives another characteristic, very important to the law concept itself. Legal solutions tend to be seen mainly as compensatory ones. Being the concept of justice so relative and difficult to define in a transcendental way,[22]

---

[22] This is the most powerful critique made by Sen to Rawls. See. A. Sen, *The Idea of Justice*, 2009.

law has always had a tendency to opt for compensatory measures. It does not interfere in the economic or social processes as such; it just compensates groups of individuals that are particularly harmed by them. Such is the case with consumer law and labor law, not to speak about ordinary private law questions, where compensation is thought of on a case by case basis.

The neo-structural approach proposes something completely different. Law is not made to compensate individuals or groups of individuals. Its aim is actually to organize the functioning of society. This can mean, in the economic arena, being able to intervene in structures of power in order to create choice and inclusion to individuals. This intervention also has its limits. It is not the scope of law to determine the results of the economic process. But it can protect values (choice and inclusion) that are instrumental to the construction of a due economic process.

Such an approach has profound consequences for the treatment of economic power. If choice and access to information are values to be pursued in a variety of fields, and not only in the markets, the theoretical instruments of antitrust law are not sufficient anymore.

On one hand, it is necessary to understand the different consequences of economic power on social and economic arenas. These different effects must be identified and dealt with separately according to the different sources of economic power. Economic power positions can be created from different sources and not just by market dynamics. They can be a product of (i) market relations, but they can also be a product of (ii) law, for example, exclusivity rights granted by law (patent law), or even of (iii) social relations, through a domination of natural resources or common goods. The expression 'social relations' here must be well understood. It is used as opposed to market relations, since the goods in question are so relevant for society in general that their attribution to a sole individual or enterprise cannot be discussed on an economic or legal traditional basis, but rather with a methodology of interest inclusion compatible with their social relevance.

Therefore, from the perspective of the source of the power, economic power originated from social relations can be better understood. In opposition to the first two sources, it refers to a market power structure based not on a position gained in the market or through a legal concession, but instead based on the possession of a good with immense social relevance to groups or communities and even (in some) to the whole species survival.

These different phenomena all have problems and instruments of regulation that cannot be found in general discussions about market rationale.

In all of these areas, economic power must be dealt with, bearing in mind that it is much more complex than just a consumer–producer relationship. It affects a series of other relations and interests (workers, community affected by the enterprise activity, the environment, etc.).

These different sources of economic power and its different effects require the application of different conceptual schemes for understanding and different methods for their regulation. These are the subjects of the next two chapters. But we must always bear in mind (and this is perhaps one of the main conclusions of this first chapter) that these different sources of power create power structures that have important things in common that, as seen above, must guide their legal treatment and justify the very elaboration of a legal theory of economic power. They all produce triple draining effects on economy and society that reach well beyond the consumer-produced relationship. And they require an intervention that is not compensatory, but rather directed at eliminating or affecting seriously the very sources of power that create these economic and social distortions.

2. Economic power structures: Creation and existence

1. IDENTIFICATION OF ECONOMIC POWER: NEW PARADIGMS

In order to understand economic power, and be able to criticize its definition, we must understand its traditional concept and systematic importance in the field of law that was classically dedicated to its study: antitrust law.[1] Once this is acknowledged, its concept can be discussed.

To determine the concept of economic power, it is important to keep in mind the famous epistemological observation by Karl Popper, according to which certain concepts are so fundamental and constitutive for a science that their definition is axiomatic. The ways in which they were conceived should be questioned, rather than attempting to define them.[2] As an example, there is the classic comparison made by B. Russell between the importance of power for the social sciences and of energy for physics. In physics, the question 'What is energy?' is a metaphysical question, with no meaning. The correct question should therefore be 'How is it revealed?' The same happens with power in the social sciences.[3]

This observation can be perfectly applied to the antitrust analysis of power in the market. It is not about defining it, but about finding in the economic theory ways of identifying the necessary conditions for its manifestation. Once these conditions are established, it becomes possible to identify, based on the

---

[1]   We must first remember that, for antitrust law, economic power is identical to market power. This statement is criticized in this book, but in order to do that, we must first understand and follow an internal critique to the concept of market power. This is what will be done here, in Chapter 2, sections 1 and 2.

[2]   V. K. Popper, *Die offene Gesellschaft und ihre Feinde*, v. I ('Der Zauber Platons'), 1957, p. 61.

[3]   The comparison between the two notions is made by B. Russell (*Power: A New Social Analysis*, 1938, p. 10), who states that power is the key concept in the social sciences, like energy is in physics. Popper's observation is a (critical) note on this famous statement by Russell; as to the latter, see F. K. Comparato, *O poder de controle*, 1983, p. 2, mentioning also the mutating character of power as a demonstration of the impossibility of defining it.

law, the illegal forms of power in the market. In this chapter we will try therefore to critically analyze the dominant views about market definition, showing that it should not be subject solely or not even mainly to quantitative measures, and try to analyze how new structures of market power influence the amount and the intensity of economic power.

2. CRITICISM OF TRADITIONAL MEASUREMENT

The observation made above, on its own, raises questions about the possibility of measuring market power. More important or useful than trying to measure it would be to identify the ways in which it is manifested.

But it is not only the epistemological matter, so to speak, that sheds doubt on the possibility of defining and measuring market power.[4] Such doubts also hover over the adequacy of the already traditional and consecrated neoclassic methodology of measurement.

This methodology will now be described with two types of reservation. One already mentioned during the description is an internal criticism, falling on the presuppositions themselves on which the neoclassic definition of market is based. In particular, the (knowingly false) presupposition of complete information will be an object of consideration.

The second line of reservations is to be made at the end and is external. It relates to the fact that not all kinds of economic power are created by market forces. Therefore, not all structures of economic power are revealed in the market and hence cannot be perceived or analyzed by theories or instruments based on market data, as is the case with marginalism. This criticism will become clearer in section 2 when the different structures of economic power will be analyzed. As will be seen, just the first of them, market power structures, can be discussed with the help of marginal concepts. For the others (legal structures and environmentally sensitive structures, both the sources of economic power and the instruments necessary to discipline it will have to be found elsewhere, with no help from economic theories, not even for the identification of structural power. It is there where antitrust theory shows its greatest shortcomings.

---

[4]   For a fresh debate on this issue, see S. Waller, 'The Story of Alcoa: The Enduring Questions of Market Power, Conduct, and Remedy in Monopolization Cases', in E. M. Fox and D. A. Crane (eds), *Antitrust Stories*, 2007, pp. 121–43; and H. Hovenkamp, 'Unreasonable Exercises of Market Power', in *The Antitrust Enterprise: Principle and Execution*, 2005, pp. 95–124.

Fundamental Marginal Concepts

According to neoclassical theory, the main manifestation of market power is the ability to raise prices through a reduction in the supply of goods or services, to the point that – reprising what was said in the introduction to this chapter – market power is defined as the power to raise prices.

For neoclassical thinkers, the possibility of increasing prices, more than the manifestation of that possibility, is a necessary consequence of the existence of market power. Raising prices is the 'rational behavior' of economic players, whose importance in the market is significant to the point of influencing prices through reducing production.

This is in fact a rather simplistic definition of market power, whose only aim is to emphasize the problem relevant to antitrust law from the neoclassical perspective. To this view, certain corrections and additional elements must, as an initial matter, be added.

In the first instance, the power to increase prices is not an absolute criterion for the definition of market power. Many times, the lack of the first may be owing to exercising the latter. It may happen that a company, being monopolistic, is already charging prices so high and abusive that it is impossible for it to increase its prices further, at the risk of consumers shifting to a substitute or simply stopping to use that product.[5]

It can be concluded, therefore, that the ability to increase prices is not a necessary condition for the existence of market power. Is it, on the other hand, a self-sufficient condition for it to take place? The answer is also negative. As will be discussed ahead, past price increases comprise only behavioral data, which should be allied to structural data to verify the real existence of market power. It is possible, for example, that the economic agent, even with no market power, may reduce prices as a result of being more efficient than its competitors (that is, capable of producing at a lower marginal cost) and thus

---

[5]   This is the main criticism manifested by scholars against the decision of the U.S. Supreme Court in *United States v. E. I. Du Pont De Nemours & Co.*, 351 U.S. 377 (S. Ct. 1956), where the Court held that here was an absence of market power owing to a high level of cross-elasticity of demand (i.e., a high level of product substitution in the event of price increases), which, according to this theory, could represent exactly the opposite: see W. Landes and R. Posner, 'Market Power in Antitrust Cases', in *Harvard Law* Review, 94, 1981. In *Eastman Kodak Co. v. Image Technical Servs., Inc.*, 504 U.S. 451 (1992), the Court noted that the price restraint caused by the capacity of the buyer to substitute the good or service does not always disprove the existence of market power once its seller may already have submitted to a monopoly price. For recent development of this discussion, see J. M. Perloff, *Microeconomics: Theory & Applications with Calculus*, 2008, p. 483; P. Krugman and R. Wells, *Microeconomics*, 2009.

hold price levels below those of competitors. Thus, price increases should always be followed by an analysis of market structure (made from a market definition) so that market power may be identified.

In theory, it should thus be concluded that the most correct definition of market power is not the ability to increase prices, but the possibility of choosing between the following alternatives: increased market share and reduced profitability, or smaller market share and greater profit margins.[6] This means of defining market power is, for instance, the only possible way of explaining monopsony and oligopsony situations. In these cases, market power is precisely about the possibility of reducing prices through reducing acquisitions, which, seen from the perspective of buyers, implies exactly the alternative defined above (this issue will be given fuller treatment later in this chapter).

The fundamental importance given to price increases is the result of the neoclassic theorist's sole concern for consumer (short-term) welfare. It is a concern solely with the effects that a determined restriction on competition may have on prices that sets the tone of the analysis, even in relations between competitors. This last aspect may also be understood as disbelief that comparison and choice itself can be means of protecting the interests of consumers. This perspective, even if characterized as 'consumer protection', many times ends up being more tolerant towards the formation and maintenance of market power, provided, however, that this power is 'efficient'. The consequence of its careless application could mean a loss for the consumer, especially in the long run.

To understand the meaning of the neoclassic conjecture, it is important to recall certain microeconomic concepts. First, one has to bear in mind that in a market with perfect competition – that is, a market in which no economic agent could on its own influence the price of a good – the seller maximizes its profits at that precise moment when it produces enough for the price to equal the marginal cost.[7] This is because, up to this point, each extra unit produced earns greater total revenue. Each unit produced from that point onwards would imply decreasing total revenue, since the marginal cost of producing it would be greater than the price. The economic foundation of this statement is that while the marginal cost is increasing, in perfect competition, marginal revenue is constant. In this way, after the intersection, the marginal cost will always be greater than the marginal revenue.

---

6   See R. Pitofsky, 'New Definitions of the Relevant Market and the Assault on Antitrust', in 90 *Columbia Law Review*, 1805, 1811 (1990).
7   The term 'marginal' always refers to the increase (in cost, income, etc.) resulting from the production or sales of an extra unit of the product.

Note that, in perfect competition, marginal price and revenue are the same; therefore, it is possible to compare them to the marginal cost. In perfect competition, the demand curve is a straight line in relation to quantity. In this way, price translates integrally to marginal revenue.

The same does not happen in a sector without perfect competition, but certain firms have market power. Imagine a situation in which a company accounts for almost the entire production in the market.[8] The company then has influence on price. The demand curve is decreasing in relation to the price offered. Nevertheless, if the demand curve is decreasing, marginal revenue is necessarily lower than the price. This is because, unless the manufacturer can differentiate between consumers (and in the simplest model, it is assumed that it cannot), it must necessarily reduce the price on all products in order to sell a larger amount. Therefore, its loss is reflected in the price of every product, and the revenue for every extra unit sold (the marginal revenue) is inferior to the price (the difference between the two represents exactly the loss in relation to the volume produced).

This is thus the explanation for the surcharge obtained by the company with market power. Rational behavior by the agent is always to equate marginal cost to marginal revenue. This is because, before this point, as seen above, any extra unit produced generates an increase in total revenue. However, with the existence of one or more economic agents with market power (in a monopoly situation, for instance), price would necessarily be greater than marginal revenue (which, in turn, is quite close, but not identical to the price in perfect competition). The price obtained by this 'rational behavior' is, therefore, necessarily greater than the actual price in a situation of perfect competition.

This economic description of the behavior of agents with market power may be understood in a much simpler manner. It is, in fact, intuitive. If the agent knows it can influence prices, it will certainly seek the combination of quantity and price that will generate the greatest profit.

Comprehending the marginal rationale in economic terms is necessary, as it has extremely important consequences for the criticism of the standard neoclassic analysis of market power to follow. Below, the two most important consequences will be explained with their respective economic foundations.

Market Power and Market Share

The first consequence of the marginal reasoning derives directly from the definition itself of market power (or its main form of manifestation). If this power

---

    [8]   In neoclassical analysis, the position of power used as a parameter is the monopoly.

is manifested by the possibility of choosing market variables in its best interest, it is not enough to observe that the agent has a large percentage of the total production or total sales of a determined product to conclude that the agent has market power. Even a company with significant market share of a certain product may not have the power to raise prices or decrease production. All that is required is (a) a substitute for the product or (b) many competitors to be ready to enter the market as soon as higher prices increase the possibilities of success and profit in that market. Letters 'a' and 'b' correspond, respectively, to the microeconomic concepts of cross-elasticity of demand and cross-elasticity of supply.

Elastic demand (elasticity > 1) occurs when the reduction in quantity demanded is more than proportional to the increase in price. In a graphic representation of the state of perfect competition, the demand curve would be a straight line parallel to the horizontal axis that represents quantities. Therefore, the demand elasticity, in this case, is infinite and the agent has no market power. The opposite, however, is not true, and that is owing to cross-elasticity. Even if demand for a product is totally inelastic and the monopolist (considering only demand for that product) can increase prices infinitely without suffering a reduction in the quantity demanded, it will not have market power if the demand and supply cross-elasticities are high. In other words, if the increase in the price of a product corresponds to a great 'escape' by consumers to substitute products (more than proportional response in the demand for the substitute product to price increases in the original product – cross-elasticity of demand > 1), the agent will not have the power to increase prices. If price is increased, the agent runs the risk of losing a large part of its sales to manufacturers of substitute products.

The same will happen if an increase in prices is followed by the mass entry of new manufacturers into the market. In this case, owing to the high cross-elasticity of supply, the manufacturer will not be able to increase its prices under the risk of seeing the market flooded by new competitors.[9] Thus, it is fundamental to find a model for determining market power that takes these factors into consideration.

---

[9] The legal and economic literature that addresses the issue of market power is vast. As an example, the description of the economic foundations for determining market power is discussed in many works in a similar manner, with varying points of focus and levels of strictness, but all, however, using the same analytical instrument of the neoclassical theory. See, e.g., in decreasing levels of neoclassic strictness, W. Landes & R. Posner, 'Market Power in Antitrust Cases', cit, p. 937, *et seq.*; P. Areeda, J. Solow and H. Hovenkamp, *Antitrust Law: An Analysis of Antitrust Principles and Their Application*, v. II A, 1995, pp. 90–93; R. Pitofsky, 'New Definitions of the Relevant Market and the Assault on Antitrust', cit., p. 1085, *et seq.*

While these factors are important, it must also be considered that, if the criticism of the marginal definition is accepted, then the focus of the definition of market power shifts to the possibility of controlling information and choice. As has been discussed above, it is not just the possibility of raising prices, but the possibility of choosing how much and at what price the producer will sell his products. With such control of the market, the producer facing high cross-elasticity rates can choose not to increase prices but to invest in the creation of barriers to entry (technical as the creation of network effects, for example) that can protect his position. Even a market with high cross-elasticity is therefore dynamic and subject to changes by an agent with high market power.

The Monopolistic Rationale

The second consequence of the marginal reasoning, which can be denominated the 'principle of monopolistic rationale', can be summarized as an important postulate: in neoclassic microeconomic theory, non-exercised market power does not exist. The economic agent acts necessarily in a way to maximize its profits. If, as was seen, the maximization of profit implies charging prices above competitive levels, this will be done. For the neoclassic economists, if economic market power is not being exercised in the sense of the monopolistic rationale, it means that it does not exist. The situation described above may happen, for example, in a company with great market share where there is nonetheless somewhat elastic demand for substitute products and also elastic cross-supply.

Consequently, a company that has a dominant market position and prices the subject product competitively in the long run, without being able to pursue any strategy of raising barriers to entry, demonstrates a lack of market power. For some, such evidence allows for an absolute assumption of the non-existence of market power. Even if such an assumption may, in certain cases, cause scholars to disregard situations in which there is effective market power, it is not possible for the law to differentiate among the companies that do and do not have such power. The 'non-rational' reasons (according to rationality standards of the economic agents in neoclassic theory) that could lead a company to not increase prices, such as the desire to increase sales and gain additional market share, or the fear of increased regulation in the sector, would be extremely rare in practice and their investigation would be very difficult and expensive. Such reasons, therefore, could not reasonably form the basis for a standard or even be taken into account by the law.[10]

---

[10]   See P. Areeda, J. Solow and H. Hovenkamp, *Antitrust Law*, v. II A, cit., p. 109.

While the principle of monopolistic rationale is useful as an indicative criterion for the probable behavior of economic agents, and is, therefore, susceptible to the formulation of (relative) assumptions, it does not lead to the result described in the previous paragraph. It is not possible to transport economic concepts directly and carelessly to the legal field. The rationale, even if it is an identifying criterion of market power from an economic point of view, is not enough to distinguish legal from illegal market power. As we will see ahead, a determination of illegal market power requires a finding of various factors of both market structure and market behavior.

To bring up only the most obvious example, when attempting to police market concentration, past behavior is a criterion of little utility. This is because, in such a case, it is not about analyzing an already existing business structure, but something that will come to exist in the future. The principle of monopolistic rationale, coherently applied, would require that, from the simple analysis of market structure as it exists after market concentration is achieved, direct conclusions about the future behavior of economic agents can be drawn.

The construction based on monopolistic reasoning can be criticized even in relation to the analysis of previously existing market power. For example, all one must do is note that, at times, market power may be manifested through the predatory reduction of prices. It is the monopolistic profit obtained in another segment of the market or obtained in the past that finances a 'price war', which, in other circumstances, would be suicidal. In fact, it was suggested in economic literature that there could be a rationale behind the apparent irrationality of predatory prices. There are three suggested explanations. First, the monopolist may wish to establish a reputation of aggressive behavior in relation to those who try to invade the subject market. Second, it may wish to transmit a false impression to the market that its costs are less than those of the competitors, discouraging entry into the market by competitors. The third explanation is based upon the monopolist's superior financial position, which leads it to believe that it can force the economically weakest competitor out of the market.[11] Apparently irrational behavior is explained, therefore, in three very rational ways.

The same can be said regarding technological predation. It may well be that prices are not being raised because the agent with market power is investing in products that are incompatible with the nets of competitors. In this sense he is trying to influence demand and supply cross-elasticities and reinforce his market power position. The new product, having no increased utility for the

---

[11]   These three hypotheses are constructed from the application of game theory; in this regard, see the pioneering work of D. Baird, R. Gertner and R. Pickner, *Game Theory and the Law*, 1994, pp. 178, *et seq.*

consumer, cannot have a higher price but the investment in technology may turn out to reinforce the power in the long run. In the dynamic sense, of controlling relevant variables in the market (especially information), a situation of power may exist.

Insufficiency of the Neoclassic Criteria: The Information Concentration Problem

One of the most important results of modern economic thinking is precisely to place doubt on the possibility of theorizing economic behavior. The main reason for such doubt is the conviction that knowledge is dispersed amongst individuals and that, consequently, in every economic relationship, different individuals will have different bits of information – information that is frequently unequal and asymmetric.[12] With this, each and every model of how the market functions that intends to suggest expected results based on ample diffusion of knowledge and information is necessarily destined to fail.

The models described above are based on contemporary economic studies and theories, especially the theory of knowledge[13] and so-called information

---

[12]   On September 22, 2009, the Federal Trade Commission (FTC) and the U.S. Department of Justice (DOJ) announced that they will solicit public comment and hold joint public workshops to explore the possibility of updating the Horizontal Merger Guidelines that are used by both agencies to evaluate the potential competitive effects of mergers and acquisitions. The goal of the workshops will be to determine whether the Horizontal Merger Guidelines accurately reflect the current practice of merger review at the FTC and DOJ, as well as to take into account legal and economic developments that have occurred since the last significant Guidelines revision in 1992 (see Press Release, FTC, Federal Trade Commission and Department of Justice to Hold Workshop Concerning Horizontal Merger Guidelines (September 22, 2009), available at http://www.ftc.gov/opa/2009/09/ mgr.shtm). The public comments are available at http://www.ftc.gov/os/ comments/horizontalmergerguides/index.shtm. One of these comments, produced by the American Antitrust Institute, sent on November 9, 2009, highlights information deficiencies as follows: '[…] The Guidelines should consider the possibility that information deficiencies and other market failures may affect the analysis of market definition and entry. Kodak recognizes that information deficiencies and other 'consumer protection' market failures can apply to businesses as well as individual consumers. Where significant information or other market imperfections exist, therefore, the Agencies should be wary of defining markets broadly to include products that are not effective substitutes because, for example, customers may be unaware of them, face high search costs, or are locked into expensive existing systems. Moreover, information deficiencies may limit the likelihood of entry.'

[13]   The best explanation of these ideas is undoubtedly found in F. Hayek, 'The Use of Knowledge in Society', cit., pp. 519–30.

economics.[14] It is interesting to note that both models, when well understood and developed, lead to profoundly reformist ideas of the structures.

All of them point to the same conclusion. Economic reasoning can no longer be directed toward the search for economic results based on theoretical models. Its objective is to ensure that economic agents acquire knowledge in economic relationships, which does not occur with traditional market instruments. In addition, no diffusion of knowledge will occur in the presence of market power, which creates immense distortions.

According to the theory mentioned above, such distortions primarily occur as a result of the asymmetries of information and knowledge. These asymmetries are more or less accentuated in varying markets, but, and this is extremely important, they do not come from natural information asymmetries. In most economies, especially the developing economies, asymmetries result from restricted access to information in such societies and the different effects such distortions have on the market and economic agents.

It is not easy to interpret and understand all of the consequences of this conjunction of factors: information that is dispersed and distributed in an asymmetrical manner.

On one hand, it is undeniable that the risk of taking advantage of information dispersion to accelerate and strengthen information asymmetries is important. The instrumentality of economic power, for the creation of such asymmetries, is evident.

But, perhaps, more important than these generic consequences, which are relatively obvious, are the specific consequences that relate to market power. The conviction that it is impossible to theorize and concentrate economic knowledge serves to question many of the neoclassic presumptions used to define the market. This is because, in the end, the definition of the market itself assumes the concentration of knowledge and information in the market.

If it is true that this concentration of information is impossible, as it is dispersed as well as placed in asymmetrical form, then the 'map' of information

---

14   Their main proponents are G. Akerloff, J. Stiglitz and M. Spence. The first author demonstrates how, in certain sectors, uncertainties about quality may lead to the disappearance of the market itself – see G. Akerloff, 'The Market for Lemons: Quality Uncertainty and the Market Mechanism', cit. The main contribution by Stiglitz, apart from systemizing information economics, shows how stock itself has signalizing effects, transmitting information – see J. Stiglitz, 'The Contributions of the Economics of Information to Twentieth Century Economics', in *The Quarterly Journal of Economics*, November, 2000, pp. 1441–7. The work by Spence concerns the development of signs theories, i.e., ways of transmitting information between agents, reducing the asymmetries – see M. Spence, 'Signaling in Retrospect and the Informational Structure of Markets', Nobel Prize Lecture, December 8, 2001.

dispersion becomes important for the definition of market and the measurement of economic power.

Therefore, traditional elements in antitrust analysis, such as defining the market and measuring market share, must also take into consideration, in some cases in a predominant manner, the level of information asymmetry. In certain cases, such as where vertical concentrations exist, the analysis of information concentration is practically the only existing criterion for measuring market power.

For this reason, the following topics will, whenever possible and relevant for the issue being discussed, address the problem of the dispersion and allocation of information.

Market Power and Definition of Market

The definition of market power presented, which emphasizes, above all, the forms in which such power is manifested, places greater importance on the problem treated in this section: the means of determining the existence of market power. There are many economic and econometric theories that address this issue. It is not necessary for the objectives of the present work to analyze them in depth, but only to describe their main features, which could be relevant for the legal analysis.

Presently, the most often used theoretical model for the determination of market power is the one based upon the definition of 'market'. This method begins the definition of the relevant market by the establishment of geographic boundaries and limits relative to the type of product, and then proceeds to the verification of market share by the agents in this market. A correct definition of the subject market should necessarily take into consideration three dimensions: the substantial (or product) dimension, the geographic dimension, and the temporal dimension. Therefore, to the traditional geographic and product dimensions is added the temporal dimension. In fact, traditional neoclassic analysis takes into consideration the temporal element in defining the market but not as a separate element. Its discussion is included in the geographic and products markets, working as a restriction in both definitions (and therefore potentially pointing in the direction of greater market power) where there is power in the temporal perspective; in other words, when there are barriers to entry that prevent erosion of the market power position in the future.

In the next topic, we will describe and discuss the neoclassic method of defining 'market', and its traditional form. This does not mean that the analysis of the temporal perspective will be skipped. On the contrary, it is regarded as so important and so little considered in the traditional neoclassic analysis that it will be the object of an independent topic, the point referring to barriers to entry. Only after analysing neoclassic rationale can we proceed to identify its shortcomings and criticize it.

Method for determining market definition

Defining the market (both in terms of products and in the geographic sense) takes into consideration two distinct elements: substitute products on the demand side and the supply side. This means that, to determine in which market an economic agent manufacturing product 'X' is placed, it is necessary to verify (a) which products the consumer (demand) sees as substitutes for 'X' and (b) which new manufacturers could reasonably enter the market of 'X' to produce it.

In both cases, and this is fundamental to understanding the method, when determining the substitutes on the supply and demand sides, it is not possible to analyze the market as it exists in that exact moment. In addition, when determining the 'market', it is not sufficient to consider only present competitors. As we have seen as a natural and necessary consequence of the formation or existence of a monopoly, a projection of the effects of a determined price increase must be undertaken. It should then be determined (from the analysis of existing data with reference to past price increases) if the consumer will substitute product 'X' for a near competitor (demand substitution) or if new manufacturers will enter the market, now manufacturing product 'X'.

For such a method to function as a measuring system, both with respect to existing market power and the projected level of market power of a conglomerate[15] of entities that is yet to be formed, the price levels over which increases will be applied must be the same. In this way, the prices over which hypothetical increases must be calculated are always competitive, even if a company is already charging monopoly prices. Only if it is impossible to obtain these values, owing to a total absence of information on past pricing behavior or pricing patterns of competitors or substitute products (with the same cost structure), can present price levels be used, reducing (eventually to zero) the price increases projected (in the event that price abuse has already been established).

Note that this apparently complicated analysis is necessary for determining the real dimension of the market and in order to evaluate market power itself. Only in a dynamic perspective can market power be correctly evaluated and measured. This is because only with the verification of the effects of a given

---

15   For information related to conglomerate effects in the European Union, see *Tetra Laval BV v. Commission*, Case T-5/02, Judgment of the Court of First Instance (First Chamber), 25 Oct. 2002, ¶ 142, 155, available at http://ec.europa.eu/smartapi/ cgi/sga_doc?smartapi!celexplus!prod!CELEXnum doc&lg=en&numdoc=62002A 0005.

price increase is it possible to observe consumer behavior, stopping consumption or substituting one product for another.

It must be noticed that the method of hypothetical price increases is based on economic assumptions that are currently accepted but that do not go without criticism. The most important of them is the assumption that market power must necessarily be exercised in furtherance of price increases. Once this premise has been accepted, the consequence is that, even in a market in which there is great concentration, the dominant market player will not stop increasing prices until they reach their point of equilibrium. If equilibrium still has not been reached, the company will soon move in that direction; if it has been surpassed, the dominant agent will be constricted by market forces to reduce its prices. The best way of evaluating market power is, therefore, to try to project the structure of this market, once the monopolistic equilibrium point has been reached.

In a given market, if it is concluded that, owing to an increase in prices, a large number of consumers will begin to choose another product or that a large number of competitors will enter the market, the economic agent, even with a large market share, would lose a large part of its market if it increased prices. In this case, it cannot be said that there is market power, since the primary means of exercising this power – increasing prices – is blocked.

There are three central problems with the application of this method that, as will be seen, transform the seemingly scientific method into a rather subjective one.

The level of price increase   How can the level of price increases be determined? As we have demonstrated, it is not possible to determine the value of the monopolistic overcharge (if it were, this entire analysis would be unnecessary, as market power could be directly calculated through the *Lerner Index*[16]).[17] On the other hand, the definition of 'market' and, consequently, a determination of whether market power exists are dependent upon a more or less correct definition of price increase. Using a very high level of price increase would imply defining a market that is excessively ample. A level that is too low creates the opposite risk. Levels used as standard, in spite of being

---

[16]   See generally A. Lerner, 'The Concept of Monopoly and the Measurement of Monopoly Power', in *Review of Economic Studies*, 157, 169, 1934; Herbert Hovenkamp, *Federal Antitrust Policy: The Law Of Competition and Its Practice*, 2005, p. 79.

[17]   To illustrate this point, see the application of this index in Brazilian case law, see, e.g., Merger No. 58/97, Companhia Cervejaria Brahma, Miller Brewing Company and Miller Brewing M 1855, Inc., judged on June 11, 1997.

necessarily arbitrary (as, in all, is the determination of market share itself), are normally fixed between 5 per cent and 10 percent.[18]

Demonstrating the existence of substitution The second problem refers to projecting the effects of such price increases. Here, the matter is more economic than legal. Without addressing the econometric details (the econometric method allows for inferences from data collected in the past), it is important to explain the different criteria for evaluating the probable reaction of buyers to price increases.[19]

The first is the proof that buyers effectively substituted or considered the possibility of substituting for the product owing to changes in prices or other competitive variables. This is, undoubtedly, the most trustworthy of all indications. Its demonstration can be made through econometric analysis of the quantitative data referring to the consumption of each product in the past as a consequence of the price increases, or even (in the absence of this data) from the comparison of price fluctuations of both products. The inexistence of parallel movement in prices between similar products is a reasonably safe indication that consumers do not see them as substitutes. After all, a steady level in prices of the product held as a substitute indicates that there is not a large enough flow of consumers from the product being substituted for (the product 'X' in our hypothetical example) to even marginally increase the

---

18   This is the percentage used by the U.S. Department of Justice in the Department of Justice Merger Guidelines of 1984 and 1992. This kind of test was established for the first time in the Guidelines of 1982, which determined the percentage increase to be 5%. Apparently affected by criticism that the percentage was arbitrary, the Department of Justice stated in the Guidelines of 1984 only that the increase should be 'small but significant and nontransitory'. With this, in fact, at the end of the 1980s, still under the strong influence of the conservative vision (also relative to economic concentrations) of the Reagan era, the Department of Justice was applying a test of 10%; this value, however, was calculated starting at competitive prices; see R. Pitofsky, 'New Definitions of the Relevant Market', pp. 1819–20. The 1992 Horizontal Merger Guidelines re-established the percentage at 5%, though with the following observation: 'However, what constitutes a "small but significant and nontransitory" increase in price will depend on the nature of the industry, and the Agency at times may use a price increase that is larger or smaller than five percent' (Section 1.11); for the complete text of the Guidelines, see P. Areeda, J. Solow and H. Hovenkamp, *Antitrust Law*, Supplement, 1994, Appendix A. Owing to this, what happens in practice is the application of the 10% test relative to competitive prices or 5% relative to prices effectively practiced in the market, when it is known that these prices are super-competitive, but it is not possible to safely infer competitive prices. See also P. Areeda, J. Solow and H. Hovenkamp, *Antitrust Law*, pp. 199–200.

19   These are the criteria used in the 1992 Horizontal Merger Guidelines of the U.S. Department of Justice (Section 1.11); see P. Areeda, J. Solow and H. Hovenkamp, *Antitrust Law*, Supplement, 1994, loc. cit.

price. The opposite, however, is not necessarily true. The existence of parallel price movement could be a result of pressure in the prices of inputs used in both products, which is indeed likely to occur when dealing with similar products.[20] Consequently, the existence of parallel price movements can be relied upon only as an indication of market power if followed by an analysis of changes in the quantities consumed of each product (which brings us back to the starting point, which makes price analysis relatively useless), or if followed by a thorough study of the history of costs incurred by the companies (which, as we have already seen, is very difficult).

The second criterion measures market power starting from the assumption that sellers base business decisions on the likelihood that some buyers will substitute products in response to price changes or other competitive variables. This is the verification of market power based on business planning, which includes analyzing the importance given by the economic agent to the behavior of its competitors. A complete lack of consideration for the existence of competitors in its planning is typical monopolistic behavior.[21] The problem is that, even here, it is not possible to draw definitive conclusions from such behavior. It is often the consideration of competitors in business planning that may indicate the existence of market power and the intention to use it in order to exclude competitors.[22]

Additionally, as we will see hereafter with the analysis of oligopoly theory, consideration of the behavior of competitors is one of the main manifestations of parallel oligopolistic behavior, which can possibly mean cartel behavior. The conclusion is that, at most, business planning may indicate market power in cases where there is the complete lack of consideration for competition. It is important to note that this is a mere indication, for we cannot be certain that failure to mention competitors is a consequence of a lack of relevant competitors. It could be owing to simple carelessness or faulty planning methods, which obviously cannot be penalized through legal instruments. The opposite is also not true. Consideration of competitors in business planning may say little or nothing about the economic agent's market power.

The amount to be included The last methodological problem consists of defining the amount of the product or the substitute production to be included. The matter is rather complicated, requiring differentiated analysis for the prod-

---

[20] See a positive criticism of inferences in R. Pitofsky, 'New Definitions of the Relevant Market and the Assault on Antitrust', cit., p. 1840.

[21] See H. J. Mestmäcker, *Das marketbeherrschende Unternehmen im Recht der Wettbewerbsbeschränkungen*, 1958, section 2, p. 15, *et seq.*

[22] See U. Immenga and H. J. Mestmäcker, *GWB Kommentar,* 2nd ed., 1992, p. 753.

ucts market and the geographic market. It can be said that, as a general rule, when dealing with demand substitutes, the entire sales volume of the substitute product must be included. In effect, if the consumer expresses preference for a certain product, there are not, in general, limits for demand expansion in the direction of the substitute product. The entire production volume of substitutes should be considered as part of the market of the main product.

About supply substitution, on the contrary, it will be possible to include only the volume that is reasonable to suppose will be redirected owing to the price increase. For this reason, it can be stated that while in the first case (demand substitution) there is a redefinition in the market, in the latter (supply substitution) there is simply a readjustment.[23] The determination of the volume to be included in supply substitution involves complex matters such as whether to include idle capacity, the issue of redirecting products in the international market, etc., which should be analyzed separately for the products market and the geographic market. For this reason, this matter will be analyzed in the following topics.

The products market
According to standard neoclassical theory, to proceed with the definition of the market it is necessary first to establish the existence of demand and supply substitutes. Here, once more, neoclassical definitions are not much more than a theoretical exercise, its explanatory power of the real world remaining very limited.

Demand substitutes There are some points that must be considered in the analysis of demand substitution. The same type of data may indicate completely different situations of market power, depending upon the cost consumers will confront in the event they wish to substitute the product. Products that for consumers have the exact same use may not be replaceable if the price differential between them is significant. They may be replaceable, provided that the price differential corresponds exactly to the difference in quality attributed to them by consumers (that is, the difference in utility between both products).

There may also be obstacles of a different variety, such as extraordinary costs to be incurred in the case of substitution. A typical example in which these costs are directly taken into consideration as a form of evaluating market power is the *lock in*. The typical case of lock in is the market for maintenance of certain equipment. The manufacturer of the equipment enjoys substantial

---

[23] The terminology is by R. Pitofsky, 'New Definitions of the Relevant Market and the Assault on Antitrust', cit., p. 1842, *et seq.*

advantage if, as frequently is the case, it wishes to supply maintenance and replacement of parts for the product. The manufacturer may charge monopolistic prices in the market for replacement parts (and, in the market for maintenance services, tie the supply of parts to maintenance services) even if the market for new equipment is competitive.[24] This is because, in relation to consumers that have already purchased equipment, the manufacturer is monopolistic in the supply of maintenance services and replacement parts (aftermarket).

The equipment manufacturer's power in the parts market and maintenance service market derives directly from the costs of substituting the product (in this case, replacement parts and/or maintenance services) for the consumer. These costs would be the value of the new equipment: to have access to competitors in the maintenance and replacement parts market, the consumer would have to buy new equipment.[25]

The lock in is an extreme case of limiting the consumer's freedom in a market through events and structures existing in another market. There are other cases in which limits upon the consumer's freedom of choice, even if egregious, cannot be ignored. A typical example is the influence exercised by a distribution network on the possibilities for replacing the products distributed. For example, the U.S. Supreme Court ruled that vegetables sold in supermarkets are a separate market from the markets for vegetables sold in warehouses, emporiums, or even by traders exclusively selling vegetables. The substitution costs, in this case, were subjective and based upon the fact that only supermarkets answer to the generic periodic needs of consumers. The

---

[24]   For Brazilian case law, see Merger No. 08012.007124/2008-54, Applied Biosystems Inc. and Invitrogen Corporation, judged on August 13, 2009.

[25]   This matter was discussed in depth by the U.S. Supreme Court in *Eastman Kodak Company v. Image Technical Services Inc.*, 112 S. Ct. 2072 (1992). The discussion addressed Kodak's power in the market for maintenance for Kodak products. In this case, as well as lock in, there was also a tying arrangement for replacement parts and maintenance services. The decision of the Supreme Court noted that there was market power (which is fundamental in the U.S. system for finding a violation of Section II of the Sherman Act – illegal market monopolization based upon insurmountable product substitution costs owing to the lock in). This decision triggered great controversy among American theorists, above all among scholars who believe that the presence of competition in the products market is an element that is sufficient to induce competition in the replacement parts market. According to these scholars, the well-informed consumer would naturally choose a product by taking into consideration the costs of the secondary market (the replacement parts market) in which there is monopoly. The problem with this position is the assumption that the consumer has complete information and bargaining power about conditions in the secondary market (replacement parts) at the moment the product is purchased, which fails to comport with reality.

majority of supermarket consumers are people who shop in one instance and who have neither the time nor the inclination to buy individual items of immediate need through specialized sellers. The substitution costs of the product (vegetables sold in supermarkets) are, therefore, excessively high for these consumers (meaning leisure time or work time lost).[26]

In fact, this case is nothing more than a differentiated application of the concept of *cluster market*.[27] A cluster market is a grouping of products that, because they are grouped, are more attractive to the consumer. In the case described above (the consumer's preference for joint purchases via supermarkets), it was deduced that supermarket vegetables were a 'different' product from vegetables sold in specialized shops, precisely because a supermarket allows for the purchase of a variety of other food products.

Note, however, that this is not the most common application of the concept. The notion of cluster markets comes from the need to aggregate and not disaggregate markets. In effect, the main consequence of the characterization of a market as a cluster is to consider the basket of products as a single product. The definition of the market should then encompass all of the products. In the case of concentrations, the definition may therefore deem two companies producing or supplying services that are apparently different as members of the same market. The definition of a market as 'clustered' would then lead to the conclusion of less market power, while in the previous case, as was seen, the conclusion was the opposite. Thus, in the case of concentrations, the greater the market power, the smaller the relevant market, and vice versa.

Supply substitutes The assumption of rationality is applied more fairly to manufacturers than to consumers. While the behavior of consumers is directed by a series of external elements (many of which result from market structuring itself, as in the case of lock in) and subjective components (e.g., the convenience of a distribution chain) that cannot be even remotely captured by the rationality paradigm, manufacturer decisions are predominantly influenced by a constant standard – the search for profits. Thus, on the one hand, past data on supply substitution is much more credible in the sense that the assumption of behavior repetition is credible. On the other hand, for the same reasons described above, more precise conclusions about the future behavior of economic agents can be drawn from structural analysis.

The consequence of this is to ensure that the most relevant issue for supply substitution analysis is not proof of substitution, but the determination of the

---

[26] *California v. American Stores Co.*, 495 U.S. 271 (1990).

[27] See generally I. Ayres, 'Rationalizing Antitrust Cluster Markets', in *Yale Law Journal*, 95, 1985; A. Gavil, W. Kovacic and J. Baker, *Antitrust Law in Perspective: Cases, Concepts and Problems in Competition Policy*, 2008, pp. 498–9.

amount that we may assume will be redirected for the manufacture of the product. There are three basic means for determining the amount of substitute production to be included in the definition of the market. The first is to include the total capacity of all manufacturers producing the good to be substituted (assuming it is possible to demonstrate, based on the criteria listed earlier, that such substitution is possible and probable). In a second alternative, it could be the inclusion of only the capacity of certain companies or only a portion of total capacity that could be reasonably deemed subject to redirection. The third alternative is to not include any part of the production or production capacity of manufacturers of the product to be substituted, but to analyze the results of the market definition in relation to the relative feasibility of market entry.

In practice, there is a preference for the first method.[28] The economic reasoning used by its adherents is quite simple: the economic agent will be willing to redirect its entire production, should this prove more profitable than its current production. This will happen each time that the price charged for the new product is greater than the price of the substituted product plus substitution costs. For members of the Chicago School,[29] however, the simple theoretical possibility is not enough. It has to be shown that production substitution has effectively taken place owing to a price increase, even if at a minimum level.

Yet, this is not the most coherent position. One cannot assume that a company would redirect in a lasting manner most or all of its production capacity to a new product, leaving its original customers unattended. If it did, and assuming that it has some market power in its original market, prices would immediately increase, which would give consumers an incentive to go back immediately. But much more convincing than this economic argument, which in any case assumes a certain market power of the company in the original market, are the reasons suggested by business logic. A place in the market obviously has value (including good will). To the economic agent's transference cost should be added the opportunity cost, which includes losing market position and consequently the loss of current and future profitability.

Not by chance, therefore, do the U.S. Department of Justice's Merger Guidelines take a fairly cautious position in relation to this issue. They state that, to determine if a party is a participant in the market, the factors to be

---

[28]   See P. Areeda, J. Solow and H. Hovenkamp, *Antitrust Law*, v. II A, cit., pp. 256–7; W. Landes and R. Posner, 'Market Power in Antitrust Cases', cit., p. 963.

[29]   For recent discussion on recent analysis of the Chicago School, see R. Pitofsky (ed.), *How the Chicago School Overshot the Mark: The Effect of Conservative Economic Analysis on U.S. Antitrust*, 2008; and E. Ehaulge, 'Harvard, Not Chicago: Which Antitrust School Drives Recent Supreme Court Decisions?', in *Competition Policy International*, 3(2), 2007.

considered are 'the costs of substitution or extension relative to the profitability of sales at the elevated price, and whether the firm's capacity is elsewhere committed or elsewhere so profitably employed that such capacity likely would not be available to respond to an increase in price in the market' (Section 1.321). The option is clear for the second method. There is a belief in the possibility of determining, even if approximately, the production volume to be effectively redirected to the market.

Actually, both hypotheses seem over-simplified and seem to exaggerate the explanatory power of the economic rationality paradigm. In fact, the construction of a coherent system requires a prior distinction between productive capacity in use and idle capacity. The first, as we have seen, is the most difficult to be redirected, owing to the resulting costs (and, above all, the opportunity cost). In relation to the productive capacity in use, so strong is the adherence of the market agent to its market that, in a complete absence of quantitative and price data that allow a less approximate definition of the amount to be included, the best method to determine the production quantity to be included in the definition of the market seems to be the last of the three methods discussed above (specifically, to not include any part of the production or production capacity of manufacturers of the product to be substituted, but to analyze the results of the market definition in relation to the relative feasibility of market entry). The results must therefore be analyzed only in light of the possibility of entry into the market. This should be done not only starting from the criteria described herein (all related to those elements that will determine whether a manufacturer is disposed to transfer its production), but also in relation to the existing barriers to entry into the new market (both structural and those resulting from the behavior of the agent that hypothetically has market power). The existence of barriers to entry is one of the key elements for identification of market dominance.

The treatment of idle capacity should be different. In relation to this, one can make the exact opposite assumption, to wit, in the absence of an explicit demonstration of barriers to entry,[30] it is convenient to simply include the entire idle capacity in the relevant market. Captive capacity should also be considered; in words, production that is used as raw material, in a certain vertically integrated business structure, but that can also be redirected to a new market should conditions in that new market become attractive. Here, the problems are clearly very similar to the ones seen previously in relation to redirecting capacity to use. The main difference is that the comparison should

---

[30]   These barriers may consist of the costs of putting this capacity to use. For this reason, the 1992 Horizontal Merger Guidelines admit the consideration of idle capacity as long as it is not 'significantly more costly to operate than capacity currently in use' (Section 2.22.).

only be the loss in profitability in trading the final product made by the vertically integrated group. This is because either the final product should stop being produced owing to the lack of raw materials, or the raw materials should be bought at a price hypothetically higher than the costs of internal production. There will therefore not be a greater loss in the form of loss of market share and good will. In this way, the situation is closer to the analysis of idle capacity than capacity in use.

The geographic market

The geographic dimension is the most important in defining the market. It is what usually allows the expansion of the market to the point of de-characterizing the presence of market power, even in the presence of high concentration levels in the original market. In addition, it is in the geographic aspects of market definition that many effects of the critical vision of standard marginalist concepts of antitrust law can be seen.

The first problem regarding the geographic element is in the greater difficulty of distinguishing between supply and demand substitution levels. In the definition of the products market, this differentiation is clear, as there is a material change that is physically measurable in the production and consumption of the goods in the market. In the definition of geographic market, however, this change is much less evident as there is simply change of regions, to wit, manufacturers begin supplying and/or consumers begin buying in a new region. As the market is exactly the point in which these two elements meet, the question arises: how do we determine which of the agents moved?

The answer is not difficult in the two extreme cases: on the one hand, where the manufacturer builds a new factory in the region at issue, which distinctly indicates supply substitution, and on the other hand, where the consumer moves to a new region in order to buy the subject product, which indicates demand substitution. In most cases, however, this is not what occurs. Normally, there is only the installation of a distribution network in the region at issue, which begins selling the products made by the manufacturer. It is important to notice that the establishment of an independent distribution network is attributed to the market, not to the manufacturers. The factors that would hence allow a distinction in the same line of products' market definition are not present.

The difficulty in distinguishing these situations creates a complex problem from the economic-judicial point of view: on the one hand, the presence of consumers suggests less care in relation to the inclusion of the entire market. From the point of view of demand substitution, there is no reason to assume that consumers would limit their desires to only one part of the new region's production. On the other hand, if the situation is analyzed as a matter of supply substitution, all of the quantitative issues faced in this type of case come to the surface. In addition, there is no denying that the need for a distribution network, especially when organized and established by the manufacturer, takes the characteristics of supply substitution.

Not coincidently, it is in the definition of geographic market that can be found the greatest, most relevant controversies among scholars in relation to the amount of 'external' production to be included. In it, there are a jumble of problems typically related to demand substitution, such as analysis of consumer preference and the general concern with whether it is necessary to include the new market, with problems typical of supply substitution, like transportation costs and the general concern with the question of the amount of 'external' production that should be included in the estimate of the relevant market.

General considerations The new wave of non-intervention after the last decade of the twentieth century, even in international trade, re-established a connection among the antitrust systems of various countries. The effects of the abolition of trade barriers in the internal antitrust systems of each country must be examined[31,32] from a critical perspective. The greatest impact is,

---

[31]   For relevant Brazilian cases dealing with the connection between the international market and internal competition see:
(i) Merger No. 08012.001885/2007-11, Owens Corning and Saint Gobain, judged on July 23, 2008, CADE disapproved the merger and recommended to the Brazilian Foreign Trade Chamber (CAMEX) to reduce the external common tariff (TEC) on continuous filament mat (CFM) from 12% to 2%;
(ii) Merger No. 08012.001637/2007-71, Hindalco Industries Ltd. and Novelis Inc., judged on August 9, 2007, CADE approved the merger and recommended to CAMEX to reduce the import tariff on aluminum sheets;
(iii) Merger No. 08012.009843/2005-67, Cimento Rio Branco S.A. and Camargo Corrêa Alimentos S.A., judged on April 11, 2007, CADE constrained a supply agreement of white cement and recommended to CAMEX to reduce the external common tariff from 4.4% to 0%;
(iv) Merger No. 08012.010195/2004-19, Suzano Bahia Papel e Celulose S.A. and Ripasa S.A. Papel e Celulose, and Merger No. 08012.010192/2004-77, Votorantim Celulose e Papel S.A. and Ripasa S.A. Papel e Celulose, judged on August 8, 2007, CADE celebrated a Performance Commitment Agreement and recommended to CAMEX to reduce the import tariff on cut size paper;
(v) Merger No. 08012.007861/2001-81, Novo Nordisk Holding do Brasil Ltda. (NN Brasil) and Biopart Ltda. (Biopart), judged on August 6, 2003. The case addressed the operation between NN Brasil and Biopart, whereby the majority of shares of Biobrás S.A., which previously belonged to Biopart and their stockholders, became the property of NN Brasil. As a result of the operation, the company Biomm S.A. was set up, spun off from Biobrás, which continued to hold the North American patent for the process of production of insulin crystals by recombinant-DNA technique carried out by means of bacteria. It is noteworthy that, in view of the existence of a non-competition clause set out in Biobrás's acquisition contract, Biomm could only operate in the

undoubtedly, in the definition of market. The importance and the effect of a market definition that includes international production are evident: the possibility of configuring market power in the internal market is eliminated or tremendously reduced. It is not by chance, therefore, that it is precisely through the definition of market that, in practice, the conservative idea of antitrust law, emphatically defended by the neoclassic Chicago School, finally prevails.

The most traditional proponent of the ideas of the Chicago School as applied to the definition of market is Richard Posner. His theory is known as *diversion approach* and its main characteristic is the absolutely undifferentiated treatment of national and foreign manufacturers. Therefore, the theory is applied, according to its creator, to both the definition of the internal market and to the definition of the international market.[33]

According to Posner, if a distant manufacturer makes sales in the local market, its entire production must be included in the definition of the market. This is because the existence of sales, even if in reduced quantity, shows that the economic agent is capable of surpassing any possible barriers in the local market. Thus, it is reasonable to assume that the manufacturer, acting rationally, is capable of redirecting its entire production to the new market, as long as the price is more attractive than in its home market.[34] Posner goes on to add

---

insulin market three years after the operation had been carried out. CADE entered into an Agreement of Preservation of Reversibility of Operation to safeguard the conditions of the relevant market so as to avoid irreversible damage occurring before the final decision. In the end, the operation was approved provided that the non-competition clause stipulated by the parties was excluded. Moreover, CADE recommended that the Brazilian Department of Commercial Defense (DECOM) should review the Price Agreement signed with Eli Lilly. As a result of the recommendation made by CADE, the Council of Ministers of the Foreign Trade Chamber, in a meeting held on March 3, 2005, decided to suspend, for one year, the Price Agreement on imports from the United States of America and from France signed with Eli Lilly.

[32] Pursuant to CADE Case Law Statement No. 01 (*stare decisis*), one should consider not only the gross turnover of the notified participants, but also that of their economic group and that posted exclusively within the Brazilian territory (published in the Official Gazette of the Federal Executive, on October 18, 2005).

[33] For current discussion on this issue, K. McMahon, 'Developing Countries and International Competition Law and Policy', in J. Faundez and C. Tan (eds), *International Law, Economic Globalization and Development*, 2010; M. Gal, 'Regional Competition Law Agreements: An Important Step for Antitrust Enforcement', 2009; J. Terhechte, 'International Competition Enforcement Law Between Cooperation and Convergence: Mapping a New Field for Global Administrative Law', 2009; A. Ezrachi, 'Merger Control and Cross Border Transactions: A Pragmatic View on Cooperation, Convergence and What's in Between', in P. Marsden, *Handbook of Research in Trans-Atlantic Antitrust*, 2007.

[34] See W. Landes and R. Posner, 'Market Power in Antitrust Cases', cit., p. 963.

two requirements so that the unlimited redirection of production can be assumed: (a) that market access is lasting and not caused by special and transitory market conditions; (b) that the foreign manufacturer is capable of reaching that specific consumer and not another consumer situated in a distant region of the country.

This last point, motivated by Posner's concern with the differing penetration of Asian products on the East and West Coasts of the United States, brings to light a very important aspect of the problem of defining the geographic market, which can be formulated as follows: including foreign manufacturers' production in the definition does not assume nor imply the inclusion of the entire national market in the 'relevant market'. All it takes for the exclusion of such domestic manufacturers and inclusion of international manufacturers to become obligatory is for interregional transportation barriers to be greater than international barriers and large enough to make the sales of domestic regional manufacturers unfeasible.

This situation is not theoretical, but very real, above all in countries occupying large geographic areas: where costs of land transportation (which a manufacturer in a rural region, for example, is obliged to use) are much greater than that of maritime transportation, many times it is preferable to import a product rather than buy it domestically. In the same way and for the same reason, in the definition of geographic market for deeply inland regions, neither products manufactured in coastal regions nor products imported by coastal regions from abroad can be included.

Posner's conservative theory was adopted by the U.S. Department of Justice as reflected in the Merger Guidelines. Both the 1984 and the 1992 editions demonstrate a rather extensive definition of geographic market and were inspired by the conservative philosophy of the Republican era, which reflected an increasing concern about the loss of competitiveness of American industry and the influx of Asian products into the U.S. market. At the very beginning of the Guidelines, it is expressly stated that the definition of market is applied to both national and foreign companies (see Section 1). Furthermore, the directives follow the all or nothing approach typical of Posner's analysis, pursuant to which, when defining geographic market, either foreign production is entirely included or entirely excluded. Once it is proved that imports are in fact coming in, even in small quantities, the entire foreign production is included.[35]

---

[35]   For a further discussion on this issue, see J. Baker and C. Shapiro, 'Reinvigorating Horizontal Merger Enforcement', in R. Pitofsky (ed.), *How the Chicago School Overshot the Mark: The Effect of Conservative Economic Analysis on U.S. Antitrust*, cit., pp. 235–88.

Criticism of Posner's approach has two very different aspects. First, in relation to the internal market, its conclusions need refinements and adjustments due to superficial consideration given to the informational asymmetrics. The biggest problems of the theory regard however the international market. Extending this approach to the international market is not acceptable, however, owing to the problem of strong overestimation of the expansion of imports into the internal market. These issues are treated below.

The international market   Normally the diversion approach general rule applied for the definition of the internal market can be formulated in the following way: the presence of substantial sales of foreign products allows for the total inclusion of its production, unless some of the economic barriers discussed above (basically, transportation costs, support and services costs and consumer preference) are clearly identifiable. The assumption, therefore, is that the occurrence of sales indicates free and unlimited entry into the market, provided that price increases occur in that region.[36]

This assumption must be formulated in the inverse way for the international market. There are certain peculiarities in foreign trade that must be considered. First, it is important to emphasize that a manufacturer's commitment to its domestic market, already mentioned as an obstacle to the application of the diversion approach, has particular application in the international environment. It is absolutely unrealistic to imagine that a manufacturer would completely abandon its domestic market, losing market position, in order to give priority to a foreign market, especially when the manufacturer knows it will be subject to uncertainties related to changes to the international political-economic environment.

It is such changes to the international politico-economic environment that represent the greatest obstacle to the acceptance of conservative theory. They result from the existence of different sovereign states, all with their respective sovereign powers, and that pursue varied economic objectives. State sovereignty influences foreign trade in two ways. First, it is not realistic to assume that competitive conditions are equal for businesses situated in regions featuring entirely different macroeconomic policies and structural situations.

---

[36]   For mergers celebrated out of Brazil that took this discussion into consideration analyzed by CADE, see Mergers No. 08012.006823/2009-68, judged on October 7, 2009; No. 08012.001312/2008-79, judged on March 4, 2009; No. 08012.010920/2007-93, judged on July 23, 2008; No. 08012.002156/2008-63, judged on May 7, 2008; No. 08012.010006/2007-42, judged on January 20, 2008; No. 08012.010392/2007-72, judged on December 12, 2007; No. 08012.001504/2007-02, judged on September 29, 2007; No. 08012.011077/2006-81, judged on February 27, 2007; No. 08012.001253/2006-77, judged on July 26, 2006.

Currency exchange is a good example. A persistent difference in inflation rates between two countries, directly influencing the exchange rate between two currencies, can suddenly make products from the country with higher inflation extremely competitive in the other country. The opposite is also true: a sudden drop in the inflation rate in one country can lead to an invasion of products from a foreign country with higher inflation. These macroeconomic differences among countries, frequent in the global scenario and inherent to the existence of multiple sovereign powers, make forecasts about imports based on marginal assumptions extremely risky.

For this reason, the coordination of macroeconomic policies is deemed a fundamental condition for the success of common markets. Without such coordination, it is not possible to fully establish an economic community, as competitive conditions remain unequal. This is exactly what is stated in the first article, third part, of the Treaty of Asunción signed by Argentina, Brazil, Paraguay and Uruguay for the establishment of the 'Mercosur' common market.[37] The coordination of macroeconomic and sector policies is mentioned as a fundamental instrument for the establishment of equal competitive conditions (see the section on the common market, below).

The existence of sovereign states has a second effect on economic relations, specifically, the ability of a state to establish restrictions on imports and exports. It is not realistic to believe that manufacturers can export without limitation to another country without any reaction by the importing country.[38] Action by the importing country can take two distinct forms. One is to exercise pressure on the government of the exporting country to establish export quotas or other restrictions on exports – this is what happened in Japan in the early 1990s with automobiles in response to pressure by the U.S. government.[39] The importing country can also increase import tariffs. This happened when, as a result of significant increases in Brazilian exports, the Argentine government was able to place on the list of exceptions to the Treaty of Asunción a series of products that were experiencing great pressure from Brazilian exports.

---

[37] Venezuela is a state party in the process of accession in Mercosur. On December 8, 2005, the Protocol of Venezuela Accession was signed, but it is not in force yet. On December 15, 2009, the Brazilian Full Senate finally approved, by 35 votes to 27, the Protocol of Venezuela Accession (PDS 430/08).

[38] Notwithstanding great international efforts to establish free trade regions, it is well known that most countries enter into them only when there are no economic and/or internal political obstacles (e.g., the need to protect a specific industry). The recent difficulties with WTO negotiations are a proof of such problems.

[39] See R. Pitofsky, 'New Definitions of the Relevant Market and the Assault on Antitrust', cit., p. 1858.

These observations are closely associated with the political perspective of market power. The influence of private interests on the state increases along-side market power. The political perspective of market power is a phenomenon that can be observed historically, which leads to the following conclusion: the greater the economic power concentration in the domestic market, the less likely it becomes that pressure to increase imports will undermine that power, as it becomes more likely that powerful domestic economic interests will persuade the national government to increase import tariffs in order to protect domestic manufacturers.

Notwithstanding the foregoing, one cannot disregard the importance of international competition to markets that are exposed to it. The decline in inflation in Brazil, for instance, derived, amongst other factors, from significant foreign imports competing with domestic products subsequent to reductions in tariffs. This confirms the importance of international competition to the establishment of closer to market conditions.

The purpose of this topic is therefore just to show the risks of counting on *substantial increases* in import levels owing to price changes. We hope to have shown that it is clearly exaggerated to exclude the entire production of foreign exporters. The alternatives are to consider only the current level of exports or, if not, to define a certain level of increase. Both alternatives are arbitrary and imprecise – the issue is to choose the one that is less arbitrary and more precise.

The solution seems simple with due regard to what was stated above. It is more realistic to assume an increase in imports exactly in the same proportion to historical levels that were attributable to previous price increases. In addition, the rate at which prices have been increasing should be preserved. This assumption, which intentionally conflicts with the results of an exclusively economic analysis, is justified by political and situational variables present in the international scenario and capable of counterbalancing, hypothetically in the same proportions, economically determinative factors. This denies the Posnerian assumption that there is an inversion point at which price becomes attractive to the point of attracting unlimited imports. According to the model suggested here, it is exactly at that point that the political pressure to establish trade barriers is so great that it ends up counterbalancing any economic pressure. The assumption, therefore, is that there is constant evolution.

The common market   The existence of an economic community comprised of countries strongly influences antitrust law. Its influence on the definition of the market deserves attention.

The first issue to be addressed concerns the position that should be attributed to the member countries of a common market. Further to the above analysis, the extent to which foreign production must be included in the definition of relevant domestic market depends upon determining the origin, domestic or foreign (in the sense of being sourced from another country), of a product. But what can be said of an economic community?

Before continuing, two other legal classifications must be distinguished that are not to be confused with the concept of 'economic community' (or common market). These are free trade zones and customs unions. Free trade zones are characterized by the abolition of national customs barriers for the circulation of goods. A customs union adds to a free trade zone a common external tariff. An example of both is Mercosur, which until 1994 was merely a free trade zone, and which, owing to the gradual harmonization of external tariffs mandated by the VI Reunion of the Mercosur Group, is increasingly closer to a customs union.[40]

An economic community, on the other hand, comprises a common economic space featuring the abolition of all restrictions, *of customs or otherwise*, on the circulation of goods. In order to achieve this goal, equal competitive conditions are imposed on all economic agents in member countries. It is not enough, however, to merely create through treaties identical competitive conditions or declare the intention to create them. Material conditions assuring equal competitive conditions must be established. It can be said that there are two fundamental conditions: (a) the convergence of macroeconomic policies of member nations; and (b) the transference of government decision making to community organizations, especially those related to domestic and foreign customs policies.

Evaluated under these criteria, the flow of goods between countries inhabiting a free trade zone and customs union is not qualitatively different from trade occurring between independent countries not related by any political or economic bond. In effect, the disparity and volatility of macroeconomic policies and the possibility of establishing barriers to imports and exports of products remain the two characteristics of sovereignty that present the greatest barriers to international trade. It could be argued that this last possibility does not exist, as a free trade zone and customs union should, at least theoretically, abolish all internal customs barriers. In reality, however, these barriers can be and are frequently re-established with pressure from member states whenever it seems expedient. This is because in many instances, as has been the case with Mercosur, community organizations comprise government representatives who lack independence from the member states. Instead of preventing member states from enacting measures that favor parochial interests at the

---

[40]   See J. Samtleben and C. Salomão Filho, 'O mercado comum sul-americano-Uma análise jurídica do Mercosul', in J. Grandino Rodas, *Contratos Internacionais*, 1995, p. 276, *et seq.*

expense of the economic community interests, such economic community institutions can serve to institutionalize political pressure from member states on their partners to establish quotas or accept new customs barriers.

This is precisely what has happened in Mercosur. Owing to the extremely volatile macroeconomic policies of certain member states, invasions of the Argentine market by Brazilian products, and vice versa, are not unusual. Integrating the markets of these countries has been possible only through the frequent reintroduction of customs restrictions by consensual decision.[41]

More stable trade relations that allow for the perfect assimilation of community structures into domestic markets exist only when member states are willing to relinquish sovereignty to independent community organizations to decide economic matters relating to antitrust law. Note that, even so, the existence of harmonized macroeconomic policies must be monitored in order to ensure the free circulation of goods in the future. Without it, migratory flows of products may be so high that there will be risks not only to competition, but also to the political existence of the community itself.

According to these criteria, it can be said that only *after* the execution of the Maastricht Treaty, did the E.E.C. (now the E.U.) become a real economic community featuring a free flow of goods within a community geographic market pursuant to the same rules that govern the flow of goods in a domestic market. In contrast, Mercosur is at best an incomplete customs union. Exports from other member states should therefore be treated, for the application of national antitrust law, according to the same criteria applicable to foreign countries, to wit, assuming the presence of a member country exporter in the domestic market of another member country, one must assume a constant increase in imports as a result of future price increases, as it is not possible to simply include the exporter's global sales in the whole of Mercosur.

It is important to make clear that the above analysis refers exclusively to the definition of market for purposes of applying domestic antitrust law. The problem is different for the application of 'community antitrust law', which is subject to different principles founded on different objectives. One of the main objectives of community antitrust law is to serve as a driving force for the creation of a common economic space. The existence of *equal conditions* for competition is an element that ensures the existence of a real freedom and not merely a formal freedom to circulate goods and capital goods.

For this reason, it is not possible to apply the definition of market in the neoclassic way to community antitrust law. If the first concern is with the

---

[41]   For more on the politics and close relationships between Mercosur community organizations and the governments of the member states, see J. Samtleben and C. Salomão Filho, 'O mercado comum sul-americano', cit., p. 248, *et seq.*

effective existence of conditions ensuring equal competition and not with the power to increase prices, the relevant market must be measured based upon whether conditions ensuring equal competition exist and not upon a hypothetical price increase. It is not surprising, therefore, that the definition of geographic market given by the Court of Justice of the European Community in the case of *United Brands v. Commission*, that is, the region where 'the conditions of competition are sufficiently homogeneous for the effect of the economic power of the undertaking to be evaluated',[42] has been adopted and refined by the E.U. Council Regulation governing the merger control.[43]

As this is the concept of relevant geographic market,[44] obviously one of the most important practical criteria for defining 'market' is the existence of barriers to entry of competitors (see below), both objective (for example, price differences, need for capital, etc.) and subjective (consumer preferences).

Attributing such significance to barriers to entry has an important consequence. The inclusion of foreign production in the relevant market becomes much more difficult, especially production outside of the community. The existence of imports, even in significant volume, is not enough to include the entire worldwide production in the relevant market where there are barriers, at least in theory, to the entry of non-community products. It is not surprising, therefore, that throughout the history of concentration control of the Commission of the European Communities, there has been only one case in which the relevant market was defined as the world market.[45]

---

[42] *United Brands vs. Commission*, Case No. 27/76, decision of February 14, 1978, in *ECR*, (1978), p. 207.

[43] Article 9, No. 7 of Regulation No. 4064/89, of December 21, 1989, provides: 'the geographical reference market shall consist of the area in which the undertakings concerned are involved in the supply of products and services, in which the conditions of competition are sufficiently homogeneous and which can be distinguished from neighboring areas because, in particular, conditions of competition are appreciably different in those areas. This assessment should take account in particular of the nature and characteristics of the products or services concerned, of the existence of entry barriers or of consumer preferences, of appreciable differences of the undertakings' market shares between neighboring areas or of substantial price differences.'

[44] For a discussion on the E.U. related to market definition, see *Volvo/Scania*, Case No COMP/M.1672, Commission Decision of March 15, 2000, available at http://ec.europa.eu/comm/competition/mergers/cases/decisions/m1672_en.pdf, *Pirelli/ BICC*, Case No COMP/M.1882, Commission decision of July 19, 2000, available at http://ec.europa.eu/comm/competition/mergers/cases/decisions/ m1882_en.pdf, *Alcatel/AEG Kabel*, Case No IV/M.165, Commission Decision of December 18, 1991, available at http://ec.europa.eu/comm/ competition/mergers/cases/decisions/ m165_en.pdf.

[45] See P. Bos, J. Stuyck and P. Wyntick, *Concentration Control in the European Economic Community*, 1992, p. 222. The decision quoted is *Aérospatiale – Alenia De Havilland* (Case IV/ M.053), October 2, 1991, in which 'the world market excluding

Such a conclusion has quite an undesirable consequence. In the event that the national legislation of a member country adopts Posner's market definition, there will again be tension between the tendency to internationalize antitrust concerns and the formation of common markets. Obviously, this tension has to be resolved in order to prevent the risk of creating an absolutely paradoxical system in which the same act of concentration or the same breach premised upon a finding of dominant position could be evaluated upon the basis of completely different criteria depending upon whether the matter is decided by national or community organizations. The even greater paradox of such a system would be that the subject concentration or illegal act, where it affected the entire economic community, would be decided according to more rigorous criteria than if it affected a national market even if the amount of concentration is greater in the national market than in the community market.

Making the two positions compatible seems, however, possible. Barriers to entry must be considered at the moment the determination is made as to *how much* of the foreign production should be included in the market, in the way just described. Barriers to entry are not a reason to discuss whether such production should be included. To adopt an extreme ordo-liberal vision, disregarding concrete data about the existence of imports and simply excluding the whole of foreign production because barriers to entry are identified, would be to take the same all or nothing approach that is so criticized in Posner's theory.

Actually, the existence of a common market or the intention of forming such a market constitutes a great legal obstacle to the use of neoclassic theory for the definition of geographic market (in its Posner version) where an inter national market is at issue. This implies the application of a theory such as the one adopted here, which, without disregarding concrete data about the existence of imports, allows a realistic analysis of the participation of the external market in the future. The common market makes imperative as a matter of law attenuations to the Posner theory described above. The only difference is that there the foundation is merely an economic rationale, while here the reason is

China and Eastern Europe' was deemed relevant. In another case that was discussed (*Aérospatiale/MBB* – Case IV/m. 053, decision of October 2, 1991), it was stated that 'the civil helicopter is from an economic point of view competition from a world market', thus concluding, in very general terms, that external competition should be taken into consideration in determining the market. It was not decided, however, if the geographic market was the world market or not. For more information, see G. Serdarevic and P. Teplý, 'Efficiency of EU Merger Control in the 1990–2008 Period', 2009; S. P. Kamerbeek, 'Merger Performance and Efficiencies in Horizontal Merger Policy in the US and the EU', October 2009, available at mpra.ub.uni-muenchen.de/18064/; and A. Christiansen, 'The Reform of EU Merger Control: Fundamental Reversal or Mere Refinement?', 2006, available at http://ssrn.com/abstract=898845.

legal. The express statement found in the first article of the Asunción Treaty renders legal what was previously an interpretation based upon an economic reasoning.

For this conclusion, however, it is not necessary for the common market to be perfectly formed. Unlike the analyses of the internal geographic markets of the countries joining the community, when dealing with a competition issue in the community context, the current state of affairs should not be observed, but rather the objectives of the integration process should be. An integration process that seeks the formation of a common market should necessarily feature in its competition rules a centrifugal force. It is thus sufficient to declare, as is the case with Mercosur, the objective of eliminating all customs and non-customs restrictions affecting the circulation of goods and production factors (Article 1) in order to make obligatory the adoption of the aforementioned definition of geographic market.

Participation in the relevant market as identification criteria

The criteria discussed above allow for the relevant market for goods and services to be defined. Once the market is defined, it is possible to apply to it a certain percentage of market share that, once attained by the economic agent, automatically subjects such agent to the supervision of the antitrust agencies.

The discussion about the percentage to be used is not very relevant. This is especially the case here because the point is to define an identification criterion, that is, to determine what type of economic structure should be subject to control and not whether a certain structure is legal. It is important to notice that, in any event, even when market participation is used as a criterion for the application of sanctions, the only existing consensus among economists is that it is impossible to define with precision the level of participation to be used.

As it is an identification criterion, the most important element seems to be the (legal-political) interest to subject the greatest number of structures to control.

The lack of a scholarly foundation and consequent predominance of political motives on the determination of percentages is reflected in national legislation. Proof of the foregoing is the different criteria used in different laws. This is the case with Brazilian law, which first set 30 per cent of the market as the standard pursuant to Law No. 8,884 (Art. 20, 3rd Section, and Art. 54, 3rd Section), only to reduce the percentage to 20 per cent via provisional measures. This lower percentage was definitively enacted into Brazil's competition law pursuant to Law No. 9,069, Art. 78, of June 30, 1995, and Law No. 10,149, Art. 1, of December 21, 2000.

Reviewed in comparative terms from a strictly numerical perspective, the percentage adopted appears reasonable. The problem is that the discussion about the requisite numerical percentage of market share, being merely arbitrary and necessarily inconclusive, masks the real problems to be resolved in order to determine market share in the relevant market. The first problem is related to the objective of the normative rule that requires a definition of market share. The second problem relates to the ways in which market power is revealed, that is, the different kinds of structures in which market power is manifested.

As to the objective of the norm, there must be a differentiation between the criteria used to identify structures and those used to classify conduct. Everything that was stated above is applied only to cases in which market power is merely one element of the criteria examined in order to determine which behavior must be subject to control. When used as a criterion to evaluate conduct, the rationale should be completely different. In such cases, adopting a fixed percentage is incorrect because, as we will see, market power, when used to assess conduct (especially abuse of a dominant position), is basically a criterion for measuring the efficacy of such conduct. There are certain types of behavior that, when undertaken by agents having no market power, have no effect on the consumer and the market in general. They cannot, therefore, be considered illegal. What happens is that the effectiveness of a given behavior depends a great deal upon the structure of each market. The criteria used for its evaluation must, therefore, be variable. Thus, even if the criteria are based exclusively on a percentage of the relevant market, they should have a certain flexibility that allows them to be adapted to every specific market structure.

Therefore, merely defining the objective of the legal provision that uses the concept of market power is insufficient. Its form of identification remains unconvincing without verification of its various structures. A monopoly is very different from an oligopoly in its very essence. In addition, the risks represented by each to the market are very different. This need for differentiation is acknowledged in other systems. German legislation uses differentiated numerical criteria to identify monopolies and oligopolies (the former are more rigorous than the latter). The U.S. system, on the other hand, uses the HHI Index as identification criteria in potentially harmful situations – the advantage of this system is that it evaluates the market as a whole, not just those market participants that are part of the concentration.

These factors emphasize the need to not only define and measure the market, but also to analyze its structure in order to correctly identify situations in which there is real market power. It is not enough, therefore, to identify the degree of market power required to trigger control under the law. It is important to characterize the specific form in which such behavior is manifested.

The concentration of information as identification criteria

The need to understand not only participation in the market, but mainly the structures of market power highlights another important shortcoming of the neoclassical theory, that is its failure to acknowledge that concentrated information about a market is a direct source of market power, even if high percentages of market share are not present. As we have seen, the natural dispersion of information tends to be used in asymmetrical form by market agents. When capable of restricting consumer choices, these agents capture information. Possessing an unequal – and bigger – share of market information ensures great power to its holders.

This power is manifested in many ways and not only through scarcity, the typical consequence of traditional neoclassic analysis. In fact, as was shown by Akerloff, in circumstances where information is lacking, scarcity can be so pronounced that it can lead to the disappearance of the market. Consequently, it is very important to study the structures that permit economic agents to capture and concentrate information, as they present a particular risk to consumer choice.

There are two basic types of concentrated information structure in the market that should be of greatest concern, since both directly affect the information: vertically integrated structures; and structures in which power is not concentrated in the hands of one individual or enterprise, but which instead concentrate information about consumption or production standards.

In fact, these structures serve not only to identify market power, but they are themselves organizing structures of market power. For this reason, it seems more logical to approach this subject in the next section.

3.   MARKET POWER STRUCTURES

In the preceding topic, different means of measuring market power have been analyzed and criticized. As we have seen, while the definition of relevant market tries to identify the environment in which market power can be effectively exercised, the definition on its own cannot determine the existence and manifestations of market power. Actually, a legal approach to market power is less interested in the identification of its mathematical intensity and more interested in its forms of manifestation.

A monopolistic structure is not identical to an oligopoly in its nature and/or its effects on the market. Consequently, a correct determination of market power is the one that allows it not only to be measured, but more than anything to be identified and distinguished in its various manifestations. This is precisely the criticism that is made of the criteria that aim only to measure market power, such as the Lerner Index or its substitute, determining market power from supply and demand curves. Such criteria, even if they correspond economically to the definition of market (since analyzing the possibility of supply and demand substitution is nothing more than determining the cross-elasticity of both), legally cannot be confused with the definition. The criteria allow only for measuring market power, but not for identifying the structure and forms by which market power manifests, elements that are fundamental for the application of antitrust law,[46] since different types of behavior are expected from different types of structure. Whereas this fact has been recognized in much of the antitrust traditional literature (see footnote 48), its consequences have not been thoroughly incorporated to the theory.

As we will see, the study of structures require not only to differentiate between monopolies or oligopolies, but to recognize structures, as the vertically integrated ones, normally forgotten by antitrust scholars but extremely important if information concentration problems are to be taken into consideration.

Monopolies

Much of the theory of monopolies has been described earlier in this book. Everything that was said in the treatment of marginal concepts is directly applicable to monopolies. The marginal theory described directly compares 'perfect competition' and 'monopoly'.

What follows, therefore, will be limited to analysis of the main aspects of monopolistic structures that can be harmful to the market and to society, allowing a comparison with oligopolistic structures.

As a threshold matter, it is important to make a reservation to avoid confusion that frequently arises from use of the word 'monopoly'. Monopoly theory is not exclusively applied to entities that hold 100 per cent market share, but also to situations in which one manufacturer has a substantial share of the market (hypothetically, more than 50 percent) and all of its competitors function in such way that none of them has any influence on market prices. These situations are, in general terms, identical in their consequences to a monopoly *stricto sensu*.[47]

There are basically three consequences of monopolies for antitrust law. The first is the *dead-weight loss*. As we have seen in the review of marginal concepts, obtaining a monopolistic position leads to an increase in prices by the monopolist. As a consequence, a certain number of consumers simply stop using the product. Dead-weight loss refers to the loss of use for such consumers owing to their failure to use the subject product, plus the opportunity cost to those consumers who continue to use the product and who pay uncompetitive high prices charged by the monopolist and who thus reduce or

---

[46]   See P. Areeda, J. Solow and H. Hovenkamp, *Antitrust Law*, v. II A, cit, pp. 156–60.

[47]   See P. Areeda and D. Turner, *Antitrust Law*, IV, 1980, p. 910.

eliminate their use of other products.[48] Note that dead-weight loss is a marginal concept. It is closely connected and in fact based on the neoclassic postulates of maximization of global wealth. Therefore, it displays no concern for the distribution of wealth (which will be analyzed separately hereafter). Dead-weight loss is thus formed exclusively of a social loss consisting of an amount of resources that is withheld from consumers and that is also not transferred to the monopolist, such resources simply being wasted.

The second great problem of monopolies consists of the destination for transferred resources. We have seen that there has been increasing concern with the destination of the extra revenue obtained by the monopolist owing to its position in the marketplace. At the rate and proportion at which such revenue grows, the value to the monopolist of its monopolistic position increases inasmuch as the monopolist will then be more willing to use some or all of this additional revenue toward maintaining its monopolistic position.[49] This expenditure is clearly a social loss. It can be assumed that a great part of it is used to capture government organizations, to finance campaigns of politicians involved with protection of the interests of the monopolist or, more generically, to lobby government agencies. In other words, it is precisely the extra income obtained by the monopolist and the objective surplus represented by its privileged position in the market that give a political dimension to market power. The concerns in relation to the political dimension of monopolies have, therefore, an economic justification.

This almost necessary consequence of the existence of monopolies also has the effect of rendering nearly useless the traditional parameter for measuring the existence of market power: the existence of extraordinary profits. The fact that monopolists do not show profits much above those of competitors is many times explained by the high costs of maintaining their monopolistic positions.

The third harmful consequence of a monopoly is the lack of motivation on the part of the monopolist to innovate and improve efficiency. This point is frequently discussed by economists and has no satisfactory solution. At most, the different theories and their philosophical foundations can be described. At issue is the principal argument offered by neoclassic theoreticians in favor of monopolies: the efficiency gained with economies of scale. What the theory

---

48   It can be assumed that substitute products do not have the same utility for the consumer, since, in the definition of market, all possible substitutions have already been taken into consideration and, even so, it can be concluded (always hypothetically) that the agent has a monopolistic position.

49   This consequence of monopolies, neglected for years, has had increasing acknowledgement since its ardent description and justification by R. Posner, *The Law and Economics of Antitrust*, 1976, p. 12, who describes the 'tendency of monopoly profits to be converted into social costs'.

presented here defends is the concomitant consideration of another side to monopolies. It might be true that monopolies may bring efficiencies owing to economies of scale at first, but it is also true that soon after comes a propensity to accommodate, where concerns about competitors disappear owing to the monopolist's privileged position in the market (hence the reason why the disregard for competitors in business planning is considered a proof of monopoly). Obviously, this only occurs if the monopolist is capable of creating barriers to entry for its competitors in a way that maintains its position in the market in spite of its increasing inefficiency. Barriers to entry therefore occupy a special position. Amongst them is included, without a doubt, the political pressure to obtain 'legal barriers to the entry of competitors'.[50]

The last point to be highlighted is the harmful effect of monopolies on the distribution of social income. A monopoly that allows for uncompetitive price increases implies the transfer of income from consumers to the stakeholders of the monopolist. Neoclassic theoreticians, believing in the invisible hand of the market, criticize this position. For them, it is not possible to maintain a monopoly unless a portion of the profits obtained is shared with consumers through a reduction in prices. Again, the response to this criticism is in the difference between the formation of the monopoly and how the monopoly is implemented later. It is conceivable that even a monopolist position reached exclusively through gains in efficiency will begin to be exercised in an inefficient manner. It takes only the existence of barriers to entry for this 'monopolistic accommodation' to take place.

But this is just the traditional discussion, based on Paretian assumption of wealth maximization. The most relevant discussion about wealth distribution is the one that takes into account distributional concerns. Regarding this one, as demonstrated in the first chapter, the negative effects of monopolies are not limited to consumer producer relations but also affect relations with the workforce and with other sectors of the economy, affecting negatively its very dynamics. That is what we called the triple draining effects of monopolies. Actually its conclusions are also applicable to other concentrating structures such as oligopolies or oligopsonies.

---

[50]   See, in the contrary sense, R. Posner, *The Law and Economics of Antitrust*, cit., p. 15, for whom competition may reduce the stimulus to invest in technology and increase efficiency, as the agent knows that any technological advance could, with the imperfections of the patents system, be promptly copied by competitors. Obviously, the argument is not convincing. If anything, this demonstrates the imperfection of the patents system and not the efficiency of monopolies. Actually, technological development occurs much more easily in dynamic markets, where companies fight for a small percentage of a point of market share, than in a market dominated by one company, whose biggest incentive is to try and keep things as they are (because they generate profits).

Oligopolies

Oligopolies have specific features that must be taken into account – they do not allow for joint and undifferentiated treatment with monopolies. The central problem is to determine whether there is 'typically oligopolistic behavior', that is, whether one can identify 'rational' behavior by the oligopolist that can justify the same assumptions that are made about monopolies.

During the 1960s, it was believed that this was the case. In 1962, D. Turner categorically stated that such behavior existed and was objectively identifiable.[51] For him, the oligopolistic rationale consists of adopting parallel behavior in relation to prices. The reciprocal power of market participants obliges them to adopt parallel behavior. There is no motivation for any of the members to reduce their prices, as it is known that their behavior will be promptly followed by the other market participants. As a result, such market participant will not gain market share – the only consequence will be the loss of profitability for all. The motivation is therefore the opposite, to wit, for a parallel and progressive price increase, following the lead (price leadership) of one of the members of the oligopoly.

Other typical behavior of oligopolists includes the differentiation between products and the maintenance of stable market share.

The differentiation between products is a direct result of the disappearance of price competition. In the absence of this competition, the difference between the market participants is established and incentives to consumers are given through product differentiation. This product differentiation and the disappearance of price competition lead to the creation of many 'market niches', that is, an exclusive market for each of the oligopolists and the consequent stabilization of market share. According to Turner, this behavior is so inherent to oligopolies that it is impossible to avoid them through financial penalties, as it is not possible to force market agents to adopt behavior that is completely irrational to them. The only solution would be direct intervention to dismantle these structures.

It does not take great effort to see the connection of this theory to the Harvard Structural School.[52] It is not by chance, therefore, that the main criticisms to this theory come from representatives of the Chicago School.

In the first place, two of its fundamental postulates are contested: the perfect information of agents and the immediate reaction. In relation to the first, it has been observed that it is possible and frequent that oligopolists feign behavior in a way to cover up knowledge (or at least full knowledge) of its

---

51   See D. Turner, 'The Definition of Agreement under the Sherman Act: Conscious Parallelism and Refusals to Deal', in *Harvard Law Review*, 75, 1962.
52   Amongst whose main representatives is D. Turner.

effects from the competition.[53] This could mean, for example, conceding indirect benefits to consumers instead of price reductions. Even if and when the competitor discovers and evaluates the effects of this behavior, it may not have the ability to react immediately. This is what would happen if the economic agent is at maximum production capacity, where an increase of production on short notice to respond to an increase in demand would be impossible.

That is not all, however. According to other scholars, empirical data does not allow one to say that parallel behavior in oligopolized industries is the rule. There are, on the contrary, many examples of high levels of competition between companies having large market shares.[54] This would be the proof that each market participant acts independently and, therefore, that the high market share held by each would be a powerful factor in the weakening of the competitor's market power. Oligopolies could not necessarily be characterized as implied cartels, as many of the Harvard Structuralists would like.

Evidently, this last criticism is rather exaggerated. The fact that there are examples of effective competition amongst oligopolists cannot lead to the conclusion that their behavior is necessarily competitive, as much as – and here is the greatest value of the neoclassic criticism – it is not possible to admit, as Harvard Structuralists would like, that parallel behavior is the rule. The imperfect transmission of information and the reaction of the oligopolists are very probable circumstances that call for a certain caution in relation to this kind of conclusion. More than that, the modern development of game theory, applied to oligopolies, shows that the behavior of market participants is not entirely predictable.

Game theory was originally developed precisely from the study of oligopolist behavior.[55] In 1950, John Nash, in his work that earned him the Nobel

---

53   See R. Posner and F. Easterbrook, *Antitrust: Cases, Economic Notes and Other Materials*, 2nd ed., 1981, p. 333.

54   See R. Bork, *The Antitrust Paradox*, 1978; Mc Millan, 1993, p. 182, *et seq.* The author supplies many examples, some of which are worthy of note, while others are less worthy. Among the latter are examples of monopolized industries that saw their prices reduced by the entry of a new competitor. Bork tries to use it as an argument in favor of oligopolies. Obviously, the example proves nothing, as it is evident that, in relation to a monopoly, the oligopoly represents a comparative improvement. A more interesting example is the American automobile industry, which, in spite of being rather concentrated, demonstrated over time competitive behavior, as shown by the frequent changes in market share of the oligopolists (p. 186, *et seq.*). Note that this simple fact does not eliminate the possibility of the existence of an agreement, express or implied, between manufacturers not to compete as to prices, but only through the differentiation of products. The fact that there were substantial changes in market share without price wars strengthens, instead of weakens, the hypothesis of an implied agreement.

55   The first known essay on game theory was by Cournot from analysis of oligopolistic behavior (hence why the Nash Equilibrium is also known as Cournot-

Prize in Economics, generalized 'game theory', defining what is now known as the *Nash Equilibrium*.[56] In this state of equilibrium, the strategy of each player should be the best response to the other player's strategy. In other words, this means that the combination of strategies that will presumably be adopted by the market players is the one in which none of the players could have a better result adopting another strategy, *considering the other player's behavior*.

The main conclusions of game theory applied to oligopolies are the following.[57] First, it is possible to identify a necessary behavior of the market participants only in the event that the 'game' is repeated only one time or, if not, a finite number of times. In the first case, the market player knows that if it increases prices, its competitors will keep its prices low and will win market share. As a consequence, the company will keep its prices low. Note that the company can only behave this way because it does not have to be concerned with the effects of its strategy on a new 'round' of the 'game'. This means that in this theoretical model, there is no possibility of the first competitor retaliating by lowering its prices in response to the behavior of the second market participant. It can, therefore, adopt an individual strategy, similar to the one in the 'prisoner's dilemma'.[58]

Nash Equilibrium). See D. Baird, C. Gertner and R. Picker, *Game Theory and the Law*, cit., p. 21, note 8.

56   There are two papers, both from 1950, in which J. Nash describes his theory: 'The Bargaining Problem', in *Econometrica*, p. 155, n. 18, and 'Equilibrium Points in N-Person Games', in *Proceedings of the National Academy of Sciences*, 36(1), p. 48, note 36.

57   For a more detailed description, see D. Baird, C. Gertner and R. Picker, *Game Theory and the Law*, cit., p. 166, *et seq.*

58   The prisoner's dilemma is one of the first theoretical models upon which modern game theory was structured. Its structure is fairly simple. Imagine two prisoners being questioned for the same crime, and suppose each one is told that if he/she confesses and turns in the other one, he/she will be pardoned and the other would receive the more severe penalty (for argument's sake, 20 years), and that if each confesses and accuses the other, both will have the less severe penalty for the crime (10 years). On the other hand, if neither one confesses, each will be sentenced to five years in connection with the simpler crime (hypothetically, the sentence that would be handed down where there is no confession). Individual strategic behavior leads both players to confess. Clearly this is the best individual strategy, since, whatever was the other player's behavior (and imagining always that the other player will adopt an individual strategy), the most convenient behavior will always be confession. If the other player does not confess, the first will be free, and if the other does confess, the first player will have avoided the more severe penalty. However, in this case, the individual strategies represent to the prisoners a worse option than the behavior that seeks maximization of collective utility (which would be the case had neither of them confessed). Read about the prisoner's dilemma and its importance to game theory in D. Baird, C. Gertner and R. Pickner, *Game Theory and the Law*, cit., pp. 48–9.

The same would happen if the 'game' was played a finite number of times. The participants in the market would not have to worry, in the last round, about the effects of their acts on future rounds. They would have, therefore, a dominating strategy in the last round that is exactly the same as the strategy described for the 'game' that is played only once. What happens is that the dominating strategy of the last round would influence the previous rounds. So, for example, if the players know that in the last round the strategy of all others will necessarily be (for the reasons stated above) to keep prices low, the one before the last round will be equivalent to the last, as the participants know that their behavior will not influence the successive round. It therefore follows successively until the first round. In simpler terms, if the number of rounds were finite and known to the participants, each one would design his/her strategy in a way so as not to lose market share, given that the strategy of both in the last round will necessarily be to keep prices low. There is therefore no incentive for cooperation between market participants.

The situation is different when dealing with an infinite number of rounds, or a finite number of rounds of uncertain duration that are unknown to the participants. Note that this is the only situation that is really relevant, as it is the only one that can be verified in practice. There are two basic differences in relation to the previous situations. First, in all 'rounds', market participants should worry about the consequences of their strategies on successive rounds. The independent behavior of competitors is riskier, because if a certain participant reduces its price to increase market share, the competitor may, in the 'following round', also reduce prices, causing losses to the first competitor. On the other hand, the possibility of inexistence of a defined end, and above all, of the inexistence of a final play by the other 'player', makes the economic agent direct its actions according to the immediately previous behavior of its competitor, which, presumably, will repeat itself. In this way, cooperation between competitors, above all through implied acceptance of so-called 'price leadership', is a lot more probable.

This conclusion brought by game theory is of extreme importance, as it can direct the actions of antitrust agencies. Any action by the antitrust authorities to avoid or prevent parallel behavior, after conduct is initiated, will be extremely effective, as not only will it avoid oligopolistic behavior in that specific situation, but it will also discourage future parallel behavior. In addition, oligopolists that have already increased prices will have to reduce them at the risk of losing market share (as the other oligopolists, who were prevented from increasing their prices, are selling at lower prices). Also in future 'games', oligopolists will resist accepting 'price leadership' to a much greater extent. To use the terminology in game theory, the 'game' will be transformed from infinite duration to a 'game' of finite duration. There will be, therefore, stimulus for independent behavior (individual strategic behavior) from oligopolists in the future.

It is precisely this implied acceptance of price leadership, or of any other kind of parallel behavior of oligopolists that characterizes an implied agreement, that is the main concern of antitrust law. This is because an implied agreement is the main characteristic of the disappearance of internal competition amongst market participants. If there is no internal competition, and as long as the group of oligopolists has market power in the larger (external) market in the sense defined at the beginning of this chapter, the oligopoly may be substantially identified, in its legal consequences, to a monopoly.

In short, for purposes of antitrust law, the oligopoly situations present one more problem in relation to monopolies. To prove the existence of market power, two tests must be applied, not just one as in the case of monopolies. First, it must be determined whether the oligopoly as a whole has market power. Here, the method applied is identical to the one used in monopoly situations. This is not enough, however. It must also be shown that the group of oligopolists may effectively be considered as one integrated bloc. For this, there cannot be competition among the oligopolists, which in turn, to be proved, requires the demonstration of intentional parallel behavior.

Obviously, the problem now is how to demonstrate the existence of 'intentional parallel behavior'. For this, attention must be paid to both elements in the expression, that is, the behavior must be both *parallel* and *intentional* (in the sense of not accidental).

Let us analyze the first element. There are many types of action that may characterize parallel behavior. Parallel price movement, joint stocking, and even the maintenance of relative market participation (exclusively among the oligopolists and not necessarily in relation to other competitors in the market) are all classic examples of parallel behavior.

This kind of activity is not, however, either sufficient or necessary to characterize an oligopoly. It just makes evident the parallel behavior. It is not possible to know for certain whether this behavior is intentional, with the aim of eliminating internal competition, or whether it only consists of a behavior determined by momentary circumstances or by the reasoning of agents who act as real competitors. When dealing with competitors in the same market, pressure as to costs is frequently identical for both, which forces a simultaneous increase in prices. On the other hand, it is possible that the parallel price movement is a direct consequence of competition. If products are plainly substitutable, the increase in prices by one manufacturer can make consumers migrate in mass to the products of the competitor, who, pressured by demand, will also increase its prices. That is precisely why, as seen in the above definition of market, parallel behavior as to prices is considered an indication that two products occupy the same market.

Parallel price movement can be considered evidence of an implied agreement only when it is done consistently in only one direction, that is, where there are price increases, and when it is not justified by any significant change in costs for market participants. This situation is incompatible with the existence of competition, as in such a case it is normal that market agents will take advantage of price reductions to gain market share, being followed immediately by their competitors.

Consistent parallel, unjustified price increases by competitors who as a whole enjoy market power, to use the reasoning of game theory, indicates that the players are adopting a behavior that aims for a collective, not individual, result (profit maximization for all). Here we see the practical application of the difference between games of determined and undetermined duration, discussed above. The behavior of the 'players', who always increase their prices together and are extremely resistant to reducing them, shows the understanding of all that a price reduction can only be profitable in that same 'round', immediately becoming unprofitable in the following 'round' (owing to the price reduction of the other player, which will follow). In a 'game' of undetermined duration, such as a market, this is clearly not the best strategy.

In the absence of constant parallel price increases by oligopolists, one must search for, in addition to suspicious behavior, structural characteristics of the market that allow for the existence of intentional behavior. As always in antitrust law, when the behavior of market agents is unclear (and in most cases it is, not being possible to draw definitive conclusions from it), the behavioral analysis must be accompanied by structural analysis. The scenario described above clearly points to the type of structure that is most worrisome.

A prerequisite for parallel behavior is the existence of a system of information that allows each competitor to promptly know the other's behavior. For this reason, trade associations (at least those that aim to supply with information only manufacturers and not consumers) that furnish information about prices and quantities sold by industry members are seen as tools to facilitate parallel behavior among competitors.[59]

Another structural element that suggests the existence of intentional behavior is the immediate reaction of economic agents to the actions of their competitors. The speed in price changes in the market is also a good indication of the existence of this behavior, as it shows that increases are not the result of demand pressure (as occurs where there is competition), but of a well-structured, institutional exchange of information[60] (it is said to be 'institutional' to avoid confusion with formal agreements such as cartels).

---

[59]   Today, there is an inclination to consider this type of information exchange, *especially when not extended to consumers*, to be an indication of an agreement. For definitive proof, the other structural elements described must also be present (see D. Baird, C. Gertner and R. Picker, *Game Theory and the Law*, cit., p. 177.
[60]   Id., p. 176.

Finally, it is fundamental to the effectiveness of parallel behavior that the number of participants is not too great and that each holds a relatively high market share. The greater the number of participants, the greater will be the difficulty of transmitting information and avoiding defections. For this precise reason, the concern with implied coordination of behavior is applicable to oligopolies.

To complete the picture of market power in oligopolies, a final element must still be introduced – it is the objective of the rule that uses the concept of oligopolistic market power. The oligopolist's power has peculiar characteristics, especially with respect to control of concentrations. The main characteristic is that, for oligopolistic structures, much more care is required with vertical or simple concentrations than is the case with monopolized markets. This is because the acquisition or merger with a retailer or with a manufacturer of substitute products made by any oligopolist may serve the oligopoly as a whole in the event that there are signs of parallel behavior. Thus, a concentration that is seemingly insignificant numerically – since only one of the oligopolists is buying a retail company or manufacturer of substitute goods – may represent great danger to the market. In these cases, the concentration serves to increase the power of the oligopolistic group as a whole. Therefore, with enough evidence of the existence of an oligopoly (that is, structural information added to signs of intentional parallel behavior in the past), the concentration should be evaluated on the basis of the market share of the oligopolists as a whole.

Monopsonies and Oligopsonies

Analysis of the different forms of market power would not be complete without the study of the phenomenon opposing the power of the seller, that is, the power of the purchaser. This analysis is particularly interesting and relevant for highlighting the impossibility of understanding antitrust law if only consumer short time interests are taken into account. If for monopolies this idea already implies serious problems in application, for monopsonies and oligopsonies it simply does not allow the identification of any illicit or potentially harmful situation to the antitrust system.

To understand the reason for this statement, a brief description of the microeconomic theory of monopsonies is required. It can be said that a monopsony represents to the demand side the same that the monopoly represents to supply. Monopsonist power means that the agent possesses the power to reduce the price of the acquired product through a reduction in the quantity demanded. Owing to the price reduction, the monopsonist's average cost of the final product is reduced. The marginal cost, however, which is the relevant one for pricing, has a tendency to increase. The formal demonstration of this postulate is complex and would require detailed explanation of many microeconomic concepts, which is beyond the purview of this work.[61]

For law application purposes, it is relevant to merely observe the following: economic theory informs us that a monopsonist that is not the final consumer, that is, who is a manufacturer that buys a product to use it in the manufacture of a final product, is not likely to pass on to consumers lower prices obtained as a monopsonist in the market in which it has monopsonist power (precisely because of marginal cost increases). The tendency is for the monopsonist to appropriate this difference as profit.

From the consumer's point of view, two situations can occur. In the first situation, the monopsonist does not have market power when it resells. It operates in a situation of perfect competition. This situation is more frequent than is believed. For example, all it takes for this to occur is that the product can be easily substituted for in the final market or that the component product to be incorporated into the final product has many substitutes. In both cases, the economic agent may have power as a buyer of component products, but be only one more competitor in the sale of the final product. However, where perfect competition exists, the price of the final product is set by the market and is only a piece of information for the manufacturer. There is therefore neither an advantage nor a disadvantage for the consumer.

On the other hand, in the event the monopsonist also has market power for sales of the final product, the tendency, contrary to what could be expected, is to increase and not reduce prices. This is because, as we have seen, the marginal cost of the monopsonist is higher than that of manufacturers who operate in perfect competition for the acquisition of component products.

Considered exclusively from the consumer's perspective, one can thus conclude that the law should be concerned only with monopsonists that are also monopolists or that maintain a certain level of market power as sellers of the final product. It is precisely from this kind of economic reasoning that the

---

[61] In a simplistic manner, this tendency of the marginal cost curve could be understood as a result of the fact that, having market power, additional acquisitions of the product made by the market actor influence the price of the entire quantity purchased (contrary to a situation of perfect competition, where the buyer does not influence the price of the product purchased). Therefore, every marginal increase in acquisitions leads to an increase in the total price of the purchases. The marginal cost of the final product is given by the ratio between the cost of the input (increasing, as shown) and its utility, i.e., how much value the input adds to the final product. This last variable is independent of the existence (or lack thereof) of a monopsony. Thus, notwithstanding the fact that the average cost of the final product of the monopsonist is reduced, the marginal cost increases. For the economic-mathematical formulation of this explanation, see R. Blair and J. Harrison, *Monopsony: Antitrust Law and Economics*, 1993, p. 36.

legal question of oligopsonies gains importance. It is argued that an oligopsonist structure implies high risk, as it increases greatly the probability of parallel behavior on behalf of oligopsonists in the retail market for the final product.[62]

As previously discussed, the key element for the functioning of an oligopolistic structure is the rapid and complete transmission of information about prices and quantity produced by the oligopolists. It is clear that, with the existence of an oligopsony, the motivation to create an oligopoly is enormous. For businesses that have already found a means of organizing themselves for the joint acquisition of component products, exchanging information about the sales conditions for the final product is very simple – the 'information cost' is quite low.

Taking exclusively the viewpoint of the consumer would mean excluding from the purview of the law the oligopsonies and monopsonies in which there is no possibility of creating an oligopoly or a monopoly, as well as the oligopsonies and monopsonies in which the economic agent is the final consumer. However, for a system that aims to stop all forms of abuse of economic power, regardless of the identity of the victim (be it consumer or manufacturer), these situations should also be the object of attention. There seems to be no dispute about the application of antitrust law to oligopsonies or monopsonies that use their power to abusively reduce prices below marginal costs, even when they cannot affect the interests of the final consumer (either because they are the final consumers themselves, or because they do not have market power in the retail market).[63]

There can hardly be a doubt that, for a legal construction that aims to find a procedural due process clause to the economic sphere, the concentration of the market through monopsonies and oligopsonies is itself a problem. Concentrating information, it leads anyhow to less choice and more draining in the economic system.

---

[62]   This generalized fear that oligopsonies can evolve into oligopolistic structures is manifested in many decisions of the U.S. Supreme Court. See, e.g., *Arizona v. Maricopa County Medical Society*, 457 U.S. 332 (1982); *American Column and Lumber Co. v. United States*, 257 U.S. 553 (1936).

[63]   This statement obviously does not imply the unlawfulness per se of monopsonies, oligopsonies, or any agreement, express or implied, aiming to unite buyers who are at the same time consumers. The per se unlawfulness of agreements between competitors, characteristic of the U.S. system, does not exist in many other countries. The analysis made here aims only to identify the structures with market power that are considered relevant for antitrust law, be it for the control of their formation or for their punishment in the event of abusive use.

Structures of Concentrated Information: Vertical Structures

A type of structure that has been subject to little research by traditional economics is the one that features the concentration of information. The natural dispersion of information tends to be used in an asymmetrical form by market agents. When the information is capable of restricting consumer choice, agents tend to try and capture information. The structure of asymmetrical distribution that results from it ensures enormous power to its holders.

This power is manifested in many ways and not only through scarcity, which is what typically garners the attention of traditional neoclassic analysis. In fact, as shown by Akerloff, in the case of lack of information, scarcity could be so extreme that it leads to the disappearance of the market. As a consequence, it is very important to study structures that are apt to capture and concentrate information, as they represent an intense risk to choice, which is the fundamental objective of competition.

The most common type of concentrated information structures naturally created by market forces, are vertically integrated structures. Most types of power structure concentrate information, as we have seen. What is peculiar with vertical is that the very and sometimes only objective of the concentration or of the existence of the structure is the concentration of information itself.

Maybe exactly because of this feature, one of the greatest gaps in current antitrust analysis concerns vertical concentrations. There are no established criteria that even define which vertical concentrations should be subject to regulation, as the neoclassic criteria for market definition are all directed to measuring horizontal power. As to the criteria for penalties, the neoclassic view still dominates, that is, only those vertical concentrations that have horizontal effects can be sanctioned.

It takes little to understand that this statement is a contradiction in terms. In effect, if the criteria for the evaluation of vertical concentrations are horizontal, it would be unnecessary to independently analyze vertical concentrations.

What these analyses overlook is that the real effect of vertical concentrations does not happen, at least not directly, to supply, demand, or relative scarcity, but rather to the level of information. The so-called transaction costs, in fact, generate an informational result that should not be disregarded. Frictions that arise among economic agents in the same productive chain result in the revelation of important information for consumers. The secondary effect of the elimination of transaction costs is therefore restrictions on information about numerous important factors affecting the market and consumer environment, such as relative scarcity, point of equilibrium, etc.

The question that now arises is how to establish criteria that identify those information restrictions that are sufficiently harmful to justify preventive or repressive antitrust measures. In fact, in a theoretical analysis, these criteria can only be formulated in general terms.

The formulation should follow the theoretical foundations of information economics. In fact, this is what is behind the famous postulation by Akerloff for the markets for used cars and health insurance. The problem of information asymmetry arises when it is capable of altering the proper functioning of the market. These alterations typically arise when possible or actual differences in information created make one of the market agents change its behavior. A very common hypothesis concerns vertical integration or concentration, which allows or implies the elimination of intra-brand competition. There should be no counterargument such as that put forth by neoclassic theoreticians to the effect that there will be no impact in the vertical line and that exclusive attention should be given to inter-brand competition. The elimination of intra-brand competition leads to a radical restriction of information for consumers. The manufacturer is capable in such a case of limiting the variety of products, restricting supply, etc. Having acknowledged the restriction of information and the possibility of change in market behavior, there is already a risk to the economic system.

But the possibilities for limiting information that results in risks to the economic system do not stop there. Many times, and this happens frequently in regulated sectors, the vertical concentration is a way of ensuring that the cost structure becomes more obscure, that is, that there is less information about costs. Again, it is the elimination of transaction costs that produces this negative effect on the flow of information.

The common element in all of these hypotheses is a restriction to information that can be called 'qualified'. In all hypotheses, this restriction has the capacity to 'self-reproduce', if not to accentuate itself with the continuation of transactions. The lack of solid information from the legal point of view is what pushes that specific market to an adverse selection, in which, as with the *lemons* of Akerloff, the lack of information always invites more and more buyers to become interested in ever-worse products, reversing the difference between the relative utility of one or the other, or the difference in price to the economic agent who now possesses the information. Therefore, each time there is an expectation that economic agents will act to restrict demand, limit supply, and leave the market owing to information restrictions, and that this situation comes to last and even reproduce itself over time, the concentration or vertical restriction will create risks for the economic system. For this evaluation, the analysis and proper understanding of series of past behavior and of the correlation between vertical restrictions and exiting of producers and consumers from the market may be useful.

Structures of Domination of Technological and Production Patterns

There is another very common type of market power structure that is rarely identified as an independent theoretical type. We refer to the structures able to impose consumption and production standards and technological formats. In fact the very recognition of this type of structure means a deep criticism of the marginalist market power definition.

For this theory, whose fundamentals were set on the nineteenth century, in truth market power is determined by the power to fix prices and/or the amount of products available in the market. In the nineteenth-century world, power is thus defined as the control of price and production. It is an economic reality directly linked to an industrial economy.

In the twenty-first-century world, attention shifts from production. The industrial sector is not any more the most relevant sector. In this new world, technology, and not the economic sector, appears to be the most important element in production. Be it for the industrial commerce or service production, relevant is not necessarily anymore just the control of price and quantity; the most relevant element is the technological standard.

Therefore, market power definition cannot include just the power of an enterprise or group of enterprises over the production of a certain good. If there is domination of a technological standard, related to production, service or even consumption, then even if it is shared by a very large number of enterprises there will be market power.

Even if this group, being composed of a variety of participants, cannot exercise control over production, it can exclude or prevent the introduction of new production or consumption patterns or technologies. It can lead then to a qualified form of information restriction, preventing people from choosing which type of product or technology they will use or consume. The reason is straightforward. If, as seen, monopolies operate a triple draining not only over consumers but also over workers and other sectors, the domination of technology can prevent completely the existence of even theoretical substitutes to the product with a similar function or use. We return to the 'liquid' characteristic of monopolies referred to by modern sociology (Z. Baumann) and discussed in the first chapter. The capability of modern monopolies to change their production in content and space is the main source of the difficulties in regulating and sanctioning them.

Through intersectoral draining, they prevent economic diversification, exactly because they prevent the existence of other production or consumption. Two good examples that will be treated later are in fields so different as information technology and agriculture.

In the first one the adoption of a unique technological standard or a sole net that imposes its technological standard is apt by itself, even in the absence of market power in the neoclassical sense, to create dominance. The holder of the technology adopted or of the net is dominant even without a high market percentage. As will be seen in the next section (4) sometimes this is the product of regulation, that is, it is a structure of power created by the law. There are instances, however, in which the dominance is the product of historical and aleatory events that lead to a technological domination at the start. Path dependence and technological predation do the rest of the job and guarantee the permanence, growth and protection of the power structure.

Something similar happens in agriculture. The existence of a dominant pattern of production, large rural property with high scale production, leads to serious effects for consumers, employees and other sectors. The low costs associated with high scales lead to the actual disappearance of a whole alternative production method, based on small proprieties and small scale production, apt to avoid rural migration, attach small peasants to the land and use alternative and environmentally friendly types of energy. This type of power can hardly be measured by market mechanism or treated based on market rationality. That is why we leave its discussion to the section about the dynamics of economics structures and their relation to the environmental problem (see Chapter 2, section 5).

The conclusion is obvious. It is necessary to guarantee the existence of choice not only between products but also between technological patterns and patterns of production. In the dynamic analysis of economic power, we will have to return to this point, trying to identify theoretical alternatives that deal with the behavior of economic power structures.

4. LEGAL STRUCTURES

As seen in the first chapter, one of the biggest shortcomings of traditional economic power analysis (antitrust analysis) is its refusal to analyze separately, with separate theoretical instruments, economic power structures that are not created by the market. We proceed now to analyze the first type of these structures, that is, the ones created by the law itself. As we shall see, the fundamentals and instruments for the control of such power positions are different from those originating from market relations.

Patents

Introduction
One of the main legal structures that allow the creation of economic power in current times is the patent. It is essential that its origins and economic function be understood so that its meaning as a concentrating juridical and economic structure may be critically analyzed.

The remote origins of patents were already present in the *Ancien Régime*. Then, privileges were granted to inventors, not to foster research and scientific progress, but rather because it was understood that they performed a duty within public interest. The master craftsmen performed a truly public duty, which was, specifically, teaching apprentices.

It is not a coincidence that the duration of the privileges was an exact multiple of the apprenticeship period in the guilds. The privileges were thus intended to guarantee exclusive use and protect that guild while the apprentices were trained in the manufacture of the product under privilege.

This remote origin completely justifies the view of patents as legal monopoly. Public interest in learning and transfer of information within the guilds justified it. Also in the late Middle Ages, the prevailing mercantilism influenced the conformation of patent law. Patents served almost as a state quality certification in distant colonies.[64]

With the end of the *Ancien Régime*, however, the economic role of the patent system underwent a deep review. This review was a direct result of the principles introduced by the Industrial Revolution, principles that transformed the organization of labor.

Central in this new order was the deterioration of the power of intermediary economical and political bodies, aiming at the strengthening of the state. The end of the monopoly of the guilds, the liberalization of practice of any profession and, consequently, free competition therefore gained fundamental significance.

This change in the economic situation induced intense transformations on economic grounds and, in the medium term, in the juridical domain of patent.

Under such a transformed economic context, the justification of patents based upon old medieval privileges lost its sense. The stimulus to creativity and invention, on the other hand, gained enormous momentousness.

In a world where inventions and technology transformation were the main stimulus for economic development and where technology was not very developed in almost all fields, privileges over inventions were an important individual and entrepreneurial stimulus. Thus, this was the period in which laws inclined towards protecting patents arose. One of the first was the French law that granted inventors the so-called '*brevet d'invention*'.[65]

In the nineteenth century, other innumerable legislations that foresaw and established the invention privilege followed. Throughout the nineteenth century, the most relevant issue, still a vestige of the corporate system, was the

---

[64]   For an in-depth description of the historical origins of patents see H. Coing, *Europäisches Privatrecht*, II, 1989, p. 160.
[65]   Cf. H. Coing, *Europäisches Privatrecht*, cit, p. 160.

recognition of foreign patents. The exclusively national system of industrial law made it possible for importers to register patents as '*brevet d'importation*'.

Obviously, the increase in global trade could not coexist with such discouragement. Hence one of the main reasons for the signature of the Paris Convention for the Protection of Intellectual Property, in 1883, giving rise to an international system of patent recognition.

The direction of the evolution seems to be towards the privatization of the interests involved. The Industrial Revolution justification of patent granting that substituted the medieval public interest principle entailed the recognition of a true privilege, derogatory of competition rules, which consisted of the exclusive right of use of the patent or brand. Therefore, no longer was it grounded in a state bestowal, but rather in the right arising from the idea's priority.

It is important to notice that this conception of patents is also historically biased. Note that the dawn of the Industrial Revolution, when it acquired its current justification and main discipline (the Paris Convention was made based on the illuminist ideal typical of the Industrial Revolution era), was a period of complete transformation in the prior state of art. The technological shift was necessary for the transformation of a society that was based on animal energy into a society based on machinery. Therefore, broad protection of patents was instrumental to this revolution.

An unlimited principle of patent recognition having as justification mainly invectives to entrepreneurial inventions could be acceptable during this period. As we will see next, our economic reality has changed and the justification to patents has to change with it. Actually, as we shall see, within a structural theory of market power the justification of patents has to be seen from a completely different perspective, closer to public interest.

Economic role and legal meaning

This brief and superficial historic overview is of great help in elucidating the current economic role of the privileges of invention, according to the view sponsored in this book.

It seems evident that the patent protection system no longer serves national protectionist objectives. In the post-Industrial Revolution era, it cannot be justified anymore as mere private incentive to inventions.

Actually its close links to technology and knowledge formation lead to the exact opposite justification for patents. Its public significance resides exactly in being a powerful means of protection of and encouragement to access information and competition, and not of private appropriation of ideas. Note that this objective is particularly delicate in regions of the world in need of development, owing to the enormous connection between development and the spread of knowledge.

If this is true, then patents should be accepted just for the extent to which they really promote technology and knowledge creation and transmission. The extent of patent granting becomes critical for the coherence of the discipline with its principles. Its unlimited granting in almost all fields to all products contradicts the idea that its purpose is really to give incentive to inventions and allow transmission of knowledge about it.[66] This is for a very simple reason.

The extent of areas that need patent protection to promote technology development is much more limited that in the Industrial Revolution era. Today, differently from the Industrial Revolution era, the required 'revolution' is much more punctual and sectoral. In most industries the state of art changes daily based on pure competition among companies.

No patents are actually needed to generate new incentives to inventions. Patents compete against patents or even against unpatented products. The Schumpeterian struggle for business survival is in these cases the true engine for innovation. There are, however, some specific sectors (for example, biotechnology, new energy sources, space technology) in which true revolutions still are and will be necessary. It is precisely in these sectors that the granting of patents is justified.

More than this, the limitation of field or sectors where patenting is accepted is important also to guarantee it as really an incentive for inventions. In a reality of scarce resources, recognizing patents in a linear manner results in a disincentive to the very sectors in which research is most difficult and costly, that is, the sectors in greatest need of a 'revolution'. Evidently, resources will eventually flow into the sectors in which invention is simplest and most imminent. If such happens, more than revolutionizing prior art, they may be aiming at the guarantee of the monopoly of use.

This sort of understanding of the meaning of patents has to have a profound effect not only on the discussion about general or sectoral recognition of patents but also on the definition of patent itself. Once transformed, the justification for patent granting, the conception of the patent institute as an exceptional body of rules, must be dismissed.

In effect, if these institutes have as main inspiration the fostering of knowledge and knowledge transmission they cannot be instrumental to the creation and protection of monopolies, but actually, to the contrary, they must incentivize the appearance and the transmission of information about new technologies, and be able to contest the existing power positions. Thus, the very

---

66   For the moment a clear sectorial limitation of patent recognition is only an academic conviction (since TRIPS states the contrary), but it is hoped that it can one day eliminate the obstacles and opposition of economic power structures and reach the real world.

achievement of the economic goals of the patents requires a more sophisticated and less linear definition.

Finally, the demonstration of the antimonopoly foundations of patent law has extremely important consequences for the position of the patent holder. Although characterized as a monopoly, it is no longer an extravagant institute, an exemption to antimonopoly laws. As a result, the right to patent cannot be seen as a privilege or property of its holder.

Understood as a means to safeguard knowledge and its transmission, the main role it performs is guaranteeing consumers access and choice. Hence, unlike what is normally believed, the understanding of industrial law within the institutional logic of choice and competition is the only understanding that is capable of providing it with the public connotation it requires. As will be demonstrated in Chapter 3, this is present in the expansion of the disclosure duties that fall upon the privilege holder as well as in the imposition to them of public functions.

Consequences on the definition of the patent: Patenting requirements

Most of the new national legislation on patents,[67] aiming at adapting to the TRIPS agreement and when applicable the Strasbourg Patent Convention,[68] sets forth three patenting requirements: novelty, inventive activity, and industrial application.

These requirements hold a profound significance and great use for the adaptation of the concept of patent aforementioned if only the interpreter of the law is ready to apply the principles discussed. The old concept of novelty – all that is not described in prior art – did not take into account the invention

---

[67] Developing countries such as Brazil, India, China, South Africa and Thailand adapted their national IP legislation, specifically patent laws, to the TRIPS Agreement making use or not from the transitional period. Brazil: Law n. 9279, of May 14, 1996 to Regulate Rights and Obligations Relating to Industrial Property; available online at http://www.wipo.int/wipolex/en/details.jsp?id=515. India: Patent (Amendment) Act, 2005, n. 15 of 2005; available online at http://www.wipo.int/wipolex/en/results.jsp?countries=IN&cat_id=1. China: Patent Law of the People's Republic of China (as Amended 2008); available online at http://www.wipo.int/wipolex/en/results.jsp?countries=CN&cat_id=1. South Africa: Intellectual Property Laws Rationalisation Act n. 107 of 1996, available online at http://www.wipo.int/wipolex/en/text.jsp?file_id=180993. Thailand: Patent Act B.E. 2522 (1979), as amended by Patent Act (No. 2) B.E. 2535 (1992) and Patent Act (No. 3) B.E. 2542 (1999), available online at http://www.wipo.int/wipolex/en/text.jsp?file_id= 129773.

[68] Strasbourg (Convention on the Unification of Certain Points of Substantive Law on Patents for Inventions (Strasbourg Convention) (November 27, 1963, ETS 47)); available at http://conventions.coe.int/Treaty/Commun/QueVoulezVous.asp?NT= 047&CM=7&DF=5/21/2007&CL=ENG.

process. It implied the necessity of an original creative activity, but did not impose any requirement regarding the creative process.

Perhaps, indeed, the reason was more practical than dogmatic. In the face of such a long list of non-patentable inventions as occurred in most countries, especially developing nations, before the effectiveness of the Strasbourg Convention, excessive rigor regarding the inventive activity was unnecessary.

The reduction of non-patentable inventions, arising from the adoption of the Strasbourg principles, resulted in the need to establish patenting requirements with clarity and dogmatic rigor.

This dogmatic rigor led to the application of antimonopoly structural principles. Requiring the existence of inventive activity means imposing that, from the scientific point of a view, there is a difficulty overcome or at least an unexpected result. It is not important, therefore, whether the invention happened by chance. On the other hand, it shall not be the mere discovery of something that already existed in nature.

From a theoretical point of view, the concept of inventive activity does nothing more than privilege the effort and encourage competition. The granting of the patent requires technological investment, effort, and the application of resources.

The requirement of inventive activity makes, therefore, the granting of the patent a major tool for stimulating investment in scientific research, preventing the action of the free rider. The consequence may be a more selective and sectoral definition of the products to be patented. The final result, on an ideal scenario, can be even the non-granting of patents in sectors where there is not real innovative activity or where the same innovations could be obtained otherwise (through competition between the economic agents).

International patent recognition: Critical analysis

The same principles that help to interpret in a more coherent manner the patent requirements suggest criticism of some of the new international rules on patents. It is debatable whether the expansion of the list of patentable products, especially in the amplitude and speed in which it was carried out, was truly necessary.

The reasons that demonstrate the lack of legal and economic foundation for this expansion are compelling, all deriving from the structural reasoning discussed above.

Firstly, it is necessary, from the start, to deviate from the hypothesis that this expansion was necessary, in all cases, to avoid free riding. This would only occur if the investment in research was made in developing countries, which rarely occurs. With these investments being made in developed countries, free riding could only be considered relevant in case it meant a disincentive to stay or to invest in the market. This is not the case.

In effect, even a standard antitrust vision of the case is sufficient to demonstrate the opposite. It has been long concluded that the effects of the so-called 'price discrimination' (which is exactly what occurs when the same company, acting in different countries, has its patent granted in some, but not in others) are not necessarily detrimental to competition and do not lead to withdrawal from the market, so long as the economic agent that implements the discrimination is capable of achieving equilibrium in both markets.

But equilibrium, even in the standard marginalist conception, can be reached both in markets where there is patent recognition, and therefore a monopoly, and in those where there is not such a recognition, in which the market is competitive.

In fact, in matters of price discrimination, there is a rare consensus. Both the Chicago and the Freiburg Schools of economic thought converge in the idea that factual price discrimination among competitors cannot be considered unlawful. What normally occurs is a mere response by the companies to different market conditions.

These different conditions may originate from the existence of different costs in each market as well as from the presence of monopoly in one of the markets, but not in the other. Penalizing discrimination in the latter is inconvenient and unnecessary.

It is inconvenient because the most probable result of this prohibition is the reduction or suppression of production in the area where there is no monopoly (and, therefore, prices are lower). No economic data exist that justify any natural reduction of production where the price is competitive. This is owing to the fact that, under ideal circumstances, price discrimination allows the producer to gain from each consumer precisely what they can afford. It allows the producer to adapt to the demand curve of the consumer and charge from each individual consumer a different price (so-called 'first degree price discrimination').

This ideal situation does not exist in the real world, but the same effect occurs in factual cases when the economic agent is able to differentiate two or three large consumer groups. Price discrimination allows the agent to maximize even more its profits, making normal profit in the regions where there is competition and monopolistic supernormal profit in the regions where there is none.

It is exactly from this last remark that the need for the differences in price arises. Price increases or reductions on the availability of the product in the monopolized area can be completely resolved by sanctioning price abuse in this market. With such purpose, the very existence of price discrimination can be used as an indication of monopoly.[69]

---

[69] Price discrimination is for this reason used within the control of the antitrust

This is the reason why the doctrine sustains, reasonably enough, that discrimination can be considered an autonomous wrongdoing only when arising from vertical relations between the seller and a determined purchaser with the aim of harming one's competitors.[70] It is, therefore, a matter of vertical collusion and should be analyzed thus.

These considerations give a powerful economic and legal justification for the existence of different patent regimes around the world. If patents are granted unlimitedly in the developed world, it has not been and need not be so in the developing world.

If this is the case, the expansion of the list of patentable products under the new patent law seems unnecessary and even ineffective in most developing countries. Imagine, as a hypothesis, the issue of medicines. From the strictly dogmatic standpoint, the admission of their patentability is inconvenient. On accepting the thesis herein defended, the prohibition of their patentability would allow their producers to be able to make only normal profits (non-monopolistic) in the area where the patent does not exist, while they would still be able to make supernormal profits (monopolistic) in areas where the patents exist.

There would be no reason for the company, operating reasonably, to abdicate this normal profit, especially bearing in mind that this fact would not be able to affect the price in the areas where the monopoly exists, since the vast majority of the industrialized countries has ample patent protection and strict regulation for protection against parallel imports.

In this sense, the expansion of the list of patentable products, especially regarding products with greater social importance, seems to be unjustifiable from the legal and economic standpoints at least in developing countries.

Under national laws of most developing countries prior to the implementation of the Strasbourg Convention principles, there was no possibility of free riding, since, on the one hand, there was no risk of disincentive to research by the companies and, on the other, no risk of the country being destitute of products with sophisticated technology.

This statement can be empirically demonstrated in the case of medicines. As a study by Hasenclever demonstrated,[71] patented drugs live very well with

---

structures, as a criterion to determine the existence of power in the market – see C. Salomão Filho, *Direito concorrencial – as estruturas*, 2007, p. 85.

70   See E. Mestmäcker, *Europäisches Wettbewerbsrecht*, cit., p. 189, who states: 'Die wettbewerbsverfälschende Wirkung lässt sich bei Regelungen in allgemeinen Geschäftsbedingungen wegen ihrer generellen Anwendbarkeit vergleichsweise einfach feststellen. Denn die Preispolitik des Unternehmens reagiert nicht auf individuelle Preissituationen, sonst sie hält Preisdifferenzen systematisch aufrecht.'

71   '*O Mercado de Medicamentos Genéricos no Brasil*, Simpósio Franco-Brasileiro,' O Novo Direito da Propriedade Intelectual no domínio da saúde e dos seres

cheaper competitors. According to this study, it is possible to verify a large number of unpatented drugs on the shelves of pharmacies in Brazil. Between 2001 and 2004, generic drug registrations increased from 81 to 1124, drugs that have been supplied in adequate conditions and side by side with patented drugs. Different prices (lower prices owing to competition by generics) are not only possible but also practiced in such circumstances.

Therefore, with regard to essential medicines, it is possible to achieve a lower pricing policy, through different legal strategies (see Chapter 3, section 3, 'Drugs patents and compulsory license') taking into account the peculiarities of developing countries and least developed countries.

The prices in the consumer markets of such countries should not have any correlation to the investment made in research, because that is fully recovered in developed countries. The price in developing countries could therefore reflect only the direct costs of production, with little or no effect on the availability of new drugs in these countries (at least in big markets such as Brazil or South Africa, for example).[72]

Regulated Sectors

The other kind of dominant concentrated structure created by the law is found in the so-called 'regulated' sectors. In order to understand how and why such situations are created in the legal system, it is necessary, at first, to identify the issues that regulation intends to address in each economic sector.

This normally happens owing to the combination of political or economical objectives, peculiar to certain sectors, which justify the creation of the dominant structures. These structures may be dominant from the start or constitute a body of legal rules that make the existence of alternatives – that is, multitude of agents – unstable. In the first case, we are dealing with the so-called *regulation of dominant positions*, and, in the second, the regulation of what will be referred to hereinafter as *regulation of markets with controlled access and permanence*.

---

vivos: Implicações para o acesso aos tratamentos anti-retrovirais', Brasília, 23–24 June 2004, available eletronically at ww.aids.gov.br; also from the same author, *Diagnóstico da Indústria Farmacêutica Brasileira*, Rio de Janeiro/Brasília, UNESCO/FUJB/ Instituto de Economia/UFRJ, 2002.

[72] We must be aware that the problem is probably different in small poor countries, where the pharmaceutical industry may not be so worried about its profits (since the market is small) and consequently might feel more inclined to teach a 'lesson' to the country using a legal strategy to provide full access to its citizens and limit the availability of the products. In this case international legal activism is required to protect the country's population from abuse.

This list, evidently, does not exhaust all regulatory hypotheses. There are innumerable others, motivated by specific reasons of public interest. Coherent systematic treatment cannot be given to all of them. The present analysis, therefore, is limited to those who have relation with the creation of economic power positions.

Regulation of dominated markets

The first structure is normally studied under the label *regulation of dominated markets*. In order to understand it, it is necessary, first, to identify the manners in which it is different from the traditional justification to regulation.

According to the theory of economic regulation, the existence of so-called 'natural monopolies' (or market failures) is the central justification of choice for regulation itself.[73]

Such a justification for regulation is unsustainable, both for the reasons it evokes and the elements that constitute it.

The reasons used change the main focus of the question. Regulation does not aim at eliminating market failure, but rather at establishing a multitude of choices and vast access to economic knowledge, which will never occur in a free market.

Also, the content is insufficient. The economic description given to natural monopoly is not able to identify the situations that make regulatory intervention necessary.[74]

The mere existence of sunk costs, which is the standard economic justification for the existence of a natural monopoly, docs not cnsure, on its own, the self-protection that the monopoly needs so that its action may not be affected by traditional antitrust action. Sunk costs draw special attention to the issue of the existence of entry barriers into the sector in which there is any economic concentration. They also draw attention towards the companies' conduct. They do not impose, however, regulatory intervention.

The same does not happen when there are structural conditions that make the position of certain economic agents protected against any erosion. In this hypothesis, we cannot rely on the traditional inefficiency or 'technological

---

[73]   See G. Stigler, 'The Theory of Economic Regulation', in *The Bell Journal of Economics and Management Science*, 2, 1971.

[74]   As another justification for the special treatment given to monopolies, it is argued that natural monopolies are defined as sectors in which competition may be ruinous or self-destructive – see R. Ely, *Outlines of Economics*, 1937. Also, the existence of sunk costs to the entry of new competitors in the market is pointed out – See W. Sharkey, *The Theory of Natural Monopoly*, 1982; J. Panzar, 'Regulation, Deregulation and Economic Efficiency: The Case of the CAB', in G. Burgess Jr., *Antitrust and Regulation*, 1992.

idleness' of the monopolies, which allow, in high-technology sectors, new and agile economic agents to be willing to threaten the dominant position of the monopolist.

The basic structural condition for this self-protection to occur is the existence of a natural or artificial network, physical or virtual, of impossible duplication, established and built (usually with governmental funding) and owned and used with exclusivity by a single economic agent.

Duplication is difficult or impossible owing to the high costs involved in it, but not exclusively for this reason. In fact, besides the high costs, the networks generate the so-called 'increasing returns to scale', that is, the bigger the number of consumers who are part of the network, the more useful it is for the next consumer.[75] Therefore, there is no stimulus for the consumer to choose

---

[75] This phenomenon occurs prominently in network services, in which all consumers are integrated into a single network, which becomes more and more complete and useful for each consumer as more consumers join it. An extreme example is the telephone network, which, in fact, is only useful in the event that all users are connected to the same network. It is important to mention, however, that recent technological advances have made the creation of wireless telephone networks possible, and consequently the partial duplication of networks for certain services. Such is the case of the WiMax system. In these special hypotheses, regulatory attention is necessary in order to avoid the consolidation of several communication media into one single market.

It is exactly owing to its utility congregating and potentiating factor that it presents two externalities (involuntary effects). The first consists of the fact that the more consumers join the network, the more useful it becomes to each consumer. This is clearly illustrated by the Internet and its growing number of users. The second is an indirect externality. In face of the existence of more consumers, more services are added to the network, making it more and more useful. It is once again the case of the Internet, which has everyday more services and information providers. The theoretical explanation of the direct and indirect externalities and their application to the natural monopoly theory can be found in M. Katz and C. Shapiro, 'Systems Competition and Network Effects', in *Journal of Economic Perspectives*, 8, 1994. The main problem in the case of increasing returns to scale occurs in the event of the network, which is the center and fundament of the increasing returns to scale and the positive externalities, not being easily accessed by all, because the odds are that the competitor that will prevail is the one that has the initiative or ways of achieving competitive advantage for its system or product before any other. This is the theory of the critical path originally elaborated by Brian Arthur ('Competing Technologies, Increasing Returns and Lock-in by Historical Events', in *Economic Journal*, 99, 1989, pp. 116–31. Certain renowned economists linked to the Chicago School maintain, even today, that there should not be any interference in cases of natural monopoly, precisely owing to its being based on natural events. Its existence would benefit the consumers' well-being. This theory is sustained by the Nobel Memorial Prize laureate Kenneth Arrow on its January 17,1995 statement in favor of the performance commitment then signed with Microsoft Corporation, which was being criticized by competitors – See J. Lopatka and W. Page, 'Microsoft, Monopolization and Network Externalities: Some Uses and Abuses of Economic Theory in Antitrust Decision Making', in *The Antitrust Bulletin*, 40, 1995.

the competing network, be it from the cost or utility standpoints. The construction of a competing network is thus inconvenient. If so, then the privately owned networks that have already been built play a fundamental role. Only within those may any sort of competition develop and only through those may the consumer be able to be served. These networks are the basic element for market dominance by the economic agents who own them.

Note that the institutional historical element is fundamental to dominate the market. It is the regulation that creates the conditions for the sector to be dominated, which means that the legal system itself creates (in most cases through privatizations) the conditions for this dominance. It is from this initial dominance that the need for regulation arises. Regulation is, therefore, at the same time cause and consequence of dominance.

It is important to use the term 'dominance' to distinguish it from monopoly. It is even possible that there may be many competitors in the market who depend on the use of the aforementioned network in order to compete. The concept of *dominance* has for its basis the broader legal concept of *dependency*,[76] whereas the economic concept of *monopoly* makes use of the strict concept of *market power*, defined on neoclassical terms.

---

[76]   Dependence is characterized by the inexistence of reasonable and sufficient alternatives for the economic agent or consumer subjected to negotiation. Therefore, unlike neoclassic market power, it is not an absolute concept. Also, unlike economic power, which necessarily encompasses all the economic agents and/or consumers who act in that determined market as a business counterpart of the monopolist (purchasers if the latter is a seller and vice versa), dependence may refer to a single economic agent who has become dependent on another owing to the specific relations between them. This definition does not and neither could make the concept of dependence subjective. The lack of alternatives is not determined according to the subjective preferences of an economic agent; it is based on rationalization that allows the empiric determination of the objective inexistence of alternatives. Hence the possibility of separating the dependence hypotheses into absolute and relative, including among the first the cases in which there is binding of all the economic agents in a specific market, and among the second the specific binding hypotheses. Among the hypotheses of absolute dependence is the one arising from economic power in the market. Among the hypotheses of relative dependence, business dependency figures prominently. The expression 'business dependency' designates those long-term contractual relations – *de jure* or de facto – that create lasting economic relations between the parties. Hence the denomination 'business dependency'. The continuity of the relation and its habitude give it obvious corporate character. A classic hypothesis of business dependency is the long-term supply agreement in which the supplier adapts its premises owing to a specific need of the buyer. From this definition results the fact that the application of the concept of business dependency is not possible in connection with new entrants. See. K. Markert, in Immenga/Mestmäcker, *GWB Kommentar*, München, 1992, sub § 26, Abs. 2, Rdn. 127, p. 1.269.

It may be said, therefore, that the basic objective of regulation in this hypothesis is the creation of a regulatory environment in an economic context where alternatives to the consumer do not exist and where strong deterrents to its establishment are present. This definition shall influence the entire construction of principles of the regulation and shall help demonstrate the need for clear differentiation between function and content of the regulation of dominated sectors.

The aforementioned evidences the necessity, in sectors characterized by the existence of networks, of preservation of choice by means of ensuring competition among networks. In the absence of any guarantee of independence between the networks, the Schumpeterian 'creative destruction' is at risk of becoming sheer destruction.

The essence of what is meant is simple. In some sectors – in the specific case of telecommunications, for example – technological change allows the creation of new networks without insurmountable fixed costs. It is therefore important to guarantee an adequate degree of competition among networks.

By means of these new networks, competitors are able to obtain increasing returns to scale much more easily than if they were to attempt to compete in networks belonging to the infrastructure owners. In such cases, from the economic standpoint, the costs curve of the incumbent (for instance, network A) reaches an immeasurably lower level than the one of the agent trying to challenge him. The latter will never be able to do so because the incumbent's price will always be lower.

The same would not happen if new technology allowed him to create a new network (for instance, network B) with competitive costs. Note that this will only be true, however, if the owner of network A is not allowed to dominate network B. If the incumbent has access to it and manages to dominate it, no competition shall be possible. Even technologic innovation will have no effects on the competition level.

More than this, the very expansion of offer to the consumer may not occur because it may be preferable for the monopolist of network A not to offer the service on network B, that is, to dominate network B merely as a means of protecting its dominant position. Here, intervention by the regulator is fundamental to prevent this cross-network dominance from occurring. Provisions must be directly inserted in rules and regulations of competitive biddings for new networks preventing such kind of dominance.[77] This is a typical example of a regulatory rule of structural nature.

---

[77]   In Brazil, the invitation to bid by ANATEL regarding the granting of services related to the WiMax technology, landline telecommunications with use of radiofrequencies, prohibited landline carriers, its controllers and companies by them controlled from participation in the bidding in the areas of their respective concession

The logic here is similar to the one developed in the notorious discussion of antitrust law in inter-brand and intra-brand competition, with competition among brands (inter-brand) being analogous to competition among networks. Traditionally, the antitrust literature tends to consider competition among brands more relevant owing to its consumer-attracting potential.[78]

This observation, although lacking certain qualifications (since intra-brand competition is important and cannot be overlooked),[79] sheds some light on a relevant issue.

It is fundamental to guarantee a market structure that stimulates the consumer to look for truly diversified alternatives. These alternatives may mean subjective or objective connection to a brand as well as patterns of service with cost and accessibility that are adequate to constitute a real alternative.

The alternatives should not be only formal or potential, but should comprise real alternatives that offer real choices to consumers. Only then will the process of information diffusion and discovery of the best alternatives really occur.

Our intention is to suggest that a real alternative comprises various factors that make necessary that the market has an adequate structural framework to ensure competition. This structural framework is, in sectors where the technological evolution has made real alternatives possible (such as, for instance, the telecommunications sector), related to the guarantees of existence of competition between networks, so that the dominant player on one existing network cannot use its deep pockets to dominate a new network.

There are direct regulatory interventions that may be implemented towards the creation of new networks. In the telecommunications sector, for example, the opening of new frequencies, incorporating new technologies, so long as accompanied by regulatory prohibition of the participation of owners of already existing networks in the competitive bidding, is an important complementary strategy.

Nothing is more legitimate than seeking structural measures that allow the offering of alternatives, especially in markets that involve high technology (the Internet and telecommunications, for example), because the fact that

---

(002/2006/SPV ITB §4.2.1 2006). This restriction aimed at avoiding market dominance. However, the topic gave rise to disputes between the agency and the Minister for Telecommunications, who declared his disagreement regarding the restrictions established by ANATEL. Meanwhile, landline carriers obtained preliminary injunctions that allowed them to participate in the bidding process before the agency.

[78]   See H. Hovenkamp, *Federal Antitrust Policy: The Law of Competition and Its Practice*, 2005.

[79]   See C. Salomão Filho, *Direito Concorrencial – As Condutas*, 2003, p. 349.

monopolies do not coexist with technological changes can be clearly demonstrated in such cases. Conversely, they seek to interrupt them or create deterrents to their introduction into the market. Monopolies seek, therefore, self-preservation.[80]

Hence the need for the creation of independent networks hostile to the influence and technological predation of monopolized networks. It becomes necessary, at this point, to resume the criticism of the purely marginal definition of market power made above (section 2). Bearing in mind that the dominance of a technological pattern, even if by different people, leads to concentration of power around the new technology, the structural attitude towards ensuring that new technologies (and the new networks that encompass them) be introduced and not absorbed by the owners of the current technologies (and the current networks) is key for the existence of alternatives and for preventing the aforementioned intersector draining.

In these high technology markets, power over the networks and information asymmetry are closely interconnected. The network dominance allows the dominant player to have extensive information on patterns of consumer habits and tastes. Having more information than any other competitor – especially a new entrant – increases the capacity of the dominant player not only to predict, but also to influence consumer behavior.

Moreover, the dominant player holds more information about the patterns of consumer usage of his services than the consumer himself will ever have, which means that the information asymmetry in favor of the dominant player is not simply related to competitors, but also to consumers. This is precisely the notorious context described by Akerloff.[81]

Exactly as in the case of the health insurance described by Akerloff, the owners of a network, once they are able to establish themselves in the network that is being created with the new technology, will have more information on the use patterns of that specific service than competitors and consumers have on the service to be rendered. This happens because, even considering that the technology is new, dominant players in competing networks will be able to use the information they have regarding the old technology to predict consumer behavior regarding the new technology.

This will allow them to offer, for example, bundled deals that reduce surcharge to a minimum for each consumer (at least the economically profitable

---

[80] See Ziebarth, J.A.B.M., 'Essential Facilities in Brazilian Telecommunications Sector', presented in Latin American Competition Forum, OECD and IADB, September 8, 2010, San Jose, Costa Rica, available at http://www.oecd.org.

[81] See G. Akerloff, 'The Market for Lemons: Quality Uncertainty and the Market Mechanism', cit.

ones) combining the services available on their established networks with the new ones. What will be left for competitors will be so insignificant (or worthless in economic terms) that, exactly as in Akerloff's model, this market (the new network) will tend to recede, reduce offer or even disappear.

Regulatory guarantee of alternative networks is, then, paramount. If the regulation is at the origin of economic dominance (as a result of specific political decisions taken at the moment of privatization, for example) it must be the source of the structural order of monopolistic activity. This structural order of monopoly is also hereby demanded for social reasons.

As elsewhere demonstrated, the monopolization by private individuals of essential services, such as most utilities sectors, is one of the main factors, especially in developing countries, of the escalation of the triple draining phenomenon described in Chapter 1.[82] The absence of structural countermeasures may, therefore, strongly contribute to the sustaining of low levels of social development.

The regulatory strategy to ensure the existence of these alternatives is complex. The best alternative is, as discussed, creating entirely new networks. When this is not possible it is necessary to identify regulatory measures that make the network more porous to competition. This porousness is necessary to ensure competition not only within the network, but also outside it.

There are two reasons for this. On the one hand, network sectioning strategies, such as unbundling, allow the rise of alternative networks within the network itself. On the other, direct strategies of reduction in the power of the dominant player, with functional separation or public ownership of the network, serve as restriction to the ability to drain and predate competitors or consumers that must use the dominant network or competitors or consumers using other networks.

Here again, structural regulatory measures, aiming at acting directly on the physical or legal structures that allow dominance, gain relevance. Such

---

[82]   In fact, the extension of the monopolistic draining to new sectors, especially sectors of public interest (telecommunications, energy, etc.) is a typical characteristic of Latin American nations as of the 1990s. It serves as a substitute for intersectoral draining, which is lessened with the sophistication of modern economies. It is socially more harmful, however, since it subjects to draining the sectors that are sensitive from the social standpoint, as the abovementioned sectors, which, by the way, served in Latin America until the 1990s as social protection (in the absence of greater intervention ability by the state). See C. Salomão Filho, *Histoire critique des monopoles – une perpective juridique et economique*, cit., p. 107.

measures can vary in format and impact, such as functional separation,[83] local and loop unbundling,[84] or even changes in the network status from private to

---

[83]   The separation of control of the network and the services that depend on it is not new to the telecommunication sector. It is illustrated by the notorious case of AT&T, which was dismembered into different operators of local services and one long distance operator (which kept the name AT&T) owing to restrictions to competition emerging from the control of the local network by an agent who also competed in the long distance market.

More recently, reduced success in the attempts at introducing competition locally has revived the idea of separation of control over the local network and the rendering of the services based on it. It is an interesting fact that this has been implemented in the United Kingdom. One of the first countries to initiate the process of the introduction of privatization in the sector ended up resorting to this solution in the face of unsatisfactory results related to competition achieved throughout two decades.

The dominant carrier in the telecommunication sector in the United Kingdom, British Telecommunications (BT), which has taken on the network of the previous state monopoly, was forced to separate into a distinct entity, named Access Services, which has taken on the commercial name Openreach, for the control over the access offer to the network in situations in which there is 'significant market power' (the details of the conditions imposed by the regulatory authority to BT can be found in the document *Final statements on the Strategic Review of Telecommunications, and undertakings in lieu of a reference under the Enterprise Act 2002*, from September 22, 2005, available at http://www.ofcom.org.uk/ consult/condocs/statement_tsr/statement.pdf). Openreach has independent management, its own workforce (whose incentives are not linked to BT results) and separate location. It must address the demands of telecommunications carriers in an unbiased and non-discriminatory manner, without being able to offer conditions distinct to those offered to BT.

There has also been a demand for the creation of an Equality of Access Board (EAB), whose function is to supervise compliance with the conditions established by the regulatory agent regarding this structural separation (including the conditions of access to the network by companies outside the BT group). The EAB comprises five members. Three of them will be independent and appointed only after BT consultations with the regulatory agent regarding the inexistence of potential conflicts in the carrying out of the functions.

Note that this separation, unlike what happened in the AT&T case, is merely functional. Therefore, there is no transfer in control over the network to a carrier subjected to a control that is different from BT's. In any case, the effectiveness of this measure (less drastic than a full structural separation) is supported by the measures that aim at ensuring management with independence from the local network activities.

[84]   As previously stated, it is the competition between the networks that matters and brings real change to the structural framework of the sector. For this reason, regulation must stimulate the rise of these alternative networks. However, in many aspects of the local network, in which there is natural monopoly, the development of alternative infra-structure tends not to be viable. The perspective offered by an inter-network competition context does not reduce, thus, the necessity of adequately regulating the access to elements of the monopolist network (i.e., local-loop unbundling).

public property,[85] with private parties serving just as service providers on a publicly owned network. All of them aim at directly intervening in the economic structure by changing the legal status that gives protection to its dominant position.

Regulation of markets with controlled access or permanence

In the absence of the aforementioned structural conditions that cause dependency on a network and, as a consequence, market dominance, it might be asked: are there other sectors where there is a need for regulation in order to ensure the spread of economic knowledge, that is, regulations that must also include the structural discipline of monopolies?

The answer is yes, these sectors exist. These are the sectors in which, for various reasons of public order, entry and permanence are controlled. The government, in order to ensure the security as well as the physical and economic integrity of its individuals (users, future users or consumers) establishes conditions to entry and permanence in the market, setting rules of behavior.

Therefore, this reference to controlled markets relates to the control of access and permanence practiced and established through regulation for some activities. This is why such structures can be classified among those 'created by regulation'.

This regulation aims at ensuring the health and security of the market and of utility users or consumers. This is the foundation of rules of control. The problem is that, in order to ensure security, it usually creates conditions that are favorable to the consolidation of dominant positions.

The functional separation described above is an instrument to realize the access to the network by all competitors. Besides the organic elements already mentioned, it must be accompanied by the definition of a minimum set of commitments to be addressed regarding the conditions in which the supply of access to disaggregated elements will be guaranteed.

This is what was done in the aforementioned British example. Various elements of the local network that would be managed by Openreach were identified. Additionally, it was established that the offer of these services should be carried out based on its cost, in a disaggregated manner (i.e. without the necessity of purchase of another type of service or access) and without discrimination between carriers. The conditions for the offer of Openreach services also figure in Chapter 5 of the *Final statements on the Strategic Review of Telecommunications, and undertakings in lieu of a reference under the Enterprise Act 2002*, of September 22, 2005, available at http://www.ofcom.org.uk/consult/condocs/statement_tsr/statement.pdf.

[85]   The transformation of networks in public property has been suggested in the doctrine through the recognition of the use and fruition of the network by third parties – see C. Salomão Filho, *Regulação da atividade econômica – princípios e fundamentos jurídicos*, cit., p. 70.

When access is limited, the sector is protected from external entry. On the other hand, the conditions of permanence in the market, aiming at ensuring the savings and security of the citizens, lead to regulation that privileges large and solid companies.

It is necessary, therefore, to develop rules or manners of drafting rules that may prevent this sort of regulatory device from leading to total market dominance by few economic agents and the consequential exploitation of other parties (consumers, workers, other sectors, etc.).

Thus, regulation, rather than creating competition, serves the purpose of preventing dominant positions to be created in an environment that generates favorable conditions for such structures.

As will be demonstrated below, the legal principles end up being similar to the principles applicable to the regulation of dominant positions, especially owing to the common need for transformation and adaptation of the antimonopoly law to situations that involve much bigger dominance risks.

In fact, the regulatory discipline faces serious problems in these sectors, which comprise the difficulty in conciliating both objectives: security and competition. This conciliation is possible as long as it is understood that, in fact, in order to protect consumers and the security and health of the market itself, it is not possible to relinquish the guarantee of existence of information and choice.

Interesting examples – of both the skew tendency that regulation has been adopting in this type of sector and also of possible solutions – can be found in the financial and airline sectors.

In the banking sector, the financial health of the market players has been the only and exclusive concern. Note that, at least in the financial sector, the tension between prudential regulation and competition is artificial, not real. Evidence of that is the conceptual confusion at its base.

In this matter, it is important not to mistake the need for antimonopoly regulation with another concern, also of great relevance, which is the study of the requirements of the internal operations of the organizations subjected to regulation. In matters of regulation of the financial system, it is common to find the idea that it is not convenient to restrict or limit the monopolistic or oligopolistic structures of great banks or financial institutions, since this would be contrary to the security and strength of the system.

This understanding is not only contrary to simple logic, but it also encompasses enormous and complex conceptual confusion regarding the purposes and effects of such sets of rules. On the one hand, the health of financial institutions is ensured through internal organizational requirements, such as rules on the minimum capital requirements of banks, maximum leverage, etc. On the other hand, regulations, with the purpose of limiting the economic power of institutions with dominant positions, are an external element that inhibits economic concentration, limits the economic power of financial institutions and, consequently, protects the consumer from abuses.

Besides, the reduction of the power of big institutions and their influence on society reduces the risk of system contamination by problems and difficulties of one particular financial institution in case of systemic problems. Most recently, in the later financial crises, this problem became very clear, and the concept of financial institutions regarded as 'too big to fail' became even an element of popular culture. More than that, the existence of such gigantic financial institutions helped to justify financial help coming from the State in favor of these financial groups, that instead of solving the real problems, helped to inflate public debt and bring government throughout the developed world close to insolvency.

In the airline sector, deregulation has been the most common trend, causing increasing risks to the operations of the sector and to the very safety of the users of the system. In both cases, there is a complete lack of commitment with the establishment of an environment of real dilution of economic power and, for various reasons, the results have been scarce and generally inconvenient, resulting in profound crises in the respective sectors.[86,87]

---

[86]   The banking regulatory measures in Brazil after Plano Real are illustrative of this problem. Once diagnosed that the banking sector in Brazil was 'swollen' owing to inflation, a series of regulatory measures were implemented with the objective of 'strengthening' the sector. Hence, the minimum capital requirements for banks increased and other similar measures were taken. Small banks were given only a very short time to adapt to these changes, and, as a result, they were not able to bear alone the requirements of higher levels of capitalization, nor the tightening on banking liquidity. The immediate result is demonstrated by R. L. Troster in his analysis of the erroneous diagnosis that gave rise to the changes mentioned above, concluding that 'the solvent and economically viable organizations had their continuity compromised' ('as instituições solventes e viáveis economicamente tiveram sua continuidade comprometida') (see R. L. Troster, 'Regulamentação bancária brasileira: situação atual e perspectivas', in *Anais do Seminário Internacional sobre Regulação e Defesa da Concorrência no Setor Bancário*, 1999. The immediate result of the post-Plano Real regulation of the banking sector was a weak performance in the period between September and December 1994, characterized as the worst crisis the sector had ever faced. The comparison of balance sheets shows that there was an asymmetric effect in the growth of deposits and credit operations, which was much bigger for larger banks (data made available by SISBACEN). From the 1990s onwards, the financial concentration policy clearly pursued by the Central Bank of Brazil has demonstrated its results: monumental increase in bank profits, at a rate incompatible with the growth of the Brazilian economy, and enormous spreads imposed by the large financial institutions, with negative consequences upon the interest rates on loans, especially to those groups who are less capable of negotiating interest rates and more in need of capital – consumers and small businesses. The negative impacts on the level of consumption and investment and, consequently, on the growth of the country, are clearly visible. For an

In both sectors, the most coherent state action should have been quite different, if based on legal structural principles. On the one hand, an active control over the correction of financial procedures and airline security in general is needed. On the other, it is necessary that the regulatory agents act directly towards the prevention of strategic behaviors in both sectors, avoiding the prevalence of dominant position, which, in itself, would represent a mechanism to prevent insecurity both in the financial and airline sectors.

In the face of these problems, the need to reconcile the protection of the security and the health of the market with the battle against the monopolistic and oligopolistic structures seems clearly evident. The protection against dominance by few agents must be stimulated on many different fronts.

Firstly, it is necessary to act upon the economic structures, creating conditions that inhibit strategic behaviors. It is necessary, then, to select the entry barriers that exist in the sector (which is exactly the opposite of what has been done in the abovementioned sectors), maintaining only the ones that are indispensable to the maintenance of the security and health of the system in the long run.

This last endeavor, although apparently limited, is of critical importance to the effectiveness of such regulatory discipline. If the objective is in fact to inhibit strategic behaviors, then it is necessary to pre-emptively tackle its most mortal enemy: the barriers to entry that block all potential competitors and their beneficial effect of new alternatives on the market in question. On the

---

econometric analysis of the relations between interest rates and market concentration, see S. M. Koyama and E. K. Toonoka, *Relação entre Taxa de Juros e Participação de Mercado segundo a Modalidade de Crédito – Avaliação de Três Anos do Projeto Juros e 'Spread' Bancário*, 2002. Although it is more difficult to identify a direct connection between market concentration and crisis in the 2008 mortgage crisis, there is no doubt that the dimension of the institutions affected at the first stages was a guarantee that the crisis would spread worldwide.

[87] The transformation carried out in the Brazilian airline sector in 1998 is another paradigmatic example. 1998 marks the opening of the airline sector (without any concern with the introduction of a coherent anti-monopoly structural regulation), the consequences of which could be verified, especially, in the fares practiced in the route between São Paulo and Rio de Janeiro. The entrance of TAM into this market put an end to the dominance of three companies who, by means of pooling, operated in this niche (VARIG, VASP and TRANSBRASIL) and caused a price war. The following period is characterized by parallel price increase, which leads to the understanding that, be it by involuntary collusion or sheer cartel, the players in the market have 'learned' that the price war can be baleful for all. The same process seems to have been triggered some years later after the entrance of GOL in the market – an initial period of strong competition followed by learning and reduction in competition. This means that the sector is probably dominated by a collusive game with competitive intermissions, structure clearly negative for consumers and for its long term perspectives of development.

other hand, it is vital to tackle in a pre-emptive manner certain strategic behaviors that tend to eliminate competitors from the market as well as those that invite collusion.

It may be said that agents would be, in these markets, structurally encouraged to anticompetitive behavior, since the existence of barriers to entry, in addition to the unstable conditions of demand, gives cause to these markets being particularly susceptible to anticompetition practices.

Collusion and attempts to drive competitors out of the market are probable behaviors. Collusion is usually accompanied by barriers to entry and the elimination of competitors, with special emphasis on predatory pricing, which are usually associated with sectors of unstable demand.

It is vital, then, to develop instruments that inhibit collusion and predation. Reflections by the literature suggest some that, if used well, may lead to interesting results, as it will be further investigated below (Chapter 3, section 2).

Evidently, only individual control of collusion and predation is not enough. Besides this, it is important that rules that ensure the health and security of the systems are developed. The less dominant the economic power of the regulated agents in each of these sectors, the more easily imposed and observed these rules shall be. This is one more demonstration of the complementary relation between the protection of security in the operation of the service and its continued subsistence (health) and the structural effort against the economic power in these sectors.

It must be remembered also that, as seen above, regulation must also have regard to structural problems regarding the access and diffusion of information. Of the sectors analysed above, at the least the banking sector has revealed that some markets are characterized by an (also structural) absence of information about the products being traded. In some markets, such as mortgage derivatives, most of the 'products' traded were the ones where 'neither' party could easily calculate the risk. More than the problem of adverse selection, these markets suffered from a structural lack of information. For other products in such markets, if information existed it was concentrated in the hands of the issuers of derivatives (the financial institutions).

In both cases, the only coherent regulation would have been and still is the prohibition to the very existence of the market.[88] Here, the only structural measure that can prevent crisis and guarantee the 'health of the system' is the one that prohibits the existence of the market itself.

---

[88]   See, from the author, the article 'Menos Mercado' (Less Market), published in Folha de São Paulo, Tendências e Debates, 15/10/2008.

5. DOMINANCE OF COMMON POOL RESOURCES

Introduction: The Problem

Besides the structures created by the market and those created by the law, there is a third type that is just as worrying, or even more so.

These are the cases in which economic power derives from the dominance of goods that cannot be easily understood within the logic of the market. They are the natural resources and the common pool resources. Their basic characteristic is the great common necessity accompanied by great relative scarcity, as a result of which the use or dominance by some excludes the fruition of the goods by the others.

Note that, in such cases, the effects of economic power may be – and are – still more harmful than the standard market power effects. There must be, then, specific concern with the conformation of economic power under these circumstances, which, besides being more harmful, cannot be well perceived by the traditional instruments of detection of economic power.

The Insufficiency of the Private Goods–Public Goods Dichotomy

In order to understand the problem, it is necessary to revisit the definition of goods, and especially to return to the distinction between public and private goods in a critical manner. This classification, adopted in its great lines by the law, has always found support in economic theory, which has even sought to justify its existence based on certain specificities.

In the classical economic theory, private goods possess two basic characteristics: they are both excludable (that is, individual A may exclude individual B from consuming) and rivalrous (that is, consumption by individual A excludes consumption by any other).[89] Public goods, on the other hand, possess the opposite characteristics. They are *non-excludable* and *non-rivalrous*.

This classification demonstrates, prima facie, two serious problems. First, there is an evident confusion between the characteristics of goods and legal discipline. While rivalry is a characteristic of the good, exclusion is a characteristic of legal discipline that is only justified in a reality of abundance of goods. The possibility of exclusion of use of the good as a characteristic of such good has as a direct consequence lack of concern with the concentration of the good in the hands of private entities (economic power). In fact, if the exclusion is admitted, so should be the power.

---

[89] P. Samuelson, 'The Pure Theory of Public Expenditure', in *Review of Economics and Statistics*, 36, 1954, pp. 387–9.

But that is not all. The abovementioned classification evidences a considerable degree of internal incoherence. It suffices to note the very enumeration of the characteristics of the referred goods. While the exclusion of usage seems to refer to a non-consumable good, the rivalry appears to refer to a consumable good.

In fact, such difficulty reveals another, deeper one. This classification does not exhaust the possible differences between goods in relation to their characteristics and, therefore, is not a good parameter for the legal discipline.

This difficulty has revealed itself long ago in the work of a well-intentioned environmentalist, who based his findings on the distinction between public and private goods. The work of Garret Hardin, in 1968, identified the existence of a 'tragedy of commons' in the use of goods that did not fit well the definition of private or public (and, therefore, could not have convenient regulation in any of the disciplines). The classic tragedy lies in the use and degrading of a common pool resource (pasture) by private individuals. Guided by their private interests, they would always have the tendency to place their interests above the interests of the group, which would result in the destruction of the pasture.[90] The absence of reflection on the possibility of specific regulation of the common pool resource is probably owing to the difficulty, at the time, of admitting anything different from public or private regulation.

A consensus was then formed with various arguments. The consensus is that there should be no special regimes for common pool resources. They should be either state property or private property, since any other regime could lead to their exhaustion. The arguments supporting it were the classical ones, both in law and in economics: on the one hand, traditional legal theory sustaining the difference between public and private law and the consequent unitary distinction between private and public goods; on the other, traditional economic theory aiming at providing foundation to such convictions.

Hence the conviction that regulation is impossible, keeping these goods and situations restricted to the static discipline of private property and public property. The growth of the concentration of private property and hence private economic power over common pool resources, which is the result of a merely static private property discipline, is hence no cause for surprise. Left on their own, such goods end up doomed to concentration and scarcity. On the other hand, the public property regime, also static and frequently incapable of taking into consideration the needs of each area and the peculiarities of each good (especially common pool resources) and its use, lacks special regulation to fit these peculiarities.

---

90   G. Hardin, 'The Tragedy of the Commons', in *Science*, 162, 1968, pp. 1243–8.

A structuralist view of how economic power reveals itself over these goods and how it is possible to regulate them in a way to minimize its effects is thus fundamental. Prior to that, however, it is necessary to clarify the very concept of common pool resources.

Common Pool Resources and Economic Power

Renowned social scientists have made a critical review of the types of good in works nowadays acknowledged. First, they substituted the categories of consumption rivalry for the ones of possibility of subtractability of use. Next, they substituted the yes and no answers to the abovementioned categories for gradations, from high to low.

At last they acknowledged a new type of good, the so-called 'common pool resource' (CPR) or, according to the denomination that shall hereon be used, common good. Note that the category of common goods solves the paradox created by the characteristics of private and public goods. Common goods are characterized by high subtractability of use and also by the high difficulty of exclusion, that is, the use by one diminishes the possibility of use by another (such as in the cases of forests, pastures and rivers) but, on the other hand, it is not possible, owing to the necessity of common use involved, to exclude the people affected by the good (participants in its communal use).[91]

This is not what occurs in the case of private goods (food, consumer goods, etc.), in which there is low difficulty of exclusion but high subtractability of use. The use by one may imply scarcity for another (as in the example of food), but the exclusion of the use by others is in the nature of the good, individualized and belonging to one person only.

On the other hand, typically public goods, such as education, health, etc., are characterized by low substractability of use and high difficulty of exclusion.

What follows is that the greater refinement of the distinction makes the problems to be solved by the discipline clearer. Common goods naturally generate greater scarcity problems than public goods, precisely for having high subtractability rates. While education (public good) for one does not

---

[91]   See V. Ostrom and E. Ostrom, 'Public Goods and Public Choices', in E.E. Savas (ed.), *Alternatives for Delivering Public Services: Towards Improved Performance*, 1977, pp. 7–49. Evidently, all these distinctions may be relativized in a world with increasing shortage of resources and services. Actually, the more scarcity there is, the more goods can be considered subtractable. In a more extreme case of scarcity most goods, even basic consumer goods, could come to be considered subtractable and get closer to the characteristics and discipline of common goods. Owing to the exhaustion of natural resources and raw materials this is not an improbable scenario for the near future.

impede (initially) education for another, the removal of trees from a forest or of animals from a reservation will impede the economic use of the forest or reservation by others. Therefore, the scarcity problems are more serious in the cases of common goods than in the ones involving public goods.

The same must be said in connection with private goods. Both have high subtractability of use but only the common good presents difficulty of appropriation (or exclusivity), which means that more people are dependent on the common goods and must have access to them (a pen cannot be used by many, but fresh water source can and must).

This creates another problem for common goods, which is the greatest possibility of scarcity. Note that, in a reality such as this, any private appropriation implies monopoly over the use of a good disputed by many. The power results from the possibility of appropriation of a good needed by many and not from production primacy. The access to a specific forest may be fundamental to the existence of a certain community, even though vast expanses of forest may exist in the same country. The community's subsistence and customs are connected to the forest and cannot be dissociated from it.

Therefore, the possession by a private individual of property and the ability to limit or restrict access to it by the community creates enormous power over such community. In fact, it creates triple draining effects similar to those of traditional monopolies.

The community will be deprived of livelihood assets and dependent on a single proprietor to obtain them. It will also depend on the single proprietor of the scarce natural resource to work. Finally, accustomed to the use of the forest for various activities, the community will have fewer economic alternatives of survival.

Note that this description is valid for a series of nature-related goods, such as forests, sea and river fishing, and even properties with water sources. Their relation with the protection of the environment is direct and immediate. Economic power or monopoly over such activities generates serious consequences. Its power to create scarcity and social destitution is enormous. Regulation must take these problems into account.

Common Goods and the Environment: Economic Power vs Cooperation

The identification of a possible regulatory framework for common goods demands, previously, the typification of the social relations likely to be more adapted to common goods and, consequently, to the use and respect of nature itself.

The law and social relations are inextricably connected and legal rules may not exist in isolation, dissociated from social relations. The reflection over common goods particularly evidences this statement.

It is extremely difficult to effectively imagine a possible discipline for a good to which many must have access but whose use by one may generate scarcity to others, without any sort of cooperation between the individuals and communities who need to use the referred good. This is an intuitive conclusion that finds vast corroboration in empiric studies carried out for a long period of time by social scientists.[92]

In order for cooperation to be feasible, however, the presence of certain requirements is essential. The theory of the so-called 'cooperative games' has been the object of much discussion in the last decades. The most complete initial formulation of this theory for the social sciences was made by Axelrod in 1984.[93] Some basic requirements for cooperation in society were then identified: i) the existence of a small number of participants; (ii) complete information between them; (iii) reciprocal dependence; and (iv) the duration of the game.

All these requirements helped to create an element considered fundamental for the operation of any cooperative structure: trust. Ulterior studies demonstrated the importance of additional questions (some already identified in the original works[94]).

They are the noise, that is, the difficulty recognizing the strategy of the other participant, and the shadow of the future, which is the effect that the duration of the interaction (the game) may have over the present behavior of the agents.

The difficulty recognizing the other's strategy hinders cooperation because it may convey defection, individualist behavior, when the objective was cooperation. Trust is once again at risk of deteriorating.

A similar situation occurs regarding the shadow of the future. Owing to the fact that there will be a moment (the final stage) in which interaction will no longer exist, behaviors may be individualistic in this round, with no thought given to the reaction by the other party. Individualism then undermines the reciprocal dependence and trust that are fundamental for cooperation even in rounds previous to the final one (due to what can be called a backward effect of individual strategies in games).

In a study of economic power, more than analyzing any of these requirements in depth, it is important to identify how the existence of power may influence their presence in social relations.

---

[92] A. Poteete, M. Janssen and E. Ostrom, *Working Together: Collective Action, the Commons and Multiple Methods in Practice*, 2010.

[93] R. Axelrod, *The Evolution of Cooperation*, 1984.

[94] R. Axelrod and D. Dion, 'The Further Evolution of Cooperation', in *Science*, 242, 1988, p. 1385.

The fairly intuitive result is that it affects negatively almost all the above-mentioned requirements. It is common knowledge that one of the main effects of monopoly is the concentration of information. Actually, as previously stated, this is one of the main characteristics of modern monopolies. It is not possible, then, to imagine any information flow between the participants of social relation.

It is also typical of the structures of economic power to create dependence without being involved in it. Thus, if there is a monopoly position, we should not consider reciprocal dependence, but unilateral dependence in relation to the strongest party. Note that, regarding common goods, oligopolies generate the same effects as monopolies. Even if present, cooperation is irrelevant (actually negative), since not only are the cooperative effects of the oligopoly felt just by its members but cooperation exists to exclude others and not to pursue interests common to the whole community. Therefore, the effects of the oligopoly over the common good are equivalent to the effects of the monopoly.

From this difficulty derive the others. Noise is a consequence of the difficulty of information. Monopolies, more than any other structure, precisely for concentrating information, are capable of transmitting false information about their strategies and consequently creating noise, which hinders cooperation.

The lack of concern of the structures of concentrated power about the future is widely known. The existence of power allows its holder to believe in the possibility of always being the last to 'play', that is, have the last reaction. This statement is particularly relevant in environmental matters. The acknowledged characteristic, even in antitrust law, of monopolies making the service life of the product shorter,[95] because there are greater profits to be made from the sales of new products (monopolistic sales) than from maintenance, demonstrates this lack of concern for the future that is typical of monopolies.

There seems to be no doubt, therefore, that a first great parameter for a structural regulation of the common goods must lie in the structural restriction to economic power.

Structural Intervention Alternatives

A simple question follows. How can the law influence this situation so as to allow more regulation over the common goods?

Firstly, it is necessary to highlight the importance of a structural intervention in such a field. Indeed, the insufficiency of compensatory solutions for the matters of nature and environment protection is evident. General traditional

---

[95]   See H. Hovenkamp, *The Antitrust Enterprise*, 2005, pp. 293–4.

principles of environmental law, such as polluter pays, precautionary principle and even preventive principle, are useless in a world of increasing scarcity and increasing overuse of resources. Some of them, like the polluter pays principle, in a way legitimize the destruction of the environment for those willing to pay for it, as if monetary compensations could be of any value in this field.[96] Rather than useful, they become a consecration and legitimization of economic power in such a sensitive field.

A discussion is called for that proposes to tackle the issue regarding the regulation of property of the common interest goods. It is in this context that a so-called 'structural intervention' is necessary.

It is necessary, however, to make some reservations. The first one is that the broad discussion of all aspects related to the common goods is obviously not to be approached here. This matter is the object of extensive treatment in the specialized literature and would have to be the object of specific study.

What is important here is the relation between economic power and regulation of common goods. As seen above, this is critical, once the economic power impedes cooperation and a convenient discipline of common goods. Thus, any regulatory apparatus to be erected must, so as to establish conditions that allow cooperation in the use and management of the goods, guarantee that power structures that may come to dominate it not be formed.

There is, however, a second reservation, as or more important than the first. It is not possible to imagine a rational and general deduction of regulatory parameters applicable to each and every case. Particularly in the matter of common goods, what is demonstrated is exactly that regulatory solutions adopted in a local situation and successful therein may not be so elsewhere.[97] Hence, more than indicating complete solutions, it is important to identify regulatory issues to be faced.

One first issue to be considered refers to the identification of the types of common goods and the key regulatory issues related to each one. Therefore, it is necessary from the start to clarify that it is no longer possible to adopt a

---

[96] As stated by G. Rist, this principle even grants the right to pollute to those who have financial resources – see *Le development – histoire d'une croyance occidentalle, 2007*, p. 327. The exacerbated individualism of this principle makes some environmentalists defend even the creation of a new principle of protector pays (protecteur payeur) to compel them financially to carry out public policies on environmental matters – cf. R. Hostiou, 'Vers um nouveau príncipe general du droit de l'énvironment – le principe protecteur-payeur', in *Pour un droit commun de l'environment – melanges em honneur de Michel Prieur*, 2007, p. 567 (575).

[97] Cf. the several cases analysed by E. Ostrom and the comparisons made in *Governing the Commons: The Evolution of Institutions for Collective Action*, 1990, p. 178.

unitary vision of property right. It is no longer the case of discussing a unitary property right and its limits, but bundles of rights composing the property.[98]

These bundles deserve special attention on their enumeration and classification. Some rights refer to the appropriation of the goods or resources arising from them; others refer to the use of the goods themselves. This enumeration and classification is important because, as will be seen, it shall have different effects regarding the key economic issues identified in relation to the goods: difficulty of exclusion and the subtractability of use.

Amongst the various rights included in the bundle of property rights, it is possible to identify: the right of access to the good; the right to withdraw products or resources from a source or property (withdrawal rights); the management right, that is, the right to transform the property and/or regulate internal patterns of use; the exclusion right, that is, the right to decide who will have the right to access, withdrawal or administration; the right to use, that is, the right to use economically the good itself (not to be confused with the withdrawal of its fruits); and the right of disposal, that is, the power to sell the good. To these is added today, in the case of many goods (especially consumer goods), the right of decision over the final destination of the byproduct of the use of such goods.

Some of these rights refer to the group (or bundle) of the rights of appropriation and others to the group (or bundle) of rights of use. Thus, in the initial description of the economic characteristics of the goods, some are connected to the idea of intensity of the subtractability of use and others to the excludability of use.

Hence, for instance, the right of access for withdrawal of resources and the withdrawal right are connected to the group of appropriation of goods. The use and disposal rights, on the other hand, are connected to the bundle of rights of use. At last, the rights related to the management of the good and the rights of decision over the residues of use refer sometimes to one, sometimes to the other group of rights.

It is not hard then to conclude that the higher the level of subtractability of use generated by the good, the greater will be the search for the right of appropriation of resources in relation to that good. Therefore, regarding the CPRs, there will be a great need to attribute rights of access and withdrawal of resources to as many members of the community that depends on them as possible. Conversely, the dominance of these rights by one single agent will generate a huge power to its holder and huge capacity of drainage of resources and utilities from the other members of the concerned community.

---

[98]   For the discussions around the idea of bundles or rights related to property see E. Schlager and E. Ostrom, 'Property rights regimes and natural resources: a conceptual analysis' in *Land Economics*, 1990, n. 68(3), p. 249 and ff.

On the other hand, in the case of goods with a high level of excludability of use, as the private consumer goods, the major concern must be about their use and abuse, especially relating to today's unlimited right of decision over the allocation of the residues of the consumption or production processes.

Appropriation: Decentralized regulation and cooperation

In relation to a significant portion of the common goods (forests, watersheds, etc.) the importance of the goods and natural resources extracted from them for the communities that surround them seems evident. It is also relevant to acknowledge that an important problem regarding natural resources lies in the predatory tendency created by large scale withdrawals, usually made by major industrial withdrawal structures. It is also not unusual for the predatory withdrawal to take place in regions distant from the ones originally explored by these economic structures. In other words, the geographical distance and the lower dependence that is created in relation to the nature or the inhabitants of that region help to make the interaction less cooperative.[99]

There is no doubt that territorial connection to goods and the structures composed by individuals depending on the existence of those good tends to make the interaction with nature more cooperative.[100]

Once more, the aim hereof is not to predefine the regulation but to identify the problems related to this kind of good. The acknowledgement of this necessity leads, as a consequence, to the imperative concession of rights of appropriation (access and withdrawal of resources) to the community that depends on them or the entities representative of this community. Obviously, the decisions over the withdrawal of resources (right of management), exactly for being a scarce resource, should be institutionalized, that is, as a rule attributed

---

[99]   A clear example takes place in the matter of ocean fishing. The well-known exhaustion of fish stock has been leading major European fishing companies (especially Spanish and Irish) to dislocate enormous fishing vessels to Senegal, carrying out activities often over the limit permitted – check the investigative journalism book by C. Clover, *The End of the Line*, 2006, p. 41 (Chapter, 'Robbing the Poor to Feed the Rich').

[100]   Notice that, from the point of view of the game theory, cooperation is more difficult in case of geographical distance for many reasons, among which because the capacity of retaliation by the local producers or by nature itself is limited, which means that the 'shadow of the future' is limited and consequently the game resembles an FRPD (finitely repeated prisoner's dilemma game), in which what prevails is individual strategy. Companies that predate or destroy the region that they are not part of or do not depend on, whether because they are able to extract from other regions or because they themselves are from other regions, cannot be retaliated against by nature, in the sense of feeling the effects of scarcity or destruction of the environment. Therefore, between them and nature, there is an FRPD game, of strictly individual strategy.

to local regulatory entities representing the community and somehow connected to a broader agency of coordination of regional regulatory policies. In fact, this large scale institutionalization in matters of regulation of common goods has been proving to be the most efficient measure in practice.[101]

Also the participation of the community in the regulation should be made in a consensual and balanced manner. Hence, it is not admissible to allow the formation of power structures influenced by the most powerful economic interests within the regulatory agencies themselves, that monopolize decisions. The effect may be lack of stimulus to natural cooperation in the use of the good, precisely owing to suspicion (noise) in relation to the appropriation strategy decided upon by the local regulatory agency. Once again, the 'game' here runs the risk of turning from a collective strategy game into an individual strategy one, which may rapidly lead to predatory or excessive use of the common good, that is, the 'tragedy of the commons' identified by Hardin.

Use: Connection between production and consumption

There is another portion of common goods and a significant portion of private goods for which the problem of use or exclusion of use is the most relevant. Exclusion in relation to productive lands is an example. This is a good whose relative scarcity and environmental importance make it increasingly more difficult to classify as a purely private good or common good.

The same may be said *mutatis mutandis* in relation to consumer goods such as food, clothes, etc. despite the fact that here there is a greater concern over the byproducts of the consumption process than the good itself (once the very use generates the consumption or disappearance of the good as it was originally, that is, the exclusion of use).

Regarding one or the other, the central problem here is the wide right of disposal of the byproducts of the production and consumption. This is or will be potentially the main cause of scarcity.

In the case of the land, it happens through environmental pollution and deterioration of rivers and lakes essential for the common interest. In the case of consumer goods, it comes through the still optional character of recycling of the byproducts of the production and consumption processes, which requires a constant increase of the scale of production and increasing insufficiency of resources.

In both cases there is a common element: concentrated economic power structures. In the case of the land, major properties dedicated to monocul-

---

101   Cf. E. Ostrom, *Governing the Commons*, cit., p. 190.

ture. The consequences of such a land property concentration are social (concentration of land exodus of peasants to big towns) and environmental (lack of concern with the effects of large scale use of fertilizer for local communities and the environment). As for consumer goods, the mass production and scale obtained by the major structures make recycling unnecessary and expensive. With a monopolized industrial circuit, it is much easier and cheaper to produce without reusing, precisely because the monopolist draining structure previously described is already assembled from the source of raw materials to the final product. Recycling, on the other hand, requires specific investment, usually of low return (because at the other end there are monopolist producers that pay little for the activity) and intensive work.

Once more, a useful proposition could be the one of selective intervention over the bundle of rights that composes the property, granting right of decision over the destination of the byproducts of the production and consumption processes to a group of individuals interested and capable of processing them. The establishment of rights (true rights, not the mere access to volunteer deposit of residues) to recycling cooperatives is in this sense an instrument with great efficiency potential. There have been successful experiments with recycling cooperatives composed of members of 'roof less' movements ('sem teto') and landless movements ('sem terra'), in Brazil. Examples like these help to prove that there can be a virtuous cycle between 'social (or anti-poverty) initiatives' and protection of the environment.

That is not all, though. Much depends also on changes to the very functioning of the industrial structure. It is then necessary for a reverse movement to the one made by the globalized economy. The production and consumption processes must be brought closer in order for more effective industrial reuse to be possible. This may only be done locally.

Also only locally and in the absence of economic power may 'industrial ecology' be sought. The aim there is to bring the industrial processes closer to the natural ecological systems in which the waste may be reciprocally reused. Companies can effectively alleviate the effects over the environment if they act closely and consume each other's waste. The objective there is to connect industrial processes producing diverse types of waste, in order to make it possible for one to make use of the byproduct of the other's industrial process, minimizing the total waste. Very successful projects in this sense exist in the creation of 'industrial ecosystem parks'.[102]

---

[102]   One of the most famous exists in 'Kolundborg', Denmark – cf. D. Gibbs, *Local Economic Development and the Environment*, 2002, pp. 97 and 129.

Once more, for this end, social and institutional support towards cooperative relationships rather than individual ones is necessary. Such environment will be more difficult to achieve the more disparity of power there is among the participants of the economic process, or, to put it more clearly, the greater the economic power of one (or some) of the members who shall easily choose an individual strategy.

3. Power structures: Dynamics and behavior

1. THE IMPORTANCE OF THE STRUCTURE OF RELATIONS FOR THE DYNAMICS OF POWER

As seen in the first chapter, the fixation with economic results is responsible for a great deal of the problems current economic law faces. A legal proposal on how to deal with the theme of economic power must be constructed around certain core values, like broad access to and distribution of economic knowledge. In order to do so, it is not enough to analyze economic structures from a static standpoint. It is also necessary to be concerned with economic relations; and for a simple reason.

In fact, when talking about structures, what we have in mind are normally legal and economic situations of power, which allow domination over consumers, other competitors, other entire sectors of the economy and even over workers, restricting the choices and/or freedom of choice.

Well, this does not happen only if there are economic structures with market power. On many occasions, even in the absence of market power, the structure of the relation between the parties generates power. In a quite relevant work on power, K. Dowding shows how, in fact, seen from the point of view of game theory, power is found a lot more in the structure of individual relations than in the unbalance of strengths between parties. This structure eventually determines the behavior of the individual (the case, for example, of the prisoner's dilemma).[1] It is, in fact, good news, as it confirms what was just suggested, that is, that

---

[1]   See K. Dowding, *Power*, 1996, p. 42. In fact, this statement deserves an explanation. For Dowding, as the prisoner's dilemma itself shows, people, in certain circumstances, decide their behavior according to the expected behavior of the other individual. Here there are two important elements. In the first place, the past, is the reputation, either of cooperation or not, built by the individual. On the other hand is the structure of the game. In the so-called zero-sum games, there are no other alternatives except for the individual behavior. So, the alternative is to structure the organizations in a way that the games are not zero-sum and that does not build a reputation of individualistic behavior. As we will see, rules like the one of conflict of interest, when well applied, favorably influence both elements (reputation and game structure).

structural modifications of relations are effective ways of limiting power in society. It also points to the need of identifying these relational ways of domination, especially when analyzing conducts of individuals and companies in the market.

The same idea might be expressed in a different manner. Law and power are alternative and mutually excluding ways of organizing economic and social relations. One withdraws from where the other is present. Therefore, it is necessary that the law be once again empowered to organize the economic relations whose discipline has been more and more dictated by relations of power. In matters of economic relations, this empowerment requires the identification of the relevant type of relation and the instruments for its legal restructuring, in a way to eliminate the power element. Note that it is eliminating or transforming the economic power element innate to the relation and not defining its objectives or instruments of action that is the core of the legal construction regarding economic relations.

Once again, it will be necessary to adopt the same division of the first chapter. Not all conducts have a similar source and, therefore, they should be treated with distinct methods.

In section 2 conducts originating from market relations will be studied. In matters of market relations, two sets of conducts seem more relevant: conducts tending to exclusion and collusive conducts. Both express relational structures that are directly defined by power, be it because the conduct aims at the construction of a situation of power or because the conduct originates from a power situation (and takes advantage of it).

Note that, in this section, what will be studied are economic relations in their pure state, acting freely in the market. It does not involve, therefore, sectors in which law creates the economic structure of power or influences the structure of the economic relation. These will be the object of section 3 and shall require special attention because, in them, the legal discipline frequently ends up consecrating the operation of power and itself creating the conditions needed for power to dominate economic relations. In such cases, the legal intervention shall be more incisive, in a way to substitute power that it (the law) has created.

Finally (section 4), the conducts in sectors characterized by dominance or possibility of dominance of public goods shall be studied. There, power dynamics and their effects have a complete different logic and demand specific treatment.

2. MARKET BEHAVIOR: EXCLUSION AND COLLUSION

Exclusion of Competitors

In this topic, two different forms of conduct will be studied: (i) predation; and (ii) compulsory negotiation.

We immediately spot one clear difference in comparison to standard antitrust theory. In the first place, the named horizontal and vertical restrictions to competition are not present. The reason is simple. The difference in results does not seem sufficient for the correct understanding and classification of the phenomena. Both in horizontal and vertical restrictions, there is the collusive element. In the case of horizontal restrictions, the aim of excluding the other competitors is, so to say, secondary. What leads to the domination of the markets is the collusion resulting from such practices and not the exclusion.

In the case of vertical restrictions, the situation is slightly different. It is important to distinguish different situations under the name of vertical restrictions. The economic nomenclature is, once again, equivocal. Under the expression vertical restrictions are included behaviors in which the element of exclusion is present as well as other conducts in which collusion is significant.

First, there can be an agreement with an economic agent in the vertical line that implies the exclusion of the others. In this case, the agreement is not the most relevant element. It is only an instrument through which exclusion will happen. This, in turn, will then lead to market domination. Furthermore, the agreement made is not the typical collusive agreement, which happens between competitors. Here are included, for example, exclusivity agreements. Exactly because the coercive element (of exclusion) prevails, these acts will be treated as a hypothesis of compulsory negotiation (the compulsory aspect is, as we will see, negative), that is, as a hypothesis of exclusion and not of collusion.

A second hypothesis of vertical restriction is the one that imposes uniformity (collusion) amongst competitors. An example would be the imposition by the supplier of retail conditions or prices. In this case, the collusive element, even if imposed, is what prevails. As we will see, domination happens, or is strengthened, through uniformity, and there is no relevant exclusion element. This second hypothesis, for this reason, will not be analyzed in the present topic, but will be included in the study of collusion.

Therefore, the legal analysis ends up being substantially different from the economic analysis of economic relations. Instead of looking for results (vertical or horizontal integration), what is relevant is the effect of economic power in the relation (through exclusion or collusion) and, in the end, the objective of replacing it as an organizing element of the relationship (even though power as such is not necessarily eliminated).

There is also a second important difference regarding traditional antitrust economic and legal studies. The exclusion as herein treated does not refer only to competitors. On many occasions, the effect of the conduct is felt in relation not only to the competitors, but also to entire sectors of the economy. A good example is the one of exclusionary conducts, which are frequently intersectoral. As we will see below, technological predation, for instance, normally aims at substituting and eliminating other economic sectors, without providing the user with a more useful alternative. Therefore, the intersectoral drainage mentioned in Chapter 1 is not only a result of structures built throughout history, but is also felt through concrete strategies. It is, therefore, also in the structure of the relations that it must be discovered and disciplined.

Predation

The term predation is the generalized denomination for various kinds of conduct in a very simple kind of practice. According to the current definition, it is the act by which the economic agent incurs losses in the expectation of eliminating the competitor from the market, hoping to recover afterwards, in many ways, the amount lost.

The first problem with this definition lies in understanding its meaning and extension. In fact, predation will take place whenever the aim of a certain conduct is not beneficial to the party practicing it, but rather implies a loss that is instrumental to the elimination of competition from the market. Thus, achieving power and not economic results appears as the main objective of the conduct.

Besides, the definition implies many theoretical and practical difficulties related to the practices. The first refers to the existence of an illegal act itself. Giving up profits, through reductions of prices or technological improvements, as long as there is no other objective, may be a profoundly pro-competitive action and beneficial to the consumer. Hence many authors simply sustain that predatory pricing should not be an object of concern.

But there is more. There is also not a convergence about the criteria to analyze such conducts. There are all kinds of doubts about them. In the first place, should the criteria be static or dynamic? The first is represented by objective and immediate economic criteria that, based on present economic data, can lead to a conclusion about the existence or not of illegal activity. The dynamic criteria, in turn, should include data on the future behavior of the agents or the future market structure.

Finally, even amongst those who defend the dynamic criteria, there is another uncertainty: whether these criteria should necessarily include the possibility of recuperation of profits lost through predation or should be composed only of elements that would indicate the strategic objective of eliminating the competition.

To answer these questions, even partially, we will attempt a critical analysis of the many existing theories on the matter, presenting, eventually, the theory that seems most compatible with a legal explanation of the phenomenon: a legal theory of strategic behaviors.

Subsequently, we will discuss the two typical cases, most frequently identified as predation, based on the theory developed here: predatory prices and predation through technological innovation.

The neoclassical economic theory and its variations The most extreme and liberal[2] theory on the practice of predatory prices is, and it could not be any different, defended by the neoclassical theoreticians.

For these authors, lowering prices is a healthy practice that should be stimulated and not punished.[3] These authors acknowledge that there may be cases in which price reduction is a strategic move, but they are so marginal it is not worth pursuing them. In the first place, because there is the risk of reaching cases in which lowering prices is pro-competitive (cases which, according to the same theoreticians, are the numerical majority). Furthermore, the proof of the practice of predatory prices is very complex. Business data on the cost of products and ways of accounting for investments in research and development are merely estimates, not offering safe elements for the elaboration of economic assumptions. They also indicate that structural data like economic power and entry barriers are also uncertain, not supplying safe indices for characterizing illegal activity.[4]

Finally, and most important of all, the practice of predatory prices, according to these same authors, would be lacking in economic reasonability for the predator, by any angle that the question is analyzed. In case the predatory prices are practiced by an economic agent who does not enjoy market power (but only financial power), the losses that should occur up until the elimination of the competitor(s) with most market share are so great to the point of making the strategy unfeasible. Inversely, if the economic agent has market power, the strategy would also be inconvenient, as the losses suffered by him are proportional to his market share and, therefore, much greater than that of the predation victims.[5]

Many of the historic cases in which there was condemnation were re-evaluated by this line of thinking, which tried to show that there was no

---

[2] The word 'liberal' when used in this book, means non-interventionist, free market oriented tendency or theory.

[3] The three most well-known and cited works in this line are by J. McGee, 'Predatory Price Cutting: The Standard Oil (NJ) Case', in *Journal of Law and Economics*, 137, 1958, p. 168 *et seq.*; R. Bork, *The Antitrust Paradox*, cit., p. 144 *et seq.*; and F. Easterbrook, 'Predatory Strategies and Counterstrategies', in *University of Chicago Law Review*, 48, 1981, p. 265 *et seq.*

[4] See F. Easterbrook, 'Predatory Strategies and Counterstrategies', cit., p. 265, who, after developing all these arguments states: 'if there is any room in antitrust law for rules of per se legality, one should be created to encompass predatory conduct. The antitrust offense of predation should be forgotten' (pp. 336–7).

[5] See R. Bork, *The Antitrust Paradox*, cit., p. 149 *et seq.*

predation. Particularly, after re-evaluating some important condemnations for predation (*Standard Oil* and *Gunpowder Trust*), the conclusion was reached that there was no price predation. Expanding the concept of predation, it was stated that there is no need to worry about predatory prices, since a company, operating rationally, will always consider it more convenient to buy the competitor rather than eliminating him through predation.[6]

It is pretty clear how simplistic these analyses are. A predator does not make a simple arithmetic sum when entering a price war. If his aim is to effectively predate, he will then consider the effects produced by the predation in other markets in which he acts, the possibility of building a reputation and, only then, the many gains, direct and indirect, which a situation of monopoly can afford him.[7]

As for the doubts of the neoclassical theoreticians on the effectiveness of the economic forecasts and the difficulty of their elaboration, there are two possible alternatives. The first is to try to elaborate economic criteria that are simple and effective for evaluating predation. The second is to question the economic criteria and try to establish legal criteria that allow the distinction of cases of predation and of pro-competitive strategies. These are the two lines of thinking that will be developed below.

The criterion based on the comparison between price and cost   In response to the challenge made by the neoclassical thinkers, other authors, convinced of the possibility of the occurrence of predation, sought to find a criterion that is strictly economic and simple to apply. For this, a rigid principle of absolute rationality by the economic agent was adopted.

The most important and influential of these works is, undoubtedly, the one by Areeda and Turner.[8] It is quoted, discussed and criticized in the main decision by the EU Commission and European Court on the subject (*Akzo* case).[9]

---

6   This is the conclusion reached by J. McGee, 'Predatory Price Cutting: The Standard Oil (NJ) Case', cit., p. 168. Also Elzinga, re-evaluating the *Gunpowder Trust* case, comes to the conclusion that, in fact, there was no predation – see H. Elzinga, 'Predatory Pricing: The Case of the Gunpowder Trust', in *Journal of Law and Economics*, 13, 1970, p. 223 *et seq.*

7   As for the argument by J. McGee, one does not even have to go very far. It is R. Bork himself who states that with the concentrations being controlled by antitrust law itself, using them as an alternative way to predatory prices cannot be considered – see R. Bork, *The Antitrust Paradox*, cit., p. 146.

8   P. Areeda & D. Turner, 'Predatory Pricing and Related Practices under Section 2 of the Sherman Act', in *Harvard Law Review*, 88, 1975, p. 697. For more recent work, see Alvin K. Klevorick, 'The Current State of the Law and Economics of Predatory Pricing', in *The American Economic Review*, 83(2), 1993, pp. 162–7; and also Massimo Motta, *Competition Policy: Theory and Practice*, 8th ed., 2007, p. 3.

9   Decision by the Commission 14/1285, 85/609 EEC in GUCE 374/1, the deci-

This is a classical work on the subject and cannot be disregarded. It was as of this work that predatory prices and sales below cost were identified in a clear manner.

What Areeda and Turner suggest is, in fact, very simple. They start from the statement that a company maximizes its profit when the price of sales is the same as the marginal cost. The marginal cost is equal to the cost of one extra unit produced. So it is quite clear that, when the marginal cost is equal to the price, this means that the last product that was possible to sell with profit was sold. From there on, and bearing in mind that the price curve is decreasing in relation to quantity and that the marginal cost curve is increasing, every extra product produced will generate a negative result. The meeting point of the two curves is where total profit is maximized (as long as the theoretical requirements for perfect competition are not configured).

For these authors, if the price of equilibrium of the economic agent is the one in which there is identity with the marginal cost, then every price above that value indicates the existence of a situation of monopoly and prices below this value indicate that the economic agent is predating. The reason for this conclusion is the pondering that, being this the point of equilibrium, it would not be rational for the economic agent to charge anything below this value. So, in this hypothesis, the objective of eliminating the competitor from the market so as to obtain monopoly profits must be present.[10]

Therefore, everything would be about the comparison between prices and marginal costs. It happens that, as the authors themselves admit, the marginal cost is very hard or almost impossible to calculate. Owing to this, the authors suggest a substitute for the marginal cost. This would be the average variable cost.[11] Even if not identical, the average variable cost would be equivalent, by measuring the average of variable costs of the company's total production divided by the number of goods produced. To eliminate uncertainties in the calculation of the average variable cost, uncertainties related to what would be fixed costs and what would be variable costs, the authors suggest a listing of what are the fixed costs. All the other costs should be considered variable.

With this series of definitions, simplifications and assumptions, the authors intend to identify a simple and definitive criterion, which would allow an easy

---

sion by the Court of Justice is from November 3, 1991 and can be found in Raccolta della Giurisprudenza della Corte di Giustizia e del Tribunale di Primo Grado I, p. 3359, C-62/86; both commented in P. Manzini, *L'esclusione della concorrenza nel diritto antitrust comunitario*, cit., p. 149 *et seq.* and 168 *et seq.*

10 P. Areeda & D. Turner, 'Predatory Pricing and Related Practices under Section 2 of the Sherman Act', cit., p. 709 *et seq.*

11 P. Areeda & D. Turner, 'Predatory Pricing and Related Practices under Section 2 of the Sherman Act', cit., p. 716 *et seq.*

decision by the courts. It is the excess of simplicity of this solution that accounts for many of its criticisms.

The possibility of recovering the costs incurred in predation   Much criticism was made of the simplistic approach of Areeda and Turner, as mentioned before. Many of them are already incorporated into the dominating neoclassical theory on predatory prices.

The first and simplest is the one that refers to the chosen parameter of prices. Many authors and many North American court decisions expressly reject the disregard (present in Areeda/Turner) of the average total cost.[12] It is stated that there is no logical reason whatsoever to imagine that a company, operating rationally, would not want to establish their prices at higher levels than their total cost. In this way, it is concluded that prices below the average total cost already deserve attention and analysis by the antitrust authorities.[13]

There is also another economic point raised, of fundamental importance for the later evolution of the theory of strategic behavior. It is on the reflection of predation as not only a strategy for leading already established competitors out of the market, but as a way of avoiding the entry of new competitors.

This possibility illustrates how it is fundamental to take into account the effects of increasing production over the prices to calculate the level of prices necessary for the suspicion of predation to arise. Prices cannot be taken, like in the Areeda/Turner model, as a variable determined exclusively by the consumers. The market and the variations in quantity supplied are, in the marginal economic theory itself, the sources of the price variation.

It is stated, then, that the mere entry of a new competitor, with the increase in supply, already has the direct effect of a drop in prices. In this way, by analyzing the level of prices practiced by the potential predator, one should bear in mind that, even if above the limit values – like the average variable cost or the average total cost – these values could be predatory, as long as

---

[12]   Note that the total cost is calculated by the sum of fixed and variable costs. Therefore, the value of the average total cost is, in general, greater than the value of the average variable cost. The immediate effect of considering this value as a reference for determining the predatory price is the inclusion of a more ample margin of values (as it included values greater than the average variable cost and not greater than the average total cost – previously not characterized as illegal) and lower than average total cost. For the concepts of variable and fixed costs, see D. Carlton & J. Perloff, *Modern Industrial Organization*, 3rd ed., 2000, p. 29.

[13]   See *McGahee v. Northern Propane Gas Co.*, 858 F.2d, 1487, 1500 (11th Circuit 1980), see also, for other decisions, H. Hovenkamp, *Federal Antitrust Policy*, cit., pp. 314–15.

they correspond, after the entry of the new potential competitor(s) to a lower price than those limits.[14]

However, still according to the neoclassical economic scholars, the information on cost and price is not enough. And here comes perhaps the most important complement to the analysis based on the comparison between price and cost of production made by neoclassical economic theory. It is the statement that, for a strategy of predatory prices to be rational, it is fundamental that it is possible for the predator to recover the losses suffered during the price war. This is considered one of the most relevant complements, above all because it accounts, in good part, for the exiguity of the condemnations related to predatory prices in the court decisions.[15,16]

---

[14] See F. Scherer, 'Predatory Pricing and the Sherman Act: A Comment', in *Harvard Law Review*, 89, 1976, p. 869 *et seq.*

[15] The possibility of recovering costs with predation, once the objectives have been reached, would be standard proof for the demonstration of predatory prices according to the Brazilian Antitrust Authorities (CADE). See *Relatório Anual 1998/1999*, Brasília, CADE, 1999, p. 46. The paradigmatic case, which established such understanding in the Brazilian courts, was representation no. 273/92, in which the plaintiff was Nogam S/A and the defendant was São Paulo Alpargatas S/A. The consolidation of this understanding came with later trials, amongst which the example is Preliminary Investigation (AP) nº 08000.018467/95-06 (plaintiff: Hot House Indústria Metalúrgica; defendant: Metalcorp Ltda.). Still along these lines, but considering the recovery of losses through abusive profits in other markets (crossed subsidies), see Preliminary Investigation (AP) nº 08000.020787/96-62 (plaintiff: Associação Brasileira da Indústria de Panificação; defendant: Associação Brasileira de Supermercados). More recently, see Averiguação Preliminar 08000.018076/94-20, plaintiff: Labnew Indústria e Comércio Ltda.; defendant: Bencton Dickson Indústrias Cirúrgicas Ltda.; Processo Administrativo 08012.003578/00-18; plaintiff: Rodobens Administração e Promoções Ltda.; defendant: Mercedes Benz do Brasil S.A. e DaimlerChrysler Administradora de Consórcios S/C Ltda.; and Processo Administrativo 08012.007104/2002-98, plaintiff: Nellitex Indústria Têxtil Ltda.; defendant: Têxtil J. Serrano Ltda., judged on April 7, 2010.

[16] The structural factors and the inability to prove the possibility of recovery have taken to nearly zero the cases of condemnation for predatory prices in the North American court decisions. See J. B. Baker, 'Predatory Pricing after Brooke Group: An Economic Perspective', in *Antitrust Law Journal*, 62, 1994, p. 585. Also in the European Court, with the exception of the *Akzo* case already described, condemnations for predatory practices are extremely rare.

Perhaps the most striking development in the US since the *Brooke* case has been the proposed Department of Transportation (DOT) Guidelines, which explicitly recognize predatory pricing as a strategic problem and would allow proof of recoupment based on reputation effects. These Guidelines focus on the ability of a major air carrier dominating a city hub to exclude competition and potential competition. For further development on this issue, see Christian Barthel, *Predatory Pricing Policy under EC and US Law*, Master Thesis, Faculty of Law, University of Lund, 2002.

So strong was the impact of this idea, that important authors even defended that the most convenient way of repressing and de-motivating the increase of prices would be to impose a prohibition on the predator of increasing his prices in a certain period following the reduction.[17] The difficulties in administrating this criterion, which would imply necessity of a strict control of prices by the antitrust authorities, led to the non-implementation of concrete policies along these lines.

Structural criteria were then developed that allowed the assumption of the possibility of recovery. They were, basically, the existence of market power (that is, large market share) on behalf of the predator and the existence of entry barriers for new competitors and re-entry of competitors that had left the market.[18]

The first criterion would be necessary to avoid the price war becoming excessively long and expensive for the predator. Effectively, with no market power, the predator would, in case he wanted to eliminate from the market the economic agent(s) with greater market share, have to enter a long and hard fight, sacrificing huge financial resources. The second, in turn, would ensure the monopolist profits that, at the end of the day, are the reason for the predation. If the competitors can easily re-enter the market when prices have already increased again to competitive prices or even monopoly prices, the strategy of predatory prices would, again, be irrational.

The first doubts: The cost of errors in the economic evaluation   The difficulties with this criterion soon become visible both in the legal literature as in the economic.

The first sign that something was really missing in the neoclassical thesis appeared in an interesting article written in partnership by an economist and a law professor.[19] The central point in this article is the analysis of the costs of errors in the evaluation of the existence of predatory costs. Still without being able to completely cut off from the neoclassic rationalistic dogma, the work contains a very important element, central for the evolution of the way of

---

[17]   W. Baumol, 'Quasi-permanence of Price Reductions: A Policy for Prevention of Predatory Pricing', in *Yale Law Journal*, 89, 1979, p. 1 *et seq.*

[18]   H. Hovenkamp, *Federal Antitrust Policy*, cit., p. 307 *et seq.* The author also develops two other criteria that would help recovery. The idle capacity of the predator would allow at any moment a greater thrust of products in the market at reduced costs, reducing, therefore, prices in the price war and the certainty that the productive factors of the victim company would leave the market, instead of being bought at low price by a competitor. Both are, however, only facilitating factors and not fundamental elements for the success of a predation.

[19]   This is the article by P. Joskow & A. Klevorick, 'A Framework for Analyzing Predatory Pricing Policy', cit., p. 213 *et seq.*

thinking on the subject: the belief in the fallibility and inconclusiveness of economic data. The authors develop a criterion whose central element is the comparison of the negative effects of the errors in the evaluation of predatory prices.

So two categories are created, respectively called false positives and false negatives. The false negatives occur when it is believed that there is no practice of predatory prices when this is, in fact, happening. The false positives occur on the opposite hypothesis.[20]

For the analysis of probabilities of errors, the traditional neoclassical theory is used in its modified form described previously. They talk, therefore, of the existence of a double test, the two-tier test, which would involve, in the first place, analysis of prices and quantities produced and, in the second place, structural analysis.

The most important element in this analysis is, however, the structural part and not the comparison of prices and costs. The latter will be relevant only in case the structural analysis shows that there is effective risk of monopolization.[21]

So market power becomes relevant, as in its presence a false negative would lead to an even greater situation of monopolization, with all the consequences generated from it. The study of entry barriers serves the same purpose.

These authors also introduce a new element: the so-called 'technological dynamics'; in other words, the analysis of the effects of concentration on technological development. If the effects are positive – that is, if it is shown that power concentration will stimulate the improvement of products through the use of new technologies (which rarely occurs), then the cost of a false negative will be small. If they are negative, the costs of a false negative will be considerably greater.[22]

Again, it is important to emphasize that, much more than the details and analytical methodology, evidently still of neoclassical inspiration, what is relevant in this theory is the critical posture in relation to the neoclassical dogma

---

[20]   Cf. P. Joskow & A. Klevorick, 'A Framework for Analyzing Predatory Pricing Policy', cit., p. 222.

[21]   In relation to the price–cost proportion, they adopt the idea that any price below the average *total* cost leads to the assumption of predation. It will then be up to the company to show that, in its specific market, the level and maximization of profit occurs below the average total cost. This will happen, for example, if the sector is operating with excess supply, as in this case average total cost is less than marginal cost – see P. Joskow & A. Klevorick, 'A Framework for Analyzing Predatory Pricing Policy', cit., p. 252 *et seq.*

[22]   See P. Joskow & A. Klevorick, 'A Framework for Analyzing Predatory Pricing Policy', cit., p. 245.

of economic rationale. This criticism goes to the point of reconstructing the entire analysis based on the possibility of error in the decisions oriented by economic reasoning and its respective consequences.

Criticism of the neoclassical notion of the rationale of the predator   The observations above seem to lead us to some kind of logical chaos. The debating and criticism of the presuppositions of the neoclassical rationalists do not seem to have been able to pave the way to the building of a coherent theory, capable of establishing a criterion for the analysis of the existence of predation other than the neoclassical marginalist rationalism.

We will now present the faults and gaps existing in the neoclassical presuppositions and, following that, the errors to which the adoption of these presuppositions lead. The criticism formulated will constitute the foundation for the elaboration of a legal theory, alternative to the economic one.

Game theory seems to provide us with instruments for a change, that is, for abandoning the neoclassical notion, which is intended. This theory provides us with different analytical instruments. It is not able, however, to formulate new criteria of identification of illegal predatory action. This definition must be based on values and is part of the legal reasoning presented below.

We do not wish, therefore, to make the same mistake as neoclassical theory, trying to deduce rules of behavior from absolute and supposedly universal economic postulates. The plan is to make good use of the economic theories and especially of game theory. For such, it must be understood that what these theories do is only to indicate possible behavior tendencies and, therefore, show us where to look, offering analytical data that allow the identification of the most relevant problems that need to be solved.[23]

In an environment governed by the market system, the main concern of the economic agent is with the behavior of its competitor. A very simple example illustrates this fact nicely. Imagine two gas stations, situated one next to the other. Suppose that these are the only two stations in the city and that there is not, at least in the short term, the possibility of the establishment of new competitors.

None of them can vary prices to gain more market share, without the other one reacting immediately. The instantaneous reaction and the possible infinite duration of a 'game' of this kind make any sort of predatory strategy on behalf of one of the competitors unfeasible. Knowing what will be the reaction of the

---

23   See, on this matter, W. Tom, stating, after an analysis of the practical application of the game theory in antitrust law: 'To the everyday antitrust practitioner, game theory offers some clues for where to look, but even more, it underscores the need to use all available tools to interpret what we find' – 'Game Theory in the Everyday Life of the Antitrust Practitioner', in *George Mason Law Review*, 5, 1997, p. 457 (469).

competitors, and seeing that the dispute will lead to a situation that will perpetuate for an undetermined period of time, economic agents necessarily tend towards cooperation.[24]

This rather simple statement, observable in the day-to-day behavior of oligopolies, gave way to the development of the entire theory of oligopolistic behavior. In formal theoretical terms, it states that every time there are an infinite or undetermined number of rounds in the game or its participants are not capable of identifying the end, there is natural motivation to cooperation. In the terminology used in game theory, this strategy is necessarily collective.

It is important to know what would happen when the competitors have an idea of the number of rounds, or at least know who will be the last one to 'play'. In this case, it is possible to draw an individual strategy. Imagine, for example, a monopolist in relation to his competitor. In case there are signs – and the disparity in economic-financial strength of both is an example – that the competitor will not be able to adequately respond to a price war, the economic agent has all the motivation for predation. Faced with a situation where a price reduction would lead to non-marketing levels (this expression is deliberately vague and will be better explained further on), the intention of predation is unmistakable.

The reason is that, in the event of being difficult to assume that the predation victim is capable of reacting indefinitely, for its economical-financial weakness relative to the predator, this 'game' should be considered to have a determined duration. Consequently, the probability that there is a dominating strategy directed at eliminating the competitor is quite high.

At this point, it is important to be sure we can intuitively understand these considerations, perhaps excessively theoretical. And here, in directing our intuition, game theory can definitely help us.

This rationale is surely not the neoclassical one, which believes that the company calculates and takes into account all the variables, including and especially the future variables – such as, for example, the possibility of recovering losses incurred. This kind of rational calculation is the example, as is shown by the theory of limited rationality, of what is unfeasible and unreal in practice. A calculation of this kind about the future implies theoretical difficulties and uncertainties (on the future itself) that prevent any kind of rational calculation.

Furthermore, as will be discussed below, the value of predation cannot be verified in merely objective terms. There are many other results, such as the

---

[24]   See for more detailed description of this example D. Carlton, R. Gertner, & A. Rosenfield, 'Communication Among Competitors: Game Theory and Antitrust', in *George Mason Law Review*, 5, 1997, p. 423 (430).

creation of a reputation of aggressiveness, which are not part of the rational calculation of the recovery value.

The rationality of the economic agent is, on the contrary, a lot simpler. It is that of the player operating with complete coherence between means and ends. As long as there is an effective possibility of making it, and success here is not conditioned to a specific numerical calculation, the economic agent will try to stay in the market. Consequently, it is up to the law to develop criteria that look for: (i) the cases in which a competitor has chances of eliminating another from the market; and (ii) when it is possible to learn from his behavior that he had the true intention of doing so.

Predation and strategic behavior: The original unlawfulness in the structure of the economic relation   Everything that was said up to now seems to point towards a presupposition of the existence of a predatory rationale of the economic agents.

This statement is, however, excessively generic and that is exactly its fault. In the first place, what was said above is that the economic agent does not always have structural incentives for predation. On many occasions, he may be motivated to cooperation (which, as we know, also requires antitrust control).

It is unquestioned and even obvious, therefore, that it is impossible to assume predatory intention.

These considerations, essentially theoretical, gain clarity when analyzing predatory behavior. In the first place, it is fundamental to define the terminology used. In terms of predation, the effect, whose verification is unnecessary (even because it is impossible), is whether the predator will be able to enjoy or not the domination he desires, that is, will the predator manage to recover the losses suffered in the price war. The reason is simple. The behavior to be punished is the one that is directed at the elimination of the other competitor from the market and not the abuse of future prices by the one who obtained monopoly through predation.

The existence of specific provisions determining the unlawfulness of price abuse in the law and its relation to predatory prices is not casual. The consequence is clearly to make illogical, also from the legal point of view, the presupposition – which in the end is what the neoclassical theoreticians do – that the only function of the unlawfulness of predatory prices is to prevent future price abuse.

However, the great problem with behavior analysis in antitrust law, in general and with particular emphasis in relation to predatory prices, is that it may have double interpretation. It may be understood as an extremely pro-competitive act as well as an anti-competitive act.

A reduction in prices is the clearest example. It may be understood as a deeply pro-competitive act or, if not, if it aims at the elimination of the competitor, as a highly anti-competitive conduct. The distinction between these two forms is and will be in the structure of the market. As we have seen, the unlawfulness is not in the behavior itself (price reductions), but in the anti-competitive strategy, inclined to the elimination of the competitor from the market; strategy that results directly from the existing legal structure for the relationship between the agents.

The legal theory of predation   A conclusion must now be attempted, explaining the meaning of the legal theory of strategic behavior.

As was shown in the first chapter, the real criticism of the myth of marginal rationale is founded in the concrete definition of legal structures from which it is possible, in the absence of certainty about the economic results, to assume the practice of abuses.

As we have also seen, it is not possible to be sure of the economic effects of the practices. It is clear, therefore, that for the definition and analysis of unlawfulness there must be, at least, the certainty that there are structures that allow the prediction of certain legal results – abuse of consumers or competitors or exclusion of entire sectors from dynamic economic activity.

That was exactly the foundation for the famous decision of the Commission and the European Court in the *Akzo* Case.[25] Analyzing the defendant's (Akzo)

---

[25]   In short, the facts of the case were the following: Akzo Chemie and its branches form the division of specialized chemical products of the Dutch multinational company AKZO NU, which produces chemical products and fibers. ECS (Engineering and Chemical Supplies) was a small company whose main activity was producing and selling additives for flour. The British branch of Akzo (Akzo UK) produced organic peroxides, reselling them in the market of plastic polymers and in the market for flour additives. In the 1970s ECS bought the peroxides produced by Akzo UK, reselling them, after processing, as flour components in the British and Dutch markets. In 1977, after a series of price increases by Akzo UK, ECS decided to produce the peroxides necessary for the flour themselves, managing in a short period of time 30% of the English market and also selling in the continent. In 1979 ECS started supplying the peroxide also in the market of plastic polymers at a price about 15% lower than what was charged by Akzo UK. Attacked in the market that earned them the best results, Akzo UK reacted, reducing the prices of the polymers not only in the market of plastic polymers, but especially in the market of additives for flour. ECS, having understood that this behavior constituted an abuse of dominating position according to article 86 of the Treaty of Rome, sued the competitor first before the High Court of London and then before the EEC Commission. In their defense Akzo pleaded, expressly quoting the Areeda-Turner article, that they never practiced prices below their average variable costs. The EEC (EU) Commission in December 14, 1985, based on article 3 of regulation no. 17, condemned Akzo Chemie BV (Controller of Akzo UK) to the payment of a fine for having, among other things, systematically offered and supplied 'at abnormally low prices with the aim of harming the commercial activity of ECS' –

defense, based on the Areeda/Turner thesis, the European Commission stated that this model ignores medium and long-term strategic behavior and other elements, like discrimination between groups of consumers.

But, above all, the Commission understood that the concept of efficiency incorporated in the economic model of predatory prices is incoherent. According to the E.E.C. (E.U.) Commission, the belief in the per se efficiency of the reduction of prices (and the concept of subliminal efficiency to a test so restrictive in relation to the characterization of predatory prices) is incompatible with the objectives of the Treaty. The simple fact that the price charged is above the average variable cost does not imply legality per se of the conduct. It must be determined whether or not it is anti-competitive, as the protection of choice is the ultimate objective of the rules of competition in the Treaty. Therefore, to determine the existence of a predatory objective, it is necessary to verify if there is a strategy that is expressly directed to the elimination of competition.

It is important to note that this difference of objectives between economic theory and legal theory has deep influence in the evaluation of behavior. Giving priority to the value of choice (and competition) necessarily leads to a concentration of unlawful elements in the intentions next to the effects and in the relations between both but not in economic results.

The practical consequence is, therefore, direct. The economic theory – neoclassical – of predation seeks economic criteria that allow the determination of what kind of behavior can lead to the elimination of efficient rivals. The

---

decision of the Commission of 14/1285, 85/609 EEC in GUCE 374/1. This decision by the Commission was confirmed by the Court of Justice of November 3, 1991, C-62/86. It can be found on the Raccolta della Giurisprudenza della Corte di Giustizia e del Tribunale di Primo Grado (1991), I, p. 3359. In this decision, in spite of everything that was said about it, the Court adopted a thesis very close to the legal theory of predatory prices. Making references to previous decisions, it stated that the notion of abuse of dominating position of the article 86 is an objective concept that embraces the behavior of a company in dominating position that has the effect of creating obstacles to the conservation of the competition level still existing in the market or the development of the referred competition. Still according to the Court, article 86 does not forbid that a company in dominating position excludes a rival, but this should take place through means that characterize a 'competition of merits'. When establishing the criteria for such it does not go a long way off from the theory of strategic behavior. It states, accepting the Areeda-Turner thesis, that prices below the average variable cost are anti-competitive per se. Prices above the average variable cost but below the average total cost, as was the case with Akzo, could be anti-competitive, in case it is shown that 'it is inserted in a plan that aims for the elimination of the competitor'. The concern is clearly systemic and not with the effects of efficiency of the referred conduct – see, for the description and analysis of the decision by the Court of Justice from a clearly liberal point of view, P. Manzini, *L'esclusione della concorrenza nel diritto antitrust comunitario*, 1994, p. 171 *et seq.*

legal theory, in turn, is not content with the mere verification of economic effects, exactly because it gives priority to a value – choice (and competition) – and not to the economic effects. It requires the verification of a behavior that could damage competition, which can be defined as every behavior unjustified by a specific business purpose and which proves to be convenient for the company only if the competition disappears. The unlawfulness, therefore, is no longer only in the pure result, but in that conduct looking for a result and capable of reaching it.[26]

In practice, in terms of predatory prices, the difference is in the proximity of the conduct required in relation to the result desired. In the economic version, only behaviors that can on their own lead directly to domination of markets are predatory. The effect that has to be shown is a direct effect of abuse of the consumer.

In the legal theory, in turn, relation with the result is intermediated by an evaluation of intentions, presumed from the concrete possibility of causing effects. So, the behavior that shows no economic sense to the agent that practices it (as the agent can suffer losses), together with structural requirements that indicate the reasonable risk of leading to the elimination of the competition, even if this does not actually happen, can also be considered unlawful.

Predatory prices and economic structures   There now must be, based on the theory developed, an analysis of the requirements for the configuration of the two main forms of predation: through prices and predation through technological innovation.

---

26   This dichotomy is particularly clear in an article by W. J. Baumol on the theme 'Predation and the Logic of the Average Variable Cost Test', in *Journal of Law and Economics*, 39, 1996, cit., p. 49 *et seq*. The author, to sustain the neoclassical thesis of the need of the average variable cost as the only possible standard of verification of unlawfulness, differentiates right at the beginning two possible justifications for predation in general: (i) the inexistence of a legitimate business purpose and (ii) the objective of causing harm to competitors. He then tries to analyze the criteria price vs marginal cost for the two justifications. The first is discarded from the start, with no further explanations (pp. 53–5; the author only makes the obvious observation that there is no way of differentiating the legitimacy of prices above marginal costs – which evidently does not settle the matter, since it must be determined if it is possible or not to consider legitimate prices below the marginal cost). Next, he goes on to describe, up to the end of the article, the incoherence of the criteria of marginal costs in case the justification for unlawfulness is the neoclassical thesis of elimination of the most efficient rival. The need of discarding the first justification clearly shows the non-acceptance of competition as a value to be protected. Once this value is accepted, every behavior that tries to harm it becomes illegitimate. So, as we will see, a behavior that doesn't bring any advantage to the economic agent unless there is elimination of the competition can be considered an act with no legitimate competitive purpose.

In the analysis of these unlawful acts, the value of choice (and competition) will become clear. Emphasis will be put, therefore, on the determination of the predatory objective and the search for structural conditions that allow us to assume that anti-competitive effects might be produced.

PREDATORY OBJECTIVE   Center of the discipline of strategic behavior, the predatory objective or intention is obligatorily the first object of analysis.

Clearly, the predatory objective does not represent greater problems when, through the company's internal material, it is possible to plainly demonstrate the predatory intention. Note, however, that this material must reveal the existence of real business planning directed to the elimination of the competitor. It is not enough to have evidence of the existence of will to do it, expressed by one or some of the directors or employees. From this documentation must result the existence of a plan, in which will be included definition of behavior and prediction of future market structures, without the competitor.

The question that follows is: but only in these cases is the existence of predatory intention admitted? Is it not possible to assume it from other behavioral and/or structural information?

The answer is, naturally, positive. Exactly for dealing with the existence of entrepreneurial planning, and not subjective intention, assumptions based on other objective data are also acceptable. There must, however, be identification of the elements that indicate the existence of this predatory intention. The theory of strategic behavior offers an excellent instrument for the objective search of intentions.

Let us take into consideration that economic agents have natural incentives to try to prevail in the market and that this may be obtained through the creation of a more efficient market strategy, or else, through unlawful strategy, prone to eliminate the competitor from the market. The reduction of prices, for example, could serve both purposes. Differentiating one objective from the other is not, however, a difficult task. The most generic standard is entrepreneurial good sense, that is, a sensible businessman does not desire losses.[27] As well as a standard of care in business relations, this entrepreneurial common sense is part of a standard of fairness in the market, very important in the analysis of the predatory purpose[28] and of economic behav-

---

[27]   This is the generic standard used by the Courts and the German scholars – see K. Kurt Markert in Immenga & Mestmäcker, *GWB Kommentar*, cit., sub § 26, Rdn 265, p. 1335, quoting decision by the BGH (BGHZ 97, 337, 348), according to which a price reduction could be considered acceptable when 'eine nach kaufmännischen Grundsätzen noch vertretbare Kalkulation erkennbar ist'.

[28]   Defending the need of using the fairness standard in the analysis of strategic behavior in general, see O. Williamson, 'Predatory Pricing: A Strategic and Welfare

ior in general.[29] This is because careless behavior cannot ever be taken as mere negligence or carelessness. It must be presumed that the businessman is aware or could foresee the losses he can inflict on his competitor. Therefore, such behavior, faced with the possibility of causing effects, inevitably indicates a predatory objective.

Entrepreneurial common sense also makes evident, *a contrario sensu*, the fairness of the conduct that is determined by an eminently comparative method.[30] One must compare the conduct practiced with what would be effectively convenient for the businessman.

The basic standard now becomes the opportunity cost. Fundamental for predation to exist is that it is possible to show that this kind of conduct will be more convenient than other alternative conducts only if the competitor (the predation victim) leaves the market or if, even if he remains, oligopolistic domination is possible on behalf of the predator (with or without the victim's participation).

This comparative standard requires two different kinds of comparison. To verify whether the alternative chosen by the businessman is better than the others – quality that will only exist if it leads to the competitor's exit – an analysis must undoubtedly be done, with the use of a static criterion that allows evaluation of the meaning of the conduct, allied to a dynamic criterion capable of understanding the potential effect over the market. These are the two criteria to be developed below.

COST AND QUANTITY OFFERED   We must therefore, in the first place, analyze the many meanings of charging prices below the cost. Selling below the cost,

---

Analysis', in *Yale Law Journal*, 87, 1977, p. 284 (337). It is very interesting to note that an economist like Williamson, when developing the theory of strategic behavior (he is, undoubtedly, one of the main designers of this theory in the economic field), has to give up ethical-legal concepts, like fairness. This fact seems to reveal the essentially legal character of the theory of strategic behavior.

29   The relation between fairness and the existence of competition is largely acknowledged, to the point of legal systems having exclusively trusted the protection of the first, believing this would naturally lead to the preservation of the latter. This is what happened in the German system and was proved insufficient. Hence the conviction of the modern line of thinking of the need for a specific discipline of the structures, which preserves and safeguards irrespective of the existence of competition – see C. Salomão Filho, *Direito concorrencial – as estruturas*, cit., p. 58 *et seq.* It is undeniable, on the other hand, that even if it is not enough, the discipline of fairness in competition is undoubtedly needed for the preservation of the existence of competition. This convergence of the two values happens exactly in the field of control of conducts.

30   See O. Williamson, for whom behavior comparison is the main element in verifying the fairness in the conduct – 'Predatory Pricing: A Strategic and Welfare Analysis', cit., p. 337.

even if the price is greater than the average variable cost is, in principle, against the common standard business behavior of the sensible businessman. Consequently, this strategy is potentially less lucrative for the businessman. It is not possible, however, to infer from that the intention or anti-competitive effect, that is, the intention to eliminate the competition.

The conduct thus generically described is, therefore, devoid of meaning. To analyze it, two kinds of competitors must be distinguished: the already established competitors and the new entrants.[31]

In the first case, a criterion of checking the existence of predation based on average variable costs makes sense only in very marginal situations. It is the situation in which the industry is operating with idle capacity. Especially in this situation, the curves of marginal cost and average variable cost are reasonably close and the curve of average variable cost is above the marginal cost. Therefore, only in this possible situation, even following the neoclassical marginal principle, can it be imagined that the average variable cost is a sure sign of predation, as no price smaller than the marginal cost will escape being caught by this test.

It so happens that this is the rarest hypothesis of predation, for a very simple reason. The idle capacity generally exists in situations of crisis. In these situations, companies are rarely willing to enter price wars, being more concerned in fighting for their own survival. The price war is a lot more probable exactly in the possibility of the absence of idle capacity, when the test cannot be applied, and should be substituted for the average total cost. The latter will always be above the marginal cost, ensuring, therefore, that all possible hypotheses of predation by price are subject to scrutiny (avoiding, therefore, the problem of false negatives already discussed).

In the second case mentioned above, predation aimed at hindering the entry of competitors, the price–cost comparison is not the most convenient. The entry of a new firm has a natural effect on the increase of supply and the consequential drop in prices, which cannot be disregarded. This makes any comparison between price and cost very risky. Strictly speaking, it would be necessary – to know if the predator's price is below cost – to calculate with a projection what the price would be after the entry of the new competitor. This price is evidently below the previous price. But only if the post entry price is below the cost can it be inferred that the price charged previously was predatory. The effectiveness of these price projections is, however, extremely risky.

Facing so many uncertainties, an alternative static criterion for the evaluation of the predatory conducts in relation to entering competitors must be

---

    [31]   See O. Williamson, 'Predatory Pricing: A Strategic and Welfare Analysis', cit., p. 285.

found. An interesting criterion is that of the quantity supplied. Imagine, for example, the case of a dominating company that witnesses the entry of a new enterprise in the market. There are three possible behaviors: maintaining the quantity supplied the same; reducing the quantity supplied as a reaction to the increase in supply resulting from the entry of the new competitor; or increasing the supply, to reduce the prices and predate the new competitor. For the reasons already explained, the third conduct is clearly predatory when compared with the others, as long as the new competitor is obliged to withdraw himself from the market.[32]

What remains to be done, therefore, is to examine in both hypotheses – predation between already established competitors and predation of entering competitors – the conditions that indicate that the elimination of a competitor is a feasible possibility. This is an indispensable requirement. Without it, the existence of a predatory intention cannot be reasonably assumed.

POSSIBILITY OF DOMINATION IN THE MARKET: THE IMPORTANCE OF STRUCTURES
The dynamic element of the legal theory of strategic behavior is profoundly different from the criteria of the possibility of recovery, elaborated by the neoclassical theoreticians.

As we have seen, the neoclassical criterion of the possibility of recovery in the end is centered in the verification of structural data, like the existence of market power and entry or re-entry barriers.

The definition of these requirements is based on the assumptions that: (i) only starting off from a position of market power could the price war be sufficiently short to allow the later recovery of its costs; (ii) only if he acquires monopolistic power could the predator recover the losses; and (iii) the recovery of losses should happen in the same market in which the predation occurs.

These assumptions, all of them, are wrong. The first one contains a false presupposition that the victim of predation can take on a price war as long as it still has market share. This is the dogma of free access to financing. It is assumed that the war would be bearable as long as the competitor remains in the market because it is possible to seek in the financial market the resources to fight it. Consequently, it will be so much longer and costlier for the predator according to the amount of the victim's market share.

This statement is doubly false. Even in economies with easy access to financing and low interest rates, it is of doubtful applicability. Typical victims of price wars are companies in precarious financial conditions, whose access to credit, in any situation, is restricted (either for not being available or for

---

[32]   For the more detailed description of these three possible kinds of behavior – see O. Williamson, 'Predatory Pricing: A Strategic and Welfare Analysis', cit., p. 338 *et seq.*

being too expensive to the point of becoming unfeasible). There is no reason to imagine that amidst a price war this situation would change.

In the reality of less developed countries, the criticism is doubled. The access to credit is restricted and/or expensive. Seeking financing in a price war would, without doubt, be an accelerating factor of the victim's disappearance.

Consequently, a price war could be shorter than imagined if the predator is a company with non-monopolistic market share, but with great financial power. This indicates that market power is not necessary, at least in the initial phase of the war. Financial power and accumulated profits, be they in the market where the predation is taking place or in another, where the predatory holds monopolist position, and, above all, financial power comparatively much greater than the victim's, are more than enough to take ahead a predation with a good chance of success.

The second presumption is also untrue. Market power is not a necessary requirement for the later recuperation of losses suffered. Today the thesis of oligopolistic recuperation is well accepted.[33] According to this theory, even with a small market share, it is possible to raise prices to supra-competitive values. It is enough for the predator to reduce the market to a situation with few participants, where there are the necessary conditions for parallel behavior between the oligopolists.

The reduction in the number of participants and, above all, the 'punishment to those who obstruct or oppose the coordination of positions in the market' could be an excellent element to motivate parallel behavior. So, the price war is a strong motivator of parallel behavior; be it because it induces the exit of rebellious economic agents, or because it shows them that aggressive behavior related to prices is not a rational strategy in that market.

This last observation suggests another weakness in recovery theory. Recovery could happen not through obtaining profits, but through eliminating a source of losses. Imagine a new competitor, who enters a market comfortably dominated by great and 'lazy' (in the sense of little concerned with costs) oligopolists. Imagine also that this company lowers the prices to levels lucrative for it, but not lucrative for the oligopolist. The strategy of the oligopolist could be to reduce prices foreseeing that the consequence will be the elimination of the competitor from the market – and in this case he will increase prices and recover his losses – or at least the lesson to this competitor that price wars, even if based on efficiency, are not convenient in this market.

---

[33]   Even in the decision of the aforementioned *Brooke Group* case, where the American Supreme Court is clearly influenced by the neoclassical postures in relation to predatory prices, the possibility of oligopolistic recovery is acknowledged. See J. B. Baker, 'Predatory Pricing after Brooke Group: An Economic Perspective', in *Antitrust Law Journal*, 62, 1994, p. 594.

For the oligopolist this could represent only the elimination of the loss he was having by losing clients, and not the production of future profits – assuming that, hypothetically, after the end of a price war, with the ('domesticated') competitor remaining in the market, there can no longer be monopoly profits. So, even eliminating losses could be a strategic objective of predation.

Finally, the last statement is also false. And here is the key point of the criticism based on the theory of strategic behavior, which would make useless even the previous criticisms. The structural characteristics enumerated by the neoclassical theoreticians to determine the possibility of recovery are not necessary.

Recovery can be done in many ways that have little to do with a direct economic recovery of losses.

It can happen through forming a reputation of *crazy firm*, which is willing to risk its own survival to gain market share or induce cooperative and non-aggressive behavior from the other competitors.[34]

It must necessarily be concluded, therefore, that predation brings direct and indirect benefits to the predator that cannot be measured in exclusively economical terms. Reputation is one of them.

But not only in the same market can this kind of non-economical benefit be obtained. It can also happen in other markets, other than where the predation took place. This is what some scholars denominate *multi-market recoupment*.[35] The reputation created in one market makes the competitors in other markets think twice before adopting aggressive competitive strategies against the predator. Even with lower production costs, they can opt for not reducing prices, fearing a counterattack from the opponent that could eliminate them from the market.

So, the possibility of direct economic recovery of costs does not and cannot make part of the planning of the predatory company. Consequently, this cannot be a requirement for the configuration of the predatory objective.

For the configuration of this objective, much more important is the effective possibility of eliminating the competition. This is indeed an indication of the objective and, according to the theory exposed here, a consequence of the strategic objective of predation. For such, the criteria of price, amount supplied, and compared financial power, previously described, are fundamental.

Differently from the neoclassical theory, therefore, the elimination of the competition and not the recovery of losses is the potential effect to be checked.

---

[34]   M. Burns, 'Predatory Pricing and the Acquisition Cost of Competitors', in *The Journal of Political Economy*, 94(92), 1996, p. 266.

[35]   For a summarized account of this theory, see J. B. Baker, 'Predatory Pricing after Brooke Group: An Economic Perspective', cit., p. 595.

But the differences from the neoclassical theory do not stop there. Even in respect to the elimination of the competition there are fundamental discrepancies. Following the theory of strategic behavior, eliminating the competition can happen either by the exclusion of these competitors (most typical effect of predation) as well as by collusion with these competitors, which are, so to speak, 'domesticated' by the price war (in other words, they understand that the 'game' will only be lucrative if it is cooperative).

Finally, the possibility of eliminating competition is not to be mistaken for the neoclassical requirement of monopoly effects (such as abusive prices and recovery of losses suffered). The effects here are relevant for the determination of the existence of intention and not as a mere requisite for the assumption of the unlawful act.

There is still one more element missing for the complete configuration of the legal theory of predation. This would be the structural element. The referred market must have natural or economic entry or re-entry barriers. This does not mean a concession to recovery theory. After all, in the neoclassical theory of recovery, entry barriers are not, on their own, enough to ensure recovery.

The sole and exclusive aim of including the requirement of the existence of entry barriers is to ensure the potential of domination of the markets, be it by monopolistic or oligopolistic domination. Evidently, if it is possible for the victim to freely re-enter the market and/or for other competitors to do it, there will not be the effective exclusion of competitors nor market domination. One cannot, therefore, attribute to the economic agent the strategic objective.

These structural and behavioral elements, added together, serve to make the assumption that the behavior is predatory.

If those elements cannot be proven, only if the price is lower than the average variable cost[36] (since such practice has a direct relation to the (possibility of) elimination of the competitor) would the conduct be presumed unlawful. It would then be up to the charged company to show that there is no risk of eliminating the competitor, because prices are temporary or promotional.

Note that, when prices are lower than average variable costs, these are, in practical terms, the only possible defense arguments. It is extremely difficult, based on structural requisites, to show that the elimination of the competitor is impossible.

---

[36] There has been the suggestion of an important refinement of the concept of average variable cost for purposes of application of the discipline of predatory prices. It has been suggested that it should include all those costs that could be avoidable in the case of exiting the market. It defines, therefore, the concept of avoidable average cost, as the sum of variable costs and fixed costs that are not irrecoverable (see W. Baumol, 'Predation and the Logic of the Average Variable Cost Test', cit., p. 55). Therefore, the concept of avoidable average cost corrects the average variable cost, adding to it the fixed costs that are not irrecoverable.

The reason is simple. The structural requisite is, in the case of predatory prices, exclusively the existence of entry barriers. Well, if the prices charged are not promotional, the fact alone that they are below the average variable cost represents an entry barrier, as they cannot be recovered. The difference between prices and costs (in the negative hypothesis) that any competitor will have to incur by the simple fact of entering the market is an irrecoverable cost (understanding by irrecoverable cost all expenditures – be they investment or expenses – that cannot be recovered by exiting the market). The amount should also be considered by the agent who plans to enter the market. Should the price be lower than the average variable cost, this loss is quite expressive, especially if the industry requires large scales to become minimally competitive. In this case it constitutes, on its own, an important entry barrier.

Technological predation: creation of structures apt for predation   Predatory practices are not restricted to strategic changes in price and output.

And it is not difficult to understand why. The elimination of a competitor through imposition of losses can also be obtained by means of changes in the other fundamental variable for the consumer: product quality. Whenever there is substantial investment in product quality and it is not desirable to transfer the amount of the investment to the price, the effect may be similar to that of unjustified price reduction.

In current times, variation in product quality is carried out basically through technological changes. Hence the reason for the denomination of such practices: technological predation. It may include the creation of different economic structures able to eliminate competition from the market (be it companies or even competing sectors). It is an interesting phenomenon because, as we will see, the elimination of competition and market dominance are a result of the economic structure created.

More than that, as previously seen (Chapter 2), technological predation has the ability of creating qualified market dominance. It is not the typical dominance of the industrial era, through control of price and output. What really happens is a direct control over the very consumption and production patterns through technology.

This means that predatory conducts, in this case, may be very effective despite the initial absence of any market power in the neoclassical sense. Power is then built without the need for great participation in the market, as dominance over a technological pattern is sufficient. As we shall see, this fact generates additional concern for the discipline.

PREDATION THROUGH INNOVATION   The first and simplest form of strategic technological behavior is the introduction of technological innovations with the sole purpose of eliminating competition from the market.

The study of such predation also serves the purpose of destroying a myth. Not all innovation is positive in itself. It can be simply a strategy to eliminate competition and dominate the markets. Innovation does not always mean evolution.

On the other hand, it is important to acknowledge a very relevant economic characteristic, without which high technology industries and technological investments would be penalized. Economically, this type of sector is characterized by the existence of high initial fixed costs, necessary for the research and development of new technology, after which, generally speaking, production is relatively inexpensive.

This means that marginal costs decrease sharply and that the curve of total average cost is, for a fairly long period, substantially superior to the marginal cost curve.

Once these characteristics are understood, it is possible to formulate the meaning of predation through technological innovation. It is a variety of predation through price change.

Imagine agents who compete fiercely against others in the market of goods with certain, reasonably similar, technological standards.

Instead of altering the price, the predator changes, without any substantial improvement, its technology, with the sole purpose of making the previous product seem 'outdated' to the eyes of the consumer and forcing competitors out of the market.[37]

In such hypothesis, and if there is a predatory agenda in the technological innovation, instead of the prices becoming lower than the costs (as occurs in predatory pricing), costs are the ones that become higher than the prices, that is, the predator will continue selling the new product for the same price as the old product, without considering the costs of research and development of the new product.

This occurs, basically, in two situations. Firstly, imagine a low investment in technology combined with price identical to the one practiced for the outdated product, which is not able to recover this investment in the long run, that is, price inferior to the total average cost for a long period.

---

[37]   The original work, mandatory reference regarding predation through technological innovation and systems predation is J. Ordover & R. Willig, 'An Economic Definition of Predation: Pricing and Product Innovation', in *Yale Law Journal*, 91, 1981, p. 8. See also, with opposing view and arguing in a strongly Chicago School manner that 'it should be obvious that liability cannot turn on whether the firm's intent was to inhibit its rivals sales, because all competition hurts competitors in this way', J. Lopatka & W. Page, 'Microsoft, Monopolization and Network Externalities: Some Uses and Abuses of Economic Theory in Antitrust Decision Making', in *The Antitrust Bulletin*, 40, 1995, p. 317 (358).

Imagine also that the new technology is evidently poor, adding little or nothing in terms of utility for the consumer. In such hypothesis, the technological introduction was very likely predatory. It is not even able to recover the necessary costs for its development; what to say of the discontinuation of the sales of its own 'old' product?

This means that, if the technology is poor, there is no reason to introduce a new product whose price to the consumer is not higher than the cost resulting from research and development (especially because the technology is poor). The market loss by the old product is only substituted by the gains with the new product; the predator cannot increase prices. Consequently, the only use of the introduction of the new product is elimination of the competition.[38]

This hypothesis is applicable to established competitors. The situation is even clearer, as usually happens with strategic behavior, in the second above-mentioned hypothesis, when predation is directed to impede the entry of a new competitor. It is the so-called 'off-the-shelf product innovation'.[39]

Imagine an agent that introduces to the market a product that competes with one supplied by the predator. The latter, then, immediately introduces a 'new' product, with technology allegedly newer than and superior to the new competitor's. The simple introduction of the product immediately after the entrance of the other is in itself sufficient indication of predatory intention. If to this are added prolonged sales below the total average cost and a low level of innovation, there is clear indication that the behavior makes no sense economically, unless the intention is to eliminate the competitor and dominate the market.[40]

---

[38]   See J. Ordover & R. Willig, 'An Economic Definition of Predation: Pricing and Product Innovation', cit., p. 49, to whom this fact demonstrates that technological innovations can be predatory even if they effectively increase utility for the consumer. As shall be seen, this is what often occurs in the software industry.

[39]   See regarding the off-the-shelf product innovations J. Ordover & R. Willig, 'An Economic Definition of Predation: Pricing and Product Innovation', cit., p. 28.

[40]   In the doctrine, the possibility of the existence of a third type of predation is evoked. It is the pre-announcement of a product aiming at impeding the entry and acceptance of the competitor's new product. A very common practice is to announce the launch of a product, supposedly superior to the competitor's product that is being launched, when, in fact, the development of the software or operational system has not even been initiated. This happened, for example, in 1990, when, one month after the launch of the DR–DOS 5.0 by DRI, Microsoft announced the launch of its MS–DOS 5.0, a launch that would only take place in July 1991. Besides, curiously, the Microsoft product had as innovations only adapted reproductions of the DR–DOS 5.0 innovations – see K. Baseman, F. Warren Boulton & G. Woroch, 'Microsoft Plays Hardball: The Use of Exclusionary Pricing and Technical Incompatibility to Maintain Monopoly Power in the Market for Operating System Software', in *The Antitrust Bulletin*, 40, 1995, p. 265 (272). See also criticism on this type of wrongfulness, in the sense that it

Here, however, as in the cases of predatory pricing, a static analysis is not sufficient. Besides the certainty of the loss, it must be possible to suppose that the predator will gain market share. When dealing with the introduction of new technology, especially of a new and fairly poor technology, as happens on most predation cases, this requirement is not easily demonstrated. Unlike the price reduction that allows us to presume increase in market share, there is no reason to suppose that the consumer will not understand, at least after some time, that this technology brings little or nothing new, ceasing to buy the product.

The existence of an incentive that is relevant to the acquisition of the new product is therefore fundamental. The structural conditions are here much more necessary than in the hypothesis of price reduction.

It might be said that, typically, these conditions exist for network products, characterized by increasing returns to scale and positive externalities. The structure and operation of these types of market will be explained below, after the study of predation through systems, since it is useful for both. For now, it suffices to state that, in such cases, it is the existence of a network that facilitates the gains in market share by the producer and almost forces the consumer to acquire the product.

This typically takes place with computers and the Internet, but other sectors characterized by the existence of networks, such as telecommunications, power supply, etc. may also be subjected to it. Not surprisingly, most cases of technological predation occur in these sectors.

Note an interesting characteristic of the so-called technological monopolies. What can be achieved by the networks is completely different from what was envisioned by Schumpeter in his concept of creative destruction. There is no true technological progress. What exists is technological innovations aiming at pushing away not only companies but also entire competing sectors. Thus, in telephony for instance, huge is the effort by the telephone companies that provide Internet connection to transform both services into one and eliminate the users' choice of an independent communication pattern (eliminating

---

brings more information to the consumer and to the competitors themselves J. Ordover & R. Willig, 'An Economic Definition of Predation: Pricing and Product Innovation', cit., p.53 and J. Lopatka & W. Page, 'Microsoft, Monopolization and Network Externalities: Some Uses and Abuses of Economic Theory in Antitrust Decision Making', cit., p. 358. In fact, it seems difficult to determine the existence of predation in this specific hypothesis. The intention is obscure, not only for the uncertainty of its effects, but also for the inexistence of losses incurred by the predator. It seems easier and more logical to classify the hypothesis as an act of unfair competition (article 195, section I of the Lei n. 9.279, of May 14, 1996) when the information made public is obviously false, therefore misleading for the consumer and illegally restrictive of competition.

Internet providers, for instance). The same can be said for the Internet companies that attempt to transform telephony into an accessory to their products. Legitimate attempts, based on effective product improvement, must be set apart from those obtained through technological and system predation.

An initial situation of monopoly is not necessary either. As the Microsoft case clearly demonstrated, it is possible, through random historical events (the choice of IBM computers as standard) followed by a great deal of path dependence and, finally, successful technological predation strategies, to obtain almost complete market dominance through the absolute control of technological standards.

PREDATION THROUGH SYSTEM INCOMPATIBILITY   The second hypothesis of technological predation is slightly more complex than the previous, but extremely common in reality.

Imagine a company B that offers components for the operation or use of the main product, another company A's system. Company A has, for example, important participation in the systems market (owing to, in the most common scenario, increasing returns to scale or the positive network externalities, which shall be addressed below). Imagine that the company also participates in the component market, competing against B.

In such a case, it is relatively easy for company A to carry out a predatory strategy against company B. It is enough to introduce a new system, incompatible with the goods produced by B.

In order for the predation to be successful, it must also ensure that its old system, compatible with the component produced by B, stops being commercialized or sold at prices high enough to make it unattractive to the consumer.

As the main objective of the new product is the elimination of the competitor, its technology is poor, adding little utility to the consumer. The research and development costs existed, but focused mainly on the discovery of new forms of incompatibility with the component produced by the competitor. Consequently, the predator cannot, or would wish not to, raise the price of the new product.

The result of all this strategy is the probable elimination of the competitor. The old systems, compatible, will stop being sold or will become economically unviable and the new ones are compatible only with the component produced by the predator itself. The static (profits reduction) and dynamic (possibility of elimination of competitor) elements are thus present.[41]

---

[41]   Another alternative way of verification of predation is the demonstration that, after the introduction of two systems, one compatible with B's products and one incompatible, the first being more lucrative than the latter, the predator opted for the second.

This type of situation may occur in any sector where there is creation of networks. The typical example, which shall be discussed below, is the actions of Microsoft in the market of operational systems, especially in the 1990s.

A reverse example can be found in the telephony sector. In theory, it would be interesting for one of the fixed (landline) telephone companies in Brazil, especially the ones who also act in mobile telephony, to make use of technical gimmicks, making the interconnection to rival companies, mobile network operators, impossible. Foreseeing this predation possibility, Brazilian telecommunications law imposed on the landline telephone companies, besides mandatory interconnection, the guarantee of compatibility between the networks – without which, as seen, the interconnection is innocuous.[42] Besides, it imposed a relatively low interconnection fee between landline and mobile operators, which led to a certain subsidy of the latter by the former. As will be seen below, the objective was to minimize the competition benefits deriving from the exclusive detention of the networks, preventing predation and allowing competition.

The result is remarkable and very illustrative of the relation between the fight against economic power and the development hereby defended. The true universalization of telecommunication services in Brazil ended up taking place not through the official agenda, set forth by law,[43] which envisions land-

---

This is referred to as evidence based on opportunity costs. In *Transamerica Computer Co. v. IBM,* 459 F. Supp 626 (1978), the plaintiff, Transamerica, tried to use this test, which was, however, rejected by the court, who understood that opportunity costs are not a good legal criterion – see critics of this decision J. Ordover & R. Willig, 'An Economic Definition of Predation: Pricing and Product Innovation', cit., p. 49, note 88. This test seems, in fact, very efficient to determine predatory intention, presumably exactly owing to the fact that the most onerous hypothesis for the company is chosen.

[42] Foreseen in Law (Act No. 9.472, of July 16, 1997), the interconnection necessarily implies network compatibility. The very definition of interconnection (article 146) states that interconnection is the connection of functionally compatible networks. The regulation of interconnection presupposes, therefore, the guarantee of compatibility. In this sense, the sections of article 146 foresee, concomitantly, the obligations of interconnection and the need of compatibility for integrated operation of the networks. Besides, article 150 of the same act states that the implementation as well as the operation and the interconnection shall be regulated by the Brazilian Telecommunications Agency, in order to ensure compatibility between networks of different companies.

[43] The Telecommunications General Act (Act No. 9,472, went into effect on July 16, 1997), in Portuguese, known as 'LGT', created the National Agency of Telecommunications (Anatel), an independent regulatory body for telecommunications sector. Prior to the creation of Anatel, Brazil's Ministry of Communications was the government body responsible for the regulation of all telecommunications services in Brazil. Upon its creation in the fourth quarter of 1997, Anatel assumed the Ministry's regulatory role (with the exception of broadcasting). In 1998, the General Plan of Universalization Goals (Federal Decree No. 2,592, of May 15, 1998) went into effect,

line telephony universalization. This, in the hands of private monopolies, became more expensive and scarce. What spread amongst the less privileged in society was mobile telephony. The so-called 'pay-as-you-go' or prepaid mobiles, which work without the payment of monthly or minimum fees, currently reach 202 million (density of 104 per cent), whereas landlines are restricted to figures of around 42 million.[44]

The conclusion is that in the Brazilian example, access to a relevant social service, with needed inclusionary effects, was obtained through fierce measures directed at introducing competition, including cross subsidies (from landline providers to mobile telecommunication companies, as a consequence of the low interconnection rates); whereas regulatory measures that did not interfere with the market power positions (as the universalisation ones), were devoid of real positive effect even if they were directed at obtaining social access to the service.

INCREASING RETURNS TO SCALE AND POSITIVE NETWORK EXTERNALITIES The study carried out in the previous sections purposefully left aside the dynamic requirement of predation, that is, how is it possible to be sure that the predatory practice will effectively exclude the competitor from the market?

The main factors for investigating the existence of such effect, absolutely sufficient to characterize the dynamic element, are the increasing returns to scale, or positive network externalities.

The increasing returns to scale constitute a new hypothesis of natural monopoly. They represent, in fact, a complete innovation in relation to the generally accepted microeconomic rule.

Until recently, the microeconomic postulate of the decreasing returns to scale was considered an undeniable truth. Its formulation is quite simple: the

---

establishing specific universal service goals for companies providing fixed telephone services under the public regime. In 2003, a new decree was enacted (Federal Decree No. 4,769, of June 27, 2003). Since 2007, the third edition of the General Plan of Universalization Goals, called, in Portuguese, 'PGMU III', has been discussed.

For further discussion on the universal access policy in the context of Brazilian telecommunications reform during the 1990s, see A. D. Faraco, *Regulação e Direito Concorrencial – uma análise jurídica da disciplina da concorrência no setor de telecomunicações*, J.S.D. Dissertation, University of São Paulo, 2001, C. M. S. Pereira Neto, 'Universal Access to Telecommunications in Developing Countries – The Brazilian Case', J.S.D. Dissertation, Yale Law School, New Haven, CT, 2005 (on file with the author). See also the Universalization Report, prepared by Anatel, 2009, available at http://www.anatel.gov.br/Portal/verificaDocumentos/documento.asp?numero Publicacao=225582&assuntoPublicacao=Universaliza%E7%E3o&caminhoRel=Cida dao-Informa%E7%F5es%20e%20consultas-artilhas&filtro=1&documentoPath= 225582.pdf.

[44]   See Anatel Annual Report, 2010.

bigger the output, the higher the level of satisfaction by the consumer and, therefore, the sale of one additional unit of the product becomes progressively harder and less lucrative.

There are some cases, however, in which the exact opposite happens. The bigger the number of users, the more useful the product becomes for the next user and, therefore, the easier and more lucrative the following sales will be.

This phenomenon typically occurs in network services, where all consumers integrate to a single network. The more users are connected to the network, the more useful it becomes for each of them. The result is that the traditional equation of the decreasing returns to scale is inverted: the bigger the output, the easier the sale of one additional unit of the product. An extreme example is the telephony system that, in fact, is only useful if all users are interconnected to the same network.

Exactly because of its congregating and utility-potentializing character, the network has two externalities (involuntary effects). The first, already mentioned, is the fact that the more consumers adhere to the network, the more useful it becomes for each of them. It suffices to imagine the Internet and the growth in the number of its users.

The second is an indirect externality. In the face of the existence of more consumers, more services are added to the network, making it more and more useful. It is, once again, the case of the Internet, which has everyday more providers of new services and information.[45]

Well, if the network, which is the center of the increasing returns to scale and the positive externalities, is not accessible to all, the competitor that will probably prevail is the one who arrives first or whose system or product has a competitive edge. Market prevalence, instead of being determined by efficiency, is fundamentally oriented by random or historical events, such as critical path theory suggests.[46]

Another matter arises that generates controversy among scholars. Certain economists connected to the Chicago School of thought still claim that, especially for being based on natural and/or historical events – as is the case of the first and only holder of the network – there should not be any interference in cases of natural monopolies. Their subsistence would serve the well-being of the consumer.[47]

---

[45]   The theoretical explanation on direct and indirect externalities and their application to the theories of natural monopolies can be found in M. Katz & C. Shapiro, 'Systems Competition and Network Effects, cit., p. 93 (96–8).

[46]   The critical path theory was originally elaborated in 1989, by Brian Arthur, in 'Competing Technologies, Increasing Returns and Lock-ins by Historical Events', in *Economic Journal*, 99, 1989, p. 116.

[47]   This theory is defended by Kenneth Arrow in his statement on January 17,

This claim faces a legal and a practical problem. The first is that legal systems normally do not foresee any antitrust immunity to natural monopolies. The rationale behind it is very simple. Even in the most liberal environment, it is impossible to deny that monopolization in a legal system is the exception and not the rule. Consequently, it is not possible to claim that any form of monopoly escapes legal control. Besides, even if it was alleged that the monopoly was obtained legally, the abuse in the exercise of the power deriving from it must, at any rate, be controlled.

But there is a second, even more serious problem. Natural monopolies, especially those based on positive network externalities, are rarely built on higher efficiency. In most cases, the events that lead to them are strongly influenced by predatory behaviors.

Experience shows that in sectors characterized by networks, especially in high technology, historical advantages are rarely sufficient to ensure market leadership. They have, however, a vicious effect. They direct all the technological effort of the agent who holds the competitive advantage towards the creation of incompatibilities for the maintenance of this initial advantage. There is no, as a rule of thumb, significant improvement in utility in such innovations.

In these markets, therefore, random historic events alongside predation determine the directions and identity of the dominant enterprise.

Relatively recent examples are the software industry, with Microsoft being penalized for technological predation,[48] and the technological convergence in telecommunications, Internet and cable television,[49] which, still in its infancy, is at risk of having its history determined by random historical facts and plenty of predation.[50]

Compulsory negotiation

The terminology used here (compensatory negotiation) is broad. That does not

---

1995, in favour of the performance commitment then signed by Microsoft Corporation, which was being criticized by competitors – see J. Lopatka & W. Page, 'Microsoft, Monopolization and Network Externalities: Some Uses and Abuses of Economic Theory in Antitrust Decision Making', cit., p. 333.

[48]   See *United States v. Microsoft Corp.*, 253 F.3d 34, 66-67 (D.C. Cir. 2001), cert. denied, 534 U.S. 952 (2001) (condemning Microsoft's 'commingling' of platform and browser code under '2 as a form of tying).

[49]   See T. W. Hazlett, 'Predation in Local Cable TV Markets', *Antitrust Bulletin*, 40, 609, 1995.

[50]   See Averiguação Preliminar 53500.004382/2003, Plaintiff: Brasil Telecom S.A.; Defendant: Empresa Brasileira de Telecomunicações S.A. – EMBRATEL, judged on July 21, 2010. In Portugal, see Processo T-340/03, *Wanadoo Interactive S.A.* available at http://eur-lex.europa.eu/LexUriServ/LexUriServ.do?uri=CELEX:62003A 0340: PT:HTML.

seem, however, to affect its precision. On the contrary, it is precisely in the mandatory (compulsory) character of negotiation that we can find the fundamental element to justify the combined treatment of the various hypotheses to be discussed below.

In a very brief and concise analysis, one can say that the mandatoriness or coercion (as it shall also be called hereinafter) consists in the determination of the key conditions of the deal by one of the contracting parties owing to the lack of economically viable alternatives for the other. The coercion may be realized through the imposition of a certain negotiation, as occurs in tied sales and reciprocal buying, or by not concluding the deal. It basically occurs through the refusal to deal and the exclusivity clauses.

In the case of compulsory negotiation, perhaps more than in any other conduct, the increase of power as a consequence of the structure of the economic relationship becomes evident. Indeed, the coercion is a direct consequence of the exercise of power in the economic relationship.

Evidently, the coercion is not the only element necessary for the existence of the compulsory negotiation. Alongside, it is necessary to study and discuss the ubiquitous goal of eliminating the competitor.

Not by chance, thus, as shall be seen in the first part of this topic, do the main doctrinal discussions, translated principally in legal terms, relate to two topics: coercion and the objective of eliminating the competitor.

In the second, third and fourth parts of this section, the main forms of compulsory negotiation will be analyzed: tied sales, reciprocal buying, refusal to deal and exclusivity clauses.

The traditional economic dispute   The issue of compulsory negotiation may be the one with the highest ability to be obscured by an exclusively economic analysis.

That is what demonstrates the dispute regarding tied sales that occurs today in doctrine and jurisprudence, which makes the former fluid and at times contradictory[51] and the latter swing in several directions.[52] Note that this clas-

---

51   These contradictions are very well demonstrated in two articles: L. Kaplow, 'Extension of Monopoly Power through Leverage', in *Columbia Law Review*, 85, 1985, p. 515 and A. Meese, 'Tying Meets the New Institutional Economics: Farewell to the Chimera of Forcing', in *University of Pennsylvania Law Review*, 146, 1997, p. 1.

52   These frequent changes are illustrated in US Supreme Court case law about 'tying arrangements'. Initially, the Court understood that the tied sale was not illicit – *United States v. United States Shoe Machinery Co.*, 247 U.S. 32 (59–67) (1918), considering licit an agreement of this kind. Four years later they changed radically their mind, beginning to consider that any tied sale that should tie a significant amount of sales would be illicit – *United Shoe Machinery Corp. v. United States*, 258 US 451, 457 (1922). Three decades later, apparently, the Court changed its positioning again, limit-

sic dispute of paradigmatic value can be generalized to all types of compulsory negotiation for having a common central element of qualification: coercion. Such is the intensity of the dispute that courts have felt compelled to deny the theories and appeal to the force of facts to implement the most just and coherent decision.

And it is not difficult to understand why. Two schools, as well known as outdated, give diametrically opposed explanations for the compulsory negotiation.

The first one is the school called classical.[53] According to its supporters, any form of coercion in the market is illicit. The fact of the seller being able to impose on to the buyer the purchase of a certain good already demonstrates its market power. Consequently, it is not necessary to demonstrate market power, once it is naturally proven by the success of the compulsory negotiation. As a result, tied sales are illicit per se precisely for being a demonstration of market power. The courts shall not, therefore, be concerned about the demonstration of this power, which is otherwise rather difficult and uncertain. There being coercion, sanction should be applied.

According to the classical school, through compulsory negotiation, the economic agent is able to transfer its power from one market to the other, doubling it. In the case of tied sales, the consumers who need its product are forced to purchase another product that they do not need or want. It is precisely this effect, of transportation of power from one market to the other, which the proponents of this theory (*leverage theory*) consider the fulcrum of the wrongdoing.[54]

---

ing the wrongdoing to the tied sales imposed by monopolists – Times – *Picayune Publishing Co v. United States*, 345 U.S. 594, (605) (1953), only to change its positioning once again five years later, stating that any tied sales, regardless of the market power held by the agent who performs it is illicit per se – *Northern Pacific Ry. Co v. United States*, 356 US 1 (11) (1958). In 1984, the Court seems to have returned to the criterion of market power – *Jefferson Parish Hospital Dist. No 2 v. Hyde*, 466 U.S. 2, (13–14) (1984). In the nineties, one more reservation is made, admitting the tying in cases of lack of accurate information and even in the absence of market power – *Eastman Kodak Co v. Image Technical Services* 112 S.Ct. 2.072 (1992).

[53] The classical theory has a clear origin in Harvard's structuralist thought. Not by coincidence, the most significant article of this line is precisely D. Turner's 'The Validity of Tying Arrangements under the Antitrust Laws', in *Harvard Law Review*, 72, 1958, p. 50; see also J. P. Bauer, 'A Simplified Approach to Tying Arrangements: A Legal and Economic Analysis', in *Vanderbilt Law Review*, 33, 1980, p. 233 and W. D. Slawson, 'A Stronger, Simpler Tie in Doctrine', in *Antitrust Bulletin*, 25, 1980, p. 671.

[54] See D. Turner, 'The Validity of Tying Arrangements under the Antitrust Laws', cit., p. 59.

As expected, the Chicago neoclassicals, argue counter to this, having developed the exact opposite of leverage theory, which is called fixed sum theory. According to this theory, and following the marginalist principles, it is argued that the monopolist will never be able to charge two monopolistic prices. As they have only one monopoly (at least initially) so as not to lose power in the original market, where they hold a monopoly, and should they already be charging a monopolistic price, they ought to ensure that the price of the main product when sold together with another (secondary product) is lower than when it is sold independently. This difference from the original to the lower price should correspond exactly to the positive difference between the utility of the secondary product to the consumer and its price.

All this corresponds to a very simple statement. The economic agents will not be able to charge two monopolistic prices unless they hold two monopolies. They shall find a combination that, in the end, always leads to the charging of one monopolistic price and the other competitive. However, this shall occur, according to the Chicago School, whether or not the secondary product is sold tied to the main product. There will not, therefore, be exercise of market power in any case. Thus, there is no need to worry about the compulsory negotiations, which should be considered lawful per se.[55]

Uncertain of their own conclusions, Chicago School scholars and their critics usually come to agree, directly or indirectly, not always willingly, even if only in theory, that the use of market power by the agent who does the tying of the market of the chief product will be the rule of reason to check the wrongfulness.[56]

It is not difficult to criticize the two constructions, classical and neoclassical. Both fail for the same reason: the attempt to explain the commercial transactions through simplified and unilateral economic theories.

The classical theory has a clear logical problem. It presents solely consequences but not causes of compulsory negotiation, and consequently ends up being effectively circular. It points out the possibility of power transfer, but does not explain how or why such a transfer would occur. The market power that could be invoked as a cause becomes a consequence of compulsory negotiation. Once it is in force, there is a demonstration of economic power. What could cause these sales to become effective remains, however, a mystery. The consequence of all this is the imposition of a rule of violation per se, insensitive to legitimate interests of the competitive system.

---

[55]   See R. Bork, *The Antitrust Paradox*, cit., p. 373; R. Posner, *The Chicago School of Antitrust Analysis*, cit., p. 925.

[56]   See in respect A. Meese, 'Tying Meets the New Institutional Economics: Farewell to the Chimera of Forcing', cit., p. 33, with reference points with mitigations and restrictions contained in between advocates of both theories.

The exact opposite happens with the arguments of Chicago. Their mistake is excessive liberalism. The fixed sum theory is target of considerable criticism. Here we focus on only two points, which are considered the most critical for addressing exactly the points with deepest root in the neoclassical thought. The first one refers to the very model used by Chicago. As stated earlier, the marginalist theory of prices is an essentially static model. It verifies what occurs at a given moment, having little or no capacity to predict the effects and/or future behaviors. Thus, the hypothesis of the fixed sum does not consider it possible that the economic agent is not concerned with maximizing profits at first, but interested in gaining power in the secondary market, so that, once he holds the monopoly, he will be able to take advantage of it. It ignores, therefore, the possibility of strategic behavior aimed at eliminating the competitor from the market.

But there is also a second mistake, concerning almost the philosophical stance of the Chicago School scholars towards economic reality. The hypothesis of the fixed sum is backed by a very relevant assumption, namely, that it is possible to identify and assess the utility of products to consumers in advance. Should that be the case, it would be possible to know how much and at what price consumers are willing to use the good. That is why, from the neoclassical point of view, every model of coercion should be necessarily based on market power. Only then would economic agents have control over the previously known demand curve, that is, over consumer utility.

There is, however, a fundamental problem. It is at least debatable, not to say unacceptable, that the utilities be measured theoretically.

The utility of a product does not have a theoretical definition, that is, a product is not acquired for being useful, but rather the opposite: it is useful because it is acquired. How is it possible then to know a priori what utility the consumer attributes to each product and, above that, what utility the consumer attributes to the two products sold together (which probably never occurred before)? The transformation of the consumer utility in monetary values leads to absurd results, precisely for disregarding the very value of the possibility of choice of the consumer.

If this is the assumption, then economic power, while remaining relevant, is no longer the center of attention. It is critical thus to understand the flow of information to consumers, which allows them to make their choices freely. It is there – and not in the imposed determination of the utilities – that economic power has influence.

Such analysis and criticism lead to two important consequences. Firstly, compulsory negotiation will not always be licit, as the Chicago School supporters might wish, and not always illicit, as the proponents of classical theory might wish. It will all depend on the effective possibility of coercion of the consumer, which may exist owing to several market imperfections, amongst which there is an undoubted highlight to imperfections in the transmission of information.

Moreover, the economic power of the agent who does the tying cannot be a central characteristic or criterion for resolving differences between the two extreme solutions. For a very simple reason: through the compulsory negotiation, more than benefiting from a particular utility for the consumer, there are intentions of creating it. A so far inexistent need is forced to emerge. Consequently, as shall be seen, compulsory negotiation does not constitute a misuse of economic power, but rather a means of gaining it.

These findings lead directly to two legal issues considered central to the analysis of compulsory negotiation: respectively, the legal concept of coercion and the correct systematic classification of compulsory negotiation.

Voluntary or compulsory negotiation　From the outset, it is important to make clear that the vast majority of practical examples offered herein will relate to the hypotheses of tying only to provide an easier and more consistent explanation. All generalizations and abstractions arising from them are, however, applicable to any case of compulsory negotiation.

Thus, for example, the element of coercion will be present in various forms of compulsory negotiation: in the tying through the obligation to acquire; in the exclusivity through the coercion to acquire; and even in the refusal to deal through coercion or negative coercion, consisting of not contracting.

Having made these initial reservations, the discussion immediately moves on to focus on the requirements to characterize the abuse. The first question is whether the element of coercion is really essential for the characterization of the abuse and why. The answer is simple and affirmative.

As seen before, the finding of the insufficiency of the marginalist explanation leads to a reaffirmation of the subjectivism of the economic choice. If so, the effective possibility of choice (competition) is the central organizing element of the overall operation of the market. It is critical that this choice be free. It cannot be determined by any external force other than the will of the consumer; hence, the value of coercion as a criterion for determining the existence of the abuse.

Previously, its broad concept was revealed. Now, it must be given substance, defining its causes and forms of disclosure. Coercion is juridical in the sense that it leads the consumer to perform a juridical act (purchase of the product), which it would not otherwise perform. Despite its effects on the juridical sphere, its source lies ultimately in the facts of economic life. Its practical verification is therefore eminently casuistic.

So it is that coercion may occur in relation to goods manufactured by only one economic agent or not. A typical example of the latter hypothesis (various economic agents) is the existence of legal or economic ties between the seller of the main product and that of the secondary product, which makes the former demand, in order to allow the sale of their product, that a third party's product also be acquired. Coercion may also be direct or indirect, that is, it may be performed either through the effective requirement of tied purchase of goods or the charging of different prices for the joint or separate acquisition of products. In the latter case, as long as the price difference does not correspond to an actual difference in cost (this last point shall be readdressed in more detail at the end of this section).

Finally, coercion does not need to be permanent. In fact, in most cases in which it is used as a means for market domination, it is temporary. Once a monopoly is obtained in the secondary market, the products may be separated, and each dominant situation independently enjoyed.

If the manifestations of coercion are highly diverse, complicating their theoretical classification and encouraging case analysis, the same does not occur with its economic sources – all are connected with the limitation of consumer choice possibilities.

As seen above, the vast majority of economic analyses of the various forms of compulsory negotiation err exactly by reducing the sources of coercion to a single concept: economic power. For the exposed reasons this concept is at once too broad and too narrow. The true competitive-legal source of coercion is economic dependence. And market power is only one possible source of dependence.

The dependence is characterized by the absence of reasonable and sufficient alternatives for the economic agent or consumer that takes part in the negotiation.[57] Therefore, unlike neoclassical market power, it is not an absolute concept. Also, contrary to economic power, which necessarily involves all economic agents and/or consumers who operate in that particular market as a monopolist's negotiating counterpart (buyers if they are the sellers, and vice versa), dependence may refer to a single economic agent that, based on their specific relationship with another, made them dependent on this other – which may occur in a series of situations illustrated below.

Here two reservations must be made. Firstly, it is important to make clear that coercion is presumed in the dependence – for one simple reason. Precisely because antitrust law is an institutional protection of competition and not an

---

[57] Thus, the German law defines Abhängigikeit (dependency), a central concept for the application of discipline for refusal to hire: 'Satz 1 gilt auch für Unternehmen und Vereinigungen von Unternehmen, soweit von ihnen kleine oder mittlere Unternehmen als Anbieter oder Nachfrager einer bestimmten Art von Waren oder geerblichen Leistungen in der Weise abhängig sind, dass ausreichende und zumutbare Möglichkeiten, auf andere Unternehmen auszuweichen, nicht bestehen' (§ 26, Abs. 2, Satz 2).

individual protection of certain economic agents, the competitive coercion is theoretical, characterized by lack of economic alternatives. It matters little if, in a concrete case, the consumer felt coerced or not. The possibility of coercion of an unknown and undetermined consumer leads to the effective limitation of competition.

The presumption is, however, relative. If it is possible to demonstrate that, even in the presence of dependence, coercion, even in theory, cannot occur regarding a particular type of business or consumer, the compulsory negotiation will be overruled. Once again, the evidence should be theoretical and economical. It is of little importance whether a consumer is ready to testify that they did not feel coerced.

The demonstration of the absence of coercion must be based on an economic argument that eliminates the possible causal relationship between dependence and the completion (or non-completion) of the negotiation, with *any reseller, distributor, consumer or competitor in that particular situation.*

The second reservation is even more important. What was said above does not and could not turn the concept of dependence into something subjective. The lack of alternatives is not determined by the subjective preferences of a particular economic agent, but is based on complex case law, which allows the empirical determination of the objective lack of alternatives.

This is how the hypotheses of dependence may be divided into absolute and relative, ranking among the former the ones that are binding for all economic agents in a given market, and among the latter the hypotheses of specific binding.

ABSOLUTE DEPENDENCE

Market power The first – but not the only, nor perhaps the most common – form of coercion is carried out through the exercise of economic power. In the face of the lack of competition, that is, the lack of choice in the market of the primary product and the unfeasibility of its replacement, the consumer or economic agent is constrained into accepting the secondary product, tied to the purchase of the principal one.

The most important element here is the classification of such practice as an abuse of dominant position or act aimed at market domination, which will be made below.

Lack of information: Secondary markets The second, and perhaps most common, form of absolute dependence arises from situations of limited information to the consumer or economic agent. The most recurrent of these situations occurs in the so-called secondary markets, targeted to serve or support the use of a core product.

The question arising here is to what extent the producer of a given good is capable of controlling the market of spare parts of such good and/or services market through the refusal to sell spare parts to the consumer without the purchase of the maintenance service, or the negative of sale of parts to 'independent' maintenance service providers, thus promoting their own 'authorized' services.[58]

Here, the compulsory negotiation is occurring in two different ways. On the one hand, for the independent service providers there is the refusal to deal. On the other, for consumers there is the tying.

Two, then, are the positions that can be undertaken. Firstly, one could argue that, in fact, the provision of maintenance services for the consumer is merely a complement to the very main good. If this occurs, the connection between them is natural and not coercive. This situation can be observed in very specific cases in which the high technological level of the products requires a highly skilled and specialized producer (and service provider), since only he can appropriately fix the good produced.

Note that in this case the consumer, highly sophisticated, will probably take into account the cost of maintenance when deciding whether to buy the product or not, precisely because they see in both, in fact, a single good.

In another hypothesis, much more common, especially when it comes to consumer goods of low or medium technological density, consumers will clearly distinguish the existence of two different products. One will be the good sold (the main product) and the other, the maintenance service. In this case, a forced connection between the two may in principle characterize illicit compulsory negotiation.

The two paragraphs above contain a typical example of what the legal translation of economic concepts mentioned earlier in this chapter means. Economically, we proceeded to simply defining the relevant market. Legally, this difference is revealed in the presence or absence of coercion.

---

[58] This issue was debated in the famous *Kodak* case, *Kodak Co v. Image Technical Services* 112 S.Ct. 2.072 (1992). Kodak took measures to limit the access of independent service providers (ISPs) to spare parts and thus force consumers to acquire maintenance services from Kodak themselves – here there is also coercion through refusal to hire. It does not take much effort to realize that the *fattispecie* is present in a countless number of authorized services for the consumers. By the breadth of its consequences and the recognition of the existence of competition infringement even in the absence of a market power, *Kodak* is considered a decision that opens the post Chicago era of legal business thought, having appeared on its trail a long literature on secondary markets – see among others C. Shapiro, 'Aftermarkets and Consumer Welfare: Making Sense of Kodak', in *Antitrust Law Journal*, 63, 1995, p. 483; S. Borenstein & J. K. MacKie-Mason, 'Antitrust Policy in Aftermarkets', in *Antitrust Law Journal*, 63, 1995, p. 455.

The legal translation of the economic postulate is particularly necessary in the matter of compulsory negotiations, because it presents the issue in due terms. Its treatment goes from marginalist to structural. If the analysis were restricted to the market definition, the decision on the existence of a single market or not would be based on abstract exercises of price increase of both products and verification of their likely effect on consumption.

In the case of a legal study of the legal acceptability or not of the connection between the two products, it is relevant to verify whether there were consumers who had been showing preference towards independent maintenance service providers. If the answer is affirmative, that service has some 'utility' for them. Consequently, the connection between the two products arises from dependence (the lack of alternative) and is not natural.

Note that, reasoning this way, the requirement of market power becomes clearly unnecessary. It is true that one could argue, as is indeed often argued, that dependence arises precisely from the monopoly that the manufacturer of the primary product has on the market of spare parts of his own good. This monopoly on the secondary market arises from the fact that the consumer is not willing to stop consuming the primary product, more expensive, only because supra-competitive prices are charged in the market of spare parts. Through this monopoly, the producer is able to promote its own maintenance services business.

Here again, the marginalist reasoning leads to a logical error. Market power is the result of existence of a successful tying and not the reverse, that is, it is possible to know that the agent holds the monopoly of the secondary market precisely because, in the presence of a tying, the consumers do not find it reasonable to replace the main product only to obtain a cheaper maintenance service. Hence the basic marginalist assumption for the definition of market power is denied, that is, the predefinition of consumer utility.

The true explanation is that dependence results from the misinformation of consumers.[59] The whole or majority of consumers does not even consider the maintenance costs upon the purchase of a consumer good. There is no way of

---

[59]   The belief in the limitation of information to the consumer over the secondary markets and their lack of consideration in the assessment of the price of the main good was the central element for the decision of the *Kodak* case. The Court, on the reasons for the decision, referred especially to the growing and recent economic literature of clear neoclassical origin, which acknowledges the flaws in the transmission of information in the market and its influence over the consumer decisions – check in respect the pioneer work of G. Stigler, 'The Economics of Information', in *Journal of Political Economy*, 69, 1961, p. 213 and H. Beales, R. Craswell, & S. Salop, 'The Efficient Regulation of Consumer Information', in *Journal of Law and Economics*, 24, 1981, p. 491. More recently, modern literature of information economics (see above Chapter 1) gave a more encompassing and scientific treatment to the problem.

knowing the frequency or the cost of maintenance, which depends on complex calculations that only the producer or some 'professional consumer' can make.[60]

The explanation of dependence based on misinformation and not market power[61] has an important applicative effect. Giving prevalence to the hypothesis of misinformation is saying that, even if it is not possible to ascertain the existence of market power according to the marginalist criteria, the economic agent may eliminate the competitor from the market by refusing to sell goods and compelling consumers to purchase the secondary product or service rendered by them.

Now, this may occur in the sale to the consumer. Imagine that the uninformed consumer, who is unable to take into account the conditions under which the maintenance service is provided at the time of acquisition, does not represent a significant portion of the demand for that good. This means that the producer, at the same time, does not have relevant market power and has little chance of gaining it. Surely that does not mean, though, that they cannot abuse their 'dominant position' (arising from lack of information rather than market power) in the face of those consumers who have less information. And note that these consumers are often those most vulnerable and economically weaker.

Deficiencies in information, it is important to remember, are greater the larger the economic inequalities in the respective regions are. Consumers with low purchasing power are not always able – even economically – to assess the secondary markets. The absolute price of the product is their only element of direction.

---

[60]   This characteristic is verifiable particularly in the franchising agreements. In franchising, the purchasers are precisely the franchisees. In the case of any obligation of purchase of products from the franchiser, it is expected that new franchisees take into account such costs upon acquiring the franchise. Also, in practice, the greatest acquirers of new franchises are the very franchisees. There is no reason to imagine that these 'corporate' consumers would not be able to compound the costs. Furthermore, in the case of franchise, it is even more likely that the mandatory binding of purchase of goods is owing to a legitimate interest of protection of reputation and not owing to a non-competitive objective – see regarding related franchise-tying G. Hay, 'Is the Glass Half-empty or Half-full?; Reflections on the Kodak Case', in *Antitrust Law Journal*, 62, 1993, p. 177 (185).

[61]   Evidently, it is also possible to accept that economic power is the central element as long as the concept of economic power is changed, to include in it not only that arising from a decreasing demand curve but also that arising from lack of information. As the results are absolutely the same, an attempt of this kind would wind up becoming a mere concept game.

<u>Increasing returns to scale</u>   In the section above, the theoretical basis of positive externalities of networks and increasing returns to scale were studied. Well, these may be used for anti-competitive purposes not only to bring forth a predatory strategy, but also to enable the illicit compulsory negotiation by creating dependence.

The networks are environments that otherwise encourage coercion of the negotiations, precisely because they create dependence.

The easy and natural introduction of the compulsory negotiation arises directly from the fact that networks create a huge problem for competitors and also, indirectly, for consumers. It is a question of compatibility. Once the network is created, the products that should be linked to it must be compatible.

It is in controlling compatibility with the network that the key to controlling the market itself lies. This competitive edge can be illicitly exploited in various ways. A first hypothesis is open predation, achieved through the introduction of a new network (main product), without significant technological improvement, whose sole purpose is to create incompatibilities with accessories (secondary products) produced by the competitor.

Another hypothesis is compulsory negotiation. The economic agent, by introducing its new main product with new technology (actually new, increasing the utility to the consumer), creates an accessory product, the only one compatible with the main product.

The difference between the two situations is less subtle than might appear at first sight. While in the former case the predatory intention is a result of the use of a harmful ploy, in the beginning harmful to the very predator – that is, the opportunistic creation of damage to himself to eliminate the competitor from the market; in the latter case, the intention of eliminating the competitors from the market is more difficult to prove.

The existence of effective technological improvement and recovery of actual costs incurred through the introduction of new products mischaracterizes predation. So for there to be abuse, it is necessary to demonstrate that the incompatibility of systems is not a natural or necessary consequence of the use of the new technology introduced, but a strategy designed intentionally to allow the exclusive sale of the good produced by the agent who created the incompatibility. For that, it is necessary to demonstrate the lack of efficiency in tying the products, proof that, especially in high technology markets, is not an easy one.

It is precisely for these reasons that, in most cases in which the incompatibility of systems occur, the corporate defendants try to lead the issue into a discussion of whether or not there is compulsory negotiation, avoiding discussion around predatory practices.

This is what happened in the case of Microsoft, in the aforementioned case of tying the Internet Explorer to the Windows operating system. Supporters of Microsoft's behavior aim to demonstrate that the matter under discussion is whether or not there is tying of sales.[62] They then deny its existence, claiming that there was a technical necessity for its association to the operating system (in the case of Windows 98) or that this tying is nothing more than the reward for the introduction of a new valuable technology. Hence the coercion is not denied; it is only claimed to be necessary or natural.

The European Commission, on an investigation carried out against very similar practices by IBM in 1984, sought to provide an answer to this question, elaborating the theory of 'implicit tying'.[63] Developed precisely to avoid a complicated, expensive and long technical analysis of the matter, this hypothesis led to the formulation of a commitment to cease with IBM, which allowed the elimination of the most harmful elements to competition (which in this case was the negative of transmission of information to competitors about their hardware, so the systems could be made compatible).[64]

According to this theory, creating incompatibilities with competitors' products results implicitly in tying, because it leaves the consumer no choice but to purchase the secondary product from the manufacturer of the primary product. The intention to eliminate competition is, then, presumed.

This assumption is legitimate, provided there is evidence of technical incompatibility and provided that there are structural elements that allow imagining that market domination will be achieved. For one simple reason. As shall be seen below, regarding compulsory negotiation, the intention is characterized exactly by the absence of other justification for the act and the structural requirements that allow us to infer that the act will achieve its objectives (market domination).

RELATIVE DEPENDENCE   The relative dependence occurs in cases in which a given agent or group of economic agents becomes, owing to specific business

---

[62]   Check in respect G. Priest, 'A Case Built on Wild Speculation, Dubious Theories', in *The Wall Street Journal*, May 19, 1998, p. A 22. In a contrary sense, defending Netscape's position and claiming that there is, in the case, technological predation R. Bork, 'The Most Misunderstood Antitrust Case', in *The Wall Street Journal*, May 22, 1998, p. A 16. It is not casual either that the North American Court of Appeal (*United States v. Microsoft Corp.* 253 F. 3d 34 C.A.D.C., 2001), acknowledged partially the existence of technological predation (item II. B.2, and II. B.5) and returned the issue of tied sales for new instruction on first instance, with severe instructions for the singular judge on the limit of the evidence to be produced, which includes concrete and mandatory demonstration of the inexistence of any efficiency in the tying of products (item IV, C).

[63]   Cf. D. C. Goyder, *E.E.C. Competition Law*, 1988, p. 316.

[64]   D. C. Goyder, *E.E.C. Competition Law*, cit., p. 315.

relations, bound without possibility of choice to the company performing the compulsory negotiation.

The main hypotheses of relative dependence are: assortment, business, and conjunctural, as we shall analyze in detail below.

Assortment dependence   This designation is home to several hypotheses, though the basic idea behind all of them is the same: the necessary presence of a particular product in the range of goods offered by the dominant agent.[65]

Imagine, for example, a retailer who must have a certain famous brand on their shelf. The producer of the brand may or may not have market power. In fact, they often do not, since many famous brands build their reputation by selling exactly a luxury image, built upon high prices and small quantities produced.[66] This does not mean, however, that the retailer or wholesaler does not feel obliged to have the product in their store.

The dependence may relate then to a certain brand, to a group of brands or, more commonly, to the very existence of an assortment. This latter hypothesis is extremely valuable for the wholesale trade, whose utility is, in many cases, precisely the congregation of several different products easily available to the retailer. Without this variety, the role of the wholesaler loses its function, being economically more attractive for the retailer to purchase the goods directly from the producer.

Now, all these situations create a clear dependence. A specific brand, a group of brands, or even the very assortment of brands may represent the value of the trader's activity itself to the consumer. In that sense, it could be stated that they have no reasonable substitute, leaving no alternative to the economic agent.

Although it may not be described perfectly as assortment dependence, the opposite hypothesis is also possible. It is often extremely convenient for some producers to have their products sold in certain stores – to the point where supermarkets charge large sums for the most attractive spaces on the shelves.

---

[65]   The concept of *Sortimentsabhängigkeit* was first used by the German BGH on the decision of the case *Revell Plastics* in *Neue Juristische Wochenschrift*, 1979, p. 2154.

[66]   It is here, as always, important to clarify that in order for the dependence to take place, it is not necessary that the luxury products market be a relevant separate market according to the neoclassical definition and that the producer of such item, therefore, have power in it. It is possible that the demand for the referred product be extremely sensitive to price variations (not creating thus a separate market) and, yet, the retailer needs to have that product on their shelf at the risk of even losing value to their business – typical examples of this situation are clothing and fashion shops, which must necessarily display products from the most famous brands.

This is also a case of dependence arising from the need of image preservation, that is, which follows the same logic of assortment dependence.[67]

Business dependence   A second – and more common – form of dependence is called business dependence. This category cannot be confused with the corporate law category of 'control'. Not even the legal categories of dominant influence and relevant influence from the competitive standpoint[68] are helpful for the concept of business dependence. All these concepts are used to identify the existence of a single corporate interest, that is, they are tools to identify structures, in which in one way or another (concentration or cooperation) there will always be a convergence of interests. They are of no use, therefore, to understand those situations in which there are effectively two opposing interests in the market, one of which is threatened to be artificially overwhelmed by the other.

This is what happens in the consumer–supplier relationship. The conflict of interest is an essential and formative part of the relationship. It is precisely this conflict that gives meaning to the concept of market relationship. The role of antitrust law is exactly to mediate this conflict, not to eliminate it. In corporate law the opposite occurs. The conflict, even existing and in fact very common, is the pathology of the relationship and not its normal course. Corporate law hence seeks to eliminate the conflict.

What follows then is another key difference between the corporate vision and the competitive vision of dependence. While corporate law accepts dependence, aiming to remedy the conflict, competition law cannot accept that kind of dependence that is able to eliminate the conflict.

With the characteristics set forth above, the term business dependence is used to designate those contractual relationships – in law or in fact – of long term, which create lasting economic ties between the parties; hence the reason for the name business dependence. The continuity of the relationship gives it a clear business nature, different from the static disciplines of one shot legal deals (as the sales contracts for example).[69]

A classical hypothesis of business dependence is that of the long-term supply agreement, in which the supplier adapts its sites according to the specific needs of the buyer.

---

[67]   This construction (*goodwill bedingter Abhängigkeit*) also belongs to the German doctrine – see K. Markert in Immenga & Mestmäcker, *GWB Kommentar*, cit., sub § 26, Abs 2, Rdn. 135, p. 1272.

[68]   On these concepts, see C. Salomão Filho, *Direito concorrencial – as estruturas*, cit., p. 243.

[69]   From this definition naturally follows that the application of the concept of business dependence is not absolutely possible in relation to the new market entrants – see K. Markert in Immenga & Mestmäcker, *GWB Kommentar*, cit., sub § 26, Abs 2, Rdn. 127, p. 1269.

Not only is it possible that the provider is dependent on the customer, but also that the distributor or dealer is often dependent on the producer, whatever its market power. What happens in these cases is that the distributor or dealer creates its reputation based on the brand of the producer. The investment is, in a sense, a sunk cost, since it is aimed at building not one's own reputation, but that of the producer in that region. The reputation of the distributor/dealer is, in these cases, closely related to the producer's. It is impossible, therefore, to dissociate from the producer, that is, there is no choice.

Conjunctural dependence   The last major group of subspecies of relative dependence comprises those cases of temporary or conjunctural dependence.

A classic hypothesis is that of scarcity. Imagine a certain retailer who is used to purchasing his products in a competitive international market, deprived of this possibility because of a momentary international shortage. Suppose, yet, that there is a national producer with an effective capacity of providing the product.

It can always be said that, during this short period of time, there is market power. That argument is indeed true. On the other hand, it is also true that this ephemeral market power does not imply any risk to the competitive system other than the use of dependence created for market domination. And this risk exists only for that client who cannot waive, nor wait for the end of the conjunctural crisis. Therefore, it is a relative and not absolute dependence.

Abuse of dominant position or act aimed at market domination   It is still prevalent in doctrine and compared jurisprudence that the various types of compulsory negotiation are classified as an abuse of the dominant position.[70]

---

[70]   A good example is once again the discussion over tying. Even though the abuse of dominant position is not yet recognized in the North American system, the classical and neoclassical theories require that market power be present, a typical requirement for the abuse of dominant position. The classical theory, for its connection with the literal concepts of the Sherman Act; and the neoclassical theory, for its unconditional adhesion to the marginalist dogma; see in the economic power the fundamental requirement for the characterization of tying. The dispute between these two schools regarding the theory of fixed sums demonstrates this hypothesis. Only in the recent decision on the *Kodak* case, clearly post Chicago, the U.S. Supreme Court seems to have given up the dogma of market power, focusing more, though without admitting it, on a hypothesis of strategic behavior. In the European Community law, on the other hand, where the category of abuse of dominant position is clearly recognized (Article 81), the link between tying and abuse of dominant position is further entrenched. The European Court and Commission only in very specific cases admit the teleological extension of Article 81 to cases in which market power is about to be conquered. It is not what happens in the case of tying, which is still seen as a typical case of abuse of dominant position, requiring the demonstration of market power – see P. Manzini,

This classification arises from a double misunderstanding. Firstly, it derives from the still prevailing conception that the pre-existence of market power is paramount for the characterization of the abuse. It was hopefully demonstrated in the previous section that such belief does not lead to convincing results.

The market power in the neoclassical sense is not required nor necessary nor sufficient for the characterization of the abuse. The compulsory negotiation may occur even when there is not market power for the primary product, and on the other hand, even when there is market power, there may not be coercion and it might not constitute an abuse.

There is still, however, a second, more obvious, problem. The simple existence of market power does not mean that the abuse subject to characterization is the abuse of economic power. Economic power may also be used strategically to build more power in that market or even create power in another one.

Nothing suggests that the goal of the performance of managers is always to maximize profits and not growth in market share of the company. And that is for two main reasons. Firstly, as supported by extensive economic literature, in environments where administration is not totally controlled by shareholders (controllers), enjoying a certain degree of independence, there would be an encouragement towards growth and not the maximization of short-term profit.[71]

This characteristic is mostly evident in economic life, to the point of being used to differentiate economic characteristics of different models of capitalism: first, the so-called Rhineland capitalism (German and Japanese), in which managers are more protected from hostile takeovers, is characterized by more long-term investments and long maturity (in technology and infrastructure); and the second, the Anglo-Saxon (U.S.), where there is a market for hostile takeovers, and where the administrators may easily be replaced in case of non-production of short-term profits, which, therefore, is oriented to maximization of short-term results.[72]

This argument is obviously not very helpful in all jurisdictions. Especially in developing countries where the market is being built, a tendency to maximize profits is generally (and mistakenly) seen as a survival strategy. There is, however, a second reason, this one universally applicable (at least in a capitalistic environment). It is the case of the already much exploited tendency

---

L'esclusione della concorrenza nel diritto antitrust comunitario, cit., p. 58, with reference to jurisprudence.

[71] Cf. L. Kaplow, 'Extension of Monopoly Power through Leverage', in *Columbia Law Review*, 85, 1985, cit., p. 515 (551), citing extensive economic literature.

[72] C. Salomão Filho & M. S. Richter Júnior, 'Interesse Social e Poderes dos Administradores na alienação de controle', in *Revista de Direito Mercantil*, 89, January–March 1993, p. 65 (75).

towards opportunism and strategic behavior by economic agents. Acting strategically, the company may decide not to maximize profit at first, but to increase its market share or to gain share in another market so that, upon reaching a monopolistic position, it may enjoy it.

And this is why leverage theory and its rival, the theory of fixed sum, are completely blurred. In the specific case of tying, for example, the company may well set its prices so that it gets a monopolistic price for the main product and a competitive price for the secondary product until it reaches a position of domination and can charge monopolistic prices.

It is possible, therefore, to acquire and not only to enjoy the dominant position through compulsory negotiation. It is much more rational and strategic for the monopolist to first increase the market share of the secondary product, then charge the monopolistic price, that is, to act towards the domination of another market and not the abuse of a dominant position not yet acquired (at least in the market of the secondary product).

ABUSE OF DOMINANT POSITION   The traditional understanding of compulsory negotiation exclusively as an unlawful abuse of dominant position is based also on a misunderstanding of the meaning of abuse of dominant position.

Generally, from the neoclassical requirement of market power arises the characterization of the compulsory negotiation as abuse of dominant position,[73] stating that the abuse is characterized by the pursuit of profit maximization (neoclassical theory) and that this may be achieved by transferring market power (classical theory) that leads to charging monopolistic prices in a new market.

The controversy, already well known, then focuses on whether or not monopolistic prices may be charged. Despite this divergence, it is always assumed that it is an abuse of dominant position and that, for the characterization of this abuse, the production of abusive or monopolistic profit is necessary.

It is true that the abuse of dominant position does not prescind, from existence, at least potentially, of an economic outcome. The arbitrary increase of profits is that result, except that this result need not be effectively produced.

---

73   This is not the appropriate place for discussion of the meaning, scope and content of the abuse of dominant position. It is important to note, however, that dominant position may not be freely associated with market power, especially if the latter holds the neoclassical sense. That is not the sense originally given to it by the ordo-liberalism that inspired the Treaty of Rome (although the current interpretation of the Court and the Commission has moved away from that original idea) and, most importantly, this is not the meaning given to the term in the Constitutional and legal system in Brazil.

Hence, for example, reducing the amount offered in the market is illicit when it is unjustified and when it is able, in theory, to lead to the increase of monopolistic profits, regardless of the actual production of that result.

If abuse of dominant position and the production of monopolistic profits are not confused, the theoretical basis for the binding between compulsory negotiation and abuse of dominant position is lost.

That does not mean the compulsory negotiation may not be used as a form of abuse of dominant position. The methods of tying and refusal to deal may also be used for the sole purpose of benefiting from market power.

In the specific case of tying, as emphasized by the doctrine, this basically occurs in two cases.

The first form is compulsory negotiation, in the form of tying in order to breach the compliance with preset prices.[74] Imagine an industry with prices set by the state (which may happen more often precisely in those sectors where there is a greater concentration of power). Unable to raise prices, the economic agent may seek to do so indirectly, through exactly the tying of a product whose price is not regulated, discharging there all monopoly overprice that will not be accepted in the regulated sector. Here both the failure to comply with government regulations, with applicable sanctions, and the antitrust illicit are evident.

Another recurring hypothesis is the practice of tying to allow price discrimination. Here too is the idea of maximization of profits that would otherwise be impossible. This hypothesis is quite interesting. In its treatment, neoclassical scholars concede, without acknowledging and without noticing, the assumptions of the legal theory of knowledge developed above. More specifically, they admit its main premise: the impossibility of theorizing over the market variables in general and the consumer utility in particular. This discovery may happen only after (and not before) the effective choice.

Consider this. The hypothesis in evidence is one where the main product and the secondary product are connected in varying proportions. Suppose, for example, the case of the copy machine and the paper used in it. Different consumers use paper in precise proportion to the utility they have for the machine.

Knowing how much paper they buy means knowing how much utility they have for the machine. That would enable the sale of the machine for each consumer at a differentiated price, greater for those who concede greater utility

---

[74] This is the classical case of tying, taken as illicit by almost all scholars, even the most extreme neoclassicals – check R. Bork, *The Antitrust Paradox*, cit., p. 376; check also H. Hovenkamp, *Federal Antitrust Policy*, cit., p. 375. For more recent work, see Erik N. Hovenkamp & Herbert J. Hovenkamp, 'Tying Arrangements and Antitrust Harm', in *Arizona Law Review*, 52, 2010, p. 925.

and so on. That being impossible, since this knowledge is acquired only after the purchase of the paper, which in turn occurs only after the purchase of the machine, an ingenious alternative was developed.

If the machine is sold at a competitive price and the paper at a monopolistic price and the sale of one is linked to the purchase of the other (through, for example, compatibility requirements – machine X only takes paper X), differentiation between consumers will be possible, case in which those who attach greater value to the machine shall pay more for it indirectly through the compulsory purchase of paper sold at a monopolistic price.[75]

The conclusion, for any mind not radically neoclassical, is that the practice is a violation of competition law and principles. There is no doubt that this is a form of exploiting a monopoly similar to the abusive increase in prices. In fact, it is a selective – and abusive – increase of prices.

Interestingly, the common element to both situations described above is that compulsory negotiation serves primarily to enable the economic agent to profit in the original market. In neither is the main goal, at least in principle, to allow the doubling of profits in the secondary market.

One can conclude, therefore, that compulsory negotiation only characterizes abuse of dominant position in cases of clear use of compulsory negotiation as a means of obtaining monopolistic prices directly and without intermediaries in the market in consideration. In any other case, it shall constitute an act aimed at market domination.

ACT AIMED AT MARKET DOMINATION   In the preceding paragraphs, much of what needed to be said about compulsory negotiation as an act aimed at market domination was already covered. Here it is only necessary to discuss its specific requirements.

The aim is to quickly set out the general principles of coercive businesses as acts aimed at market domination.

As aforementioned, the main characteristic of such acts is the strategic behavior. There is not, as in predatory pricing, the open loss in order to eliminate the competitor. There is, here, the use of a market situation, of power, lack of information or increasing returns to scale to limit the consumer's freedom of choice and prevail in the market.

From this definition, the two main characteristics of compulsory negotiation as an act aimed at market domination will derive. Firstly, the effective coercion of the consumer or economic agent in a situation of dependence upon

---

75   On a very similar hypothesis, only involving paint guns for civil construction and their respective cartridges (which contain fixation pins to be fixed by the firing of that gun) the CEE Commission found the company Hilti guilty for the illicit tying – check Decision of 22/12/87 in G.U.C.E. L 65/19 of 11/3/88.

purchasing the product, and secondly, the intention of thereby eliminating competitors from the market, thus dominating it.

Just as in predatory pricing, such intention is measured by objective data that demonstrates the actual possibility of achieving domination. They vary, therefore, for each specific type of conduct.

As a rule, the presence of structural data (especially entry barriers) enables the assumption that the strategy will actually lead to domination and, consequently, that such a strategy would be part of business planning for an economic agent acting opportunistically.

Moreover, it is necessary that there be no other justification for the behavior. As much as the structural data, the justifications allowed here are only the ones that are able to overrule the possibility of producing effect. Therefore, within a system that links the intention to the possibility of producing effects, the latter becomes a part of the subjective element (intention).

Here, the legal, and not the economic, nature of the analysis appears in one of its most interesting manifestations. The economic data, rather than determining the legality or not of the conduct, are a mere index of intention, of the goal of eliminating the user's choice and alternative.

The value of choice, directly linked to social and redistributive objectives, gains prominence in comparison with the economic data.

Exclusionary practices and underdevelopment

It is not hard to intuitively understand the links between exclusion as a standard business conduct and underdevelopment.

The structuring of economic relations based on market power and exclusion (consequent to it or derived from it) has many effects on development patterns. First, it clearly leads to an intensification of the triple draining effect and therefore of worse redistributive patterns in society.

Both violations studied (predation and compulsory negotiation), if well interpreted in a legal theory, lead to draining of resources, choice and information from the consumer. In predation, his choice is eliminated in the medium or long run, and prices and/or technological patterns can be imposed to him. In compulsory negotiation, the choice and the profits are directly extracted from the consumer.

Both practices have strong intersectoral potential draining effects: predation, through the imposition of entire technological patterns across sectors that are beneficial to the monopolies; and compulsory negotiation, through the cross-market extension of market power that it allows.

But here, again, this is just the smallest part of the damage. A business environment built on predation and coercion is not prone to creative development. New technologies are not developed but imposed. Market articulation and dynamics are not possible.

The structuring of relations around power and its typical behaviors (coercion, predation, etc.) is a powerful element not only to induce worse distributive patterns in society but also to restrain social and economic innovation. This is why the legal intervention is so necessary.

Collusion

The second great group of conducts that may lead to market dominance is the one of collusive conducts. Collusive conducts, as predatory ones, are behaviors commonly found in social relationships. The gathering of some in their own benefit and to damage others is as common as predatory behavior, directed to the exclusion of others.

Therefore its study, even if limited here to the economic collusion by structures with market power, can serve, in a more general structural theory of law, to discuss social relations in general.

But collusion can be a form of cooperation between people. Cooperation in its turn is one of the basic forms of human socialization. Therefore collusion to the creation of market power must be carefully distinguished from positive cooperation.

When dealing with collusive conducts, agreement between competitors, the so-called cartel agreement, naturally springs to mind. The 'joint game' (collusion) is co-natural to the relations between competitors.

However, collusion is not restricted to that. The reason is clear. As previously discussed, since the pioneer works of Coase, it is an accepted result in modern theoretical economics that vertical relations between producer and distributor or supplier imply enormous transaction costs. This result is accepted, even if the exact relevance its elimination must have to the law is far from being clear.

Well, if this is true and if the elimination of the abovementioned costs is convenient to the competitors, then (i) the agents will tend to eliminate such costs, making vertical agreements, and (ii) it is necessary that the antitrust law undertake such agreements, whether to punish them or admit them when pro-competitive.

Vertically, there is still another issue besides the one identified in horizontal collusion: agreements often lead to the exclusion of companies from the market, whether competitors of the producer or the distributor. A question naturally arises: why not treat them as exclusionary practice? The answer is simple. Exclusion is only a side effect of the conduct. It is not this effect, however, that causes concern. The immediate effect, anti-competitive, is the adjustment of behaviors between participants in the market.[76]

---

[76]   Here what happens is the opposite of the hypothesis of involuntary collusion

This is what happens in the hypotheses of discrimination between competitors and imposition of resale conditions, for different reasons. In discrimination between competitors, the legal element, the agreement between certain participants in the market to discriminate, is necessary.

On the one hand, as seen in Chapter 2, the mere factual discrimination between competitors is not illicit. On the other, the anti-competitive effect of discrimination lies in the agreement that results in privileges for a specific distributor or supplier to the detriment of its competitors.

As will be demonstrated, true corporate planning tending to eliminate in a stable manner the contractual tension that is typical of the buyer–seller relation (or, to use economics terminology, eliminate the costs of transaction) is necessary for the violation to take place; hence the reason why this hypothesis might be compared to vertical integration.

In the second hypothesis, imposition of resale prices, there is no agreement, but behavior parallelism (even if imposed) between resellers and distributors.

In both cases, for distinct reasons, there is a common element.[77] The collusion – voluntary or imposed – is the central factor that leads to an increase in market participation and/or the exclusion of competition. Consequently – and this is the most important abovementioned characteristic – such acts could not be punished as anti-competitive if they were not understood as collusive, since there is no exclusionary practice.

The goals and therefore the ultimate justification of collusion are also in line with the legal character of the theory on economic power. To the legal observer, concerned as he must be with the values reflected in the conducts, it is necessary to find in them elements that hold legal significance. In collusion, be it horizontal or vertical, it is in the agreement that they can identify the objective of driving the competitor out of the market and dominating it.

But this is not all. The inclusion of vertical collusion alongside horizontal collusion has another important consequence. It implies recognition of the idea that market power is not exerted by a sole market agent, but several agents, even if in different markets and lacking mutual dependence relation, may exert power through the control of information and choice. From this legal perspective, economic power gains, therefore, different dimension and scope.

---

that derives from the adoption of the exclusivity clause. There, the conduct is clearly of exclusion – the prohibition of making a contract with the competitor – and the collusion (involuntary) is the consequence.

[77]   Note that also here vertical collusion is parallel to the horizontal. As will be seen later, also horizontally the generic hypotheses of violation are (i) express agreement and (ii) parallel behavior of the competitors.

Horizontal collusion

Horizontal collusion is considered, basically, any form of agreement, express or tacit, made between competitors. The many forms of agreement that this definition implies and its specificities will be analyzed below. Here, by way of introduction, it is only important to mention the different objects that such agreements may have.

In order to understand them correctly, it is necessary to make a reservation. Horizontal collusion herein dealt with is restricted to the hypotheses of pure agreements, in which the objective is primordially the joint fixation of one of the competition variables. For the reasons exposed, those cases in which the agreement on competition variables is part of a structural shift of the relations between competitors, who begin to cooperate with objectives that exceed (or may exceed) competition interests, shall not be considered. These hypotheses, which may and must be cause for antitrust concern, are dealt with within the control of structures.[78]

If the agreements herein covered are the pure ones, the object of such agreements can only be the main competition variables. They are, beyond any doubt, price, quantity, quality and market. Agreements on price and quantity are substantially equivalent since, as preached by microeconomics, they are reciprocally determinative.

As for technological agreements, they deserve a distinct classification. The objective here is not to discuss the associations for the promotion of investments in technology. These are also part of the control of structures. Here, the object is an agreement over the sharing of technology to be used and the creation of products with distinct qualities. It is, therefore, an indirect form of market sharing by means of creation of different products, with different technologies.

The last form of pure agreement is the one that directly divides the markets, be it geographically or by products. Note that this may also take distinct forms. The sharing of the consumer market may happen based on its geographical aspect, products or both. There may also be a supplier division. The possibilities are as numerous as the possibilities of variations in competition in the market.

It is with the analysis of the requirements and hypotheses of violation of the referred agreements that the following sections shall deal. The reference to hypotheses of violation is intentional. The non-treatment of any conduct as wrongful per se is currently accepted and is an acquired result of legislation. All are subject to some rationality criterion that may link them to the production of some effect.

---

[78] See C. Salomão Filho, *Direito concorrencial, as estruturas*, cit., p. 305 ('A cooperação empresarial').

Following this logic, the analysis of violation that shall be subsequently conducted will imply the study of the types of conduct and the (structural) conditions necessary for the effects of horizontal collusion to be produced. Finally, the justifications that may lead to the acceptance of such conducts will be analyzed.

Horizontal collusion may occur either owing to express agreement or intentional parallel behavior, which, as will be demonstrated, may be understood as tacit agreement.

The basic distinguishing feature between them is not only the existence of a written or express agreement, but also, or even more importantly, the content of the agreement.

Express agreements   The main characteristic of the express agreement, as well as the most dangerous, is its stability. These agreements usually end up unifying or allowing predictions on the competitors' corporate policy.[79]

The agreement may have as its content the exchange of information on the competitors' pricing policy. In such hypotheses, the most frequent indicator of an agreement is the pre-announcement of price increase, usually by the cartel leader, so the others can follow.

The list of possible agreements and most common ways of attempting to conceal them is virtually endless. More than studying or describing each agreement, it is necessary to understand the true competitive content of such agreements.

EXISTENCE AND EVIDENCE OF AGREEMENT   In order to do so, it is key to understand the extent to which reference to agreements in the sense bestowed on them by private law can – or must – be made. No barriers exist to the use of private law concepts. Conversely, such use is convenient. Not in the formalist sense of verifying the presence of validity and effectiveness requirements of the act to ensure the enforceability of the provisions therein, but rather its existence requirements.

There being an agreement, regardless of its consequences or legal effects from the private law standpoint, there is legal certification of the intention of conferring durability and extension to the bond being created so that companies may take advantage of this situation. The idea of durability, essential for the antitrust notion of agreement, is present in the very idea that the violation is 'fixing prices in accordance with competitors'.

Therefore, we may be certain that the bond being created is relevant to antitrust law. Thus, the existence of express convergence, oral or written, of

---

[79]   See E. Mestmäcker, *Europäisches Wettbewerbsrecht*, cit., p. 189.

intentions is relevant evidence, not the way in which those intentions are expressed. Hence the search, sometimes exaggerated, for factual evidence of intention pacts, furtive encounters and such.

It is important to observe, however, that this natural and vital search for evidence may lead to relevant legal problems. Recently, this has been the tendency in the Brazilian practice. Cartel investigations have been reduced to search for evidence of agreement.[80]

Owing to that, the discipline only weakens. On the one hand, the *fattispecie* gains formal and non-systematic definition. It inevitably becomes restrictive, since it encompasses only the hypotheses of express and formalized agreements.

On the other hand, in order to compensate for this restriction, the tendency is and has been to greatly expand the list of what can be considered evidence of agreement. Mere assumptions, not even signs of agreement, are frequently considered enough. Therefore, individual rights are infringed and investigations are often fruitless.

Note that, if any encounter between competitors is considered an evidence (or sign) of the existence of a cartel, the agents will be punished for the simple act of meeting. There is clear violation of the constitutional freedom of assembly – which is represented by the restriction to the meeting itself, and not its

---

[80]   An important indicator of this concern is the presidential decree that broadened the investigative powers of the Secretariat of Economic Law ('SDE'). The Medida Provisória 2.055 from August 11, 2000 added to clause 35 of Act No. 8.884/94 the following paragraphs, which illustrate the concern about the matter of evidence: '§ 2º Respeitado o objeto de averiguação preliminar, de procedimento ou de processo administrativo, compete ao Secretário da SDE autorizar, mediante despacho fundamentado, a realização de inspeção na sede social, estabelecimento, escritório, filial ou sucursal de empresa investigada, notificando-se a inspecionada com pelo menos vinte e quatro horas de antecedência, não podendo a diligência ter início antes das seis ou após as dezoito horas. § 3º Na hipótese do parágrafo anterior, poderão ser inspecionados estoques, objetos, papéis de qualquer natureza, assim como livros comerciais, computadores e arquivos magnéticos, podendo-se extrair ou requisitar cópias de quaisquer documentos ou dados eletrônicos'. Leniency deals, introduced in our antitrust legislation by this presidential decree, also illustrate this concern (see article 35-B). The proposals of alteration of Act No. 8.884/94 presented in the bill proposal by the Chief of Staff that created the Agência Nacional de Defesa do Consumidor e da Concorrência (ANC) are even more radical. They intend to eliminate any sort of debate over licit and illicit behavior between competitors. The new legislation classifies the actions *exercised through agreement, deal or collusion between competitors* as absolute infringement (new proposed wording of the article 20), that is, violation per se. The classification of the conducts in absolute and relative (and the classification of agreements between competitors as absolute conducts) is nothing but an attempt to overcome the problems related to evidence.

content.[81] On the other hand, it must be remembered that the protected value is competition (and freedom of choice) and not absence of meeting between competitors.

Another blatant example involves associations between competitors. The belief that associations between competitors are not and cannot be per se illicit is widely accepted by the doctrine.[82] Moreover, such associations must be subjected to structural control.[83] A consequence of this is that, once the statutes of such associations are scrutinized, the normal exertion of its statutory duties cannot be considered antitrust wrongdoing. State interference, to the detriment of the constitutional right of assembly, would be characterized by the ruling of wrongfulness of the association that was legally constituted

---

[81]   The freedom of assembly, besides being condition for the exercise of other rights (right to petition, freedom of speech and thought, political freedom) is itself also a right. Owing to this, its exercise depends on the content of the gathering. Therefore, the mere impediment to physical meeting of people, be it direct or indirect, is already contrary to the constitutional protection. In this sense, the remarks by Pontes de Miranda are elucidating: 'O que importa é o fato de se reunirem as pessoas, porque, se se quer apreciar o conteúdo do que se discute, ou que vão ou vêm fazer, já se introduz elemento novo. Entra em causa, forçosamente, outra liberdade, e.g., a de pensamento, ou a de não emitir pensamento' (Pontes de Miranda, *Comentários à Constituição de 1967*, V, São Paulo, RT, 1968, p. 558). Thus, the meeting – whose elements are the following: (i) plurality of participants, (ii) unlimited duration and episodic character, (iii) determined purpose (see Jean Rivero, *Les libertés públiques*, v.2, Paris, PUF, 1989 p. 335) – cannot be considered, per se, indication of collusion (included here are meetings between competitors) otherwise there would be violation of the Constitution (in this case Brazilian Constitution is taken as an example but the same is valid for most occidental constitutional traditions).

[82]   More recent CADE jurisprudence already acknowledged the legitimacy of meeting between competitors. In this sense, PA n. 58 (1987) and PA n. 94 (1990), in which the following understandings are mentioned, respectively: cooperatives can only be condemned when there is distortion of the corporative objectives; and the occurrence of abuse of power by cooperatives also entails condemnation. More recent jurisprudence has followed such understanding. See in this sense the decision in the PA n. 61/92, n. 155/94 and n. 26/96, which point at the fact that the constitutional protection to class associations confers licit character to them, as long as they are not infringing antitrust law. In this sense, it is worth mentioning the 1997 ruling on the Processo Administrativo n. 145/93: 'Não estão incluídas nas prerrogativas constitucionais da entidade sindical atentar contra a ordem econômica, servindo de intermediário para que as empresas concorrentes no mercado de produtos e serviços hospitalares negociem, discutam e concertem suas estratégias de mercado, notadamente através da fixação uniforme de preços.' On the other hand, all construction of the article 81 of the CEE Treaty, explicit base for the article 54 of the Brazilian bill, points towards acknowledging the rule of reason for cooperative structures, including associations. Well, this is completely incompatible with the application of the per se violation rule for associations.

[83]   See Calixto Salomão Filho, *Direito Concorrencial – as estruturas*, cit., p. 319.

and whose statutes have already been approved. Here the reasoning is the opposite of the right of assembly. The existence of previous scrutiny (carried out by the structural control) of the scope of the association leads to the unconstitutionality of the intervention if the association acts within the strict limits of its object (already pre-approved), at least in the cases where the wrongfulness is identified in the very existence or social object of the association rather than in subsequent behavior.

POTENTIAL EFFECTS OF THE AGREEMENT   If this is the case, the legal discussion on the agreements cannot be restricted to the matter of its evidence. Its precise meaning must be researched. In order to precisely understand the legal notion of agreement in the antitrust field, the presence of another element is necessary. If the agreement, to be relevant to antitrust law, must be qualified by the effect, then this effect, obviously, is not internal to the agreement, but external. Once again, the difference between the legal and economic analyses is evident. In the first, unlike in the latter, the legal moment and its economic effect are clearly separated. This ulterior effect (or potentiality of its achievement) may be either contained in the corporate realm of society or derive from the structural conditions of the market.

Note, however, that despite being distinct, intention and effect are correlated. In fact, in order to understand the idea of valid intention for economic law, it is necessary to deepen the relation between intention and effect. In economic law, both elements are not mutually exclusionary, but rather interrelated.

From the study of this mutual relation, more concrete and profound concepts of intention and effect in antitrust law arise. In both cases, it implies making the referred concepts coherent to the structuralist concept of competition.

The understanding of the influence of potential effects over the market in the reasoning and planning by the rational economic agent implies radical changes to the study of the intentions. It completely loses its subjective bias, which makes its application usually uncertain and arbitrary. It goes beyond investigating the intention of the directors of the company and addresses the corporate sector of society.[84] It is the corporate plan revealed by contracts, acts and practical reactions that distinguishes its intention.[85] This provides justifi-

---

[84]   See E. J. Mestmäcker, *Europäisches Wetlbewerberecht*, cit., p. 226.

[85]   The word used by the German doctrine in order to make clear that the intention derives from the action and not from any subjective element is interesting. Instead of talking about intention, the doctrine says that the analysis of objectives must look for the tendency (Tendenz) of the act. Well, this is nothing else than its ability to produce effects – see V. Emmerich in Immenga & Mestmäcker, *EWG Kommentar*, cit., sub art 85 (1), Rdn. 240 241, p. 185.

cation to the application of sanctions to the corporate entity. The administrative responsibility of the corporate entity is perfected and gains logical consistency. The effect also gains new and more consistent theoretical qualification. It distances itself from the political or even ideological definition when it ceases to represent real economic data (efficiency) and starts being defined as potential risk to competition.

This new meaning of the effects in antitrust law explains the rationale behind the frequent reference by the doctrine to reasonability or the rule of reason. The rule of reason is nothing but an unconscious way of searching for a criterion of social reprimand. Once the importance of the existence of choice and alternative is acknowledged, only the acts that have potential effects on it shall be reprimanded.

In the face of this richer meaning of intention, the practical questions over price changes may be regarded from a different perspective. Mere discussion over price by companies with no market power, therefore, does not generate any danger to competition since they lack the capacity of harming competition. For the agreement on prices between these companies to be illicit, they must possess a minimum degree of market power. Without it, the agreement does not represent any risk and cannot be punished simply because the most likely result is that the companies will self-destruct, completely losing the market, if they try to raise their prices as a consequence of such agreement.

There are cases, however, in which it is possible to infer risk to competition from the agreement and their implicit intentions. These are borderline cases – maybe the most numerable among the ones of interest here. In such hypotheses, the possibility of obtaining this ulterior effect derives from specific characteristics of the agreement: (i) stability, that is, its permanence especially when compared to a merely factual reaction to the others' conducts, which can be verified in intentional parallel behavior; and (ii) its content, which must make the corporate policy of the companies involved predictable.

In the presence of these characteristics, it must be acknowledged that the agreement generates reasonable risk of market dominance, even in the absence of structural elements that absolutely ensure such dominance. When one or more corporate policies of economic agents are announced or made available to competitors, with guarantee of their durability, there is true invitation to join the incipient cartel.

Thus, even if the current participants do not jointly hold market power and there are no relevant barriers to the entrance of competitors (barriers to entry) it is possible to infer risk to competition.

This is the reason why the doctrine traditionally states that the more extended and stable the agreement, the smaller is the need to use structural elements that demonstrate the risk of market dominance.[86] Conversely, when there is no express agreement, such structural conditions are fundamental.

Intentional parallel behavior   The central issue in matters of tacit agreement involves the questioning of the reasons for regarding as anti-competitive the tacit agreements over competition positions in the market.

This verification is essential for a legal theory of economic power. Here, as in the case of compulsory negotiation, the power reveals itself in the structure of the relation. Unlike that case, however, the structure of the relation helps to create rather than exercise the economic power.

DE FACTO CONTRACTUAL RELATIONS   The possibility and the hypotheses in which it would be reasonable to infer the existence of agreements from a chain of facts have been the object of discussion in the doctrine for a long time.

The matter is more disputed and disputable in connection with the general theory of private law. Its starting point and denomination are given by the German doctrine in the 1940s, by the famous work of G. Haupt (*Über faktische Vertragsverhältnisse*).[87] A formulation of a true general theory of de facto contractual relations, 'social behaviors' capable of giving rise to a contractual relation regardless of the existence of formal binding, is therein sought. The great problem in this attempt, as demonstrated by the doctrine, is the use of

---

[86]   See K. Kuhn, *Abgestimmtes und sogennantes bewußtes Parallelverhalten auf Oligopolmärkten – Bedeutung, Unterscheidungsproblematik und Konsequenzen für die Wettbewerbspolitik*, 1978, p. 195. See also the Harvard structuralist school position discussed in Chapter 2. Note that this position is not identical to the very pragmatic position adopted by R. Bork regarding agreements between competitors. The American author states that any agreement, even those between competitors with no market power, must be prohibited. The reason is simply to avoid that authorities responsible for the application of antitrust law have to make the complicated calculations that allow the evaluation of market power and therefore evaluate which deals result in risk for competition and which do not – see R. Bork, *The Antitrust Paradox*, cit., pp. 267–8. Here, there is a very dogmatic reason for stating that a certain type of agreement may itself create risk of market dominance, which has nothing to do with the pragmatic posture by Bork per se. What happens is that, if the deal allows the agent to foresee the competition policies and the business plans of its competitor, it is capable, on its own, of generating incipient dominance. Imagine an agreement on price between two bakeries that have no market power. It is absolutely ineffective. There is no chance of one obtaining market dominance. Conversely, the most likely consequence of such a deal is loss of market by the bakeries and their eventual disappearance. On the other hand, imagine that two bakeries, besides making agreement regarding prices, start advertising their price policy. This allows business planning by the others. It is an invitation for the others to join the agreement, even though it does not involve them.

[87]   See *Festschrift für Heinrich Siber*, vol. II, 1943, p. 5.

disparate criteria for the identification of the cases that constitute de facto contractual relations.[88]

This criticism does not invalidate the theory, but simply tries to find a unifying element. This unifying element is the so-called 'negotiating declarations', i.e. formal declaration or behavior that indicates the existence of an intention directed at the production of a certain result. This means that the fact that the contractual discipline must be applied to these situations is not under dispute. What is stated is simply that such behaviors do not exclude negotiating declaration, being capable of allowing the inference of the existence of the declaration.

This criticism is, in fact, useful to solve two formal problems. Firstly, it eliminates the paroxysm of the expression 'de facto contractual relation'.[89] The many forms of de facto relation are not equivalent to the contractual ones, constituting mere indication of the existence of a declaration of negotiation.

The difference seems merely theoretical at this point, but it is not. The criticism also ensures the existence of a single criterion – declaration of negotiation – to which all the indications of fact must make reference. This allows the non-application – at least in its integrity – of the contractual discipline to the cases in which the factual indications do not allow the presumption of existence of the declaration.

The more it is possible to demonstrate that the acts or facts with legal implications are rationally addressed or may lead to a single objective, the more this assumption can be made.[90] It is the chain of acts and its inclination towards a potential objective that induces the assumption of business declaration or socially typical behavior.

It is the law that creates this assumption in commercial matters. The socially typical behavior is, in fact, legally typical behavior. The habitude of the relations between traders has always been considered indication of agreement. Therefore, traditionally, the traders' statutes establish that the traders' books constitute evidence of agreement. Evidently, the emphasis lies in the habitude of the relation. Being the requirement not necessarily reciprocal entries (which on its own would denote the existence of agreement), the unilateral entry has no value as such, but as proof of a continuous relation. It is in the habitude of the relation, evidenced in the books of the dealer, that the commitment to a determined objective and, therefore, the indication of contract lie.

---

[88]   See N. Nery Junior (org.), *Código Brasileiro de Defesa do Consumidor – Comentado*, 1999, p. 297, with interesting bibliographic references.

[89]   See K. Larenz, *Allgemeiner Teil des deutschen Bürgerlichen Rechts*, 7th ed., 1989, p. 333 and A. Junqueira Azevedo, *Negócio jurídico e declaração negocial*, 1986, p. 45.

[90]   See K. Larenz, *Allgemeiner Teil*, cit., p. 333.

If this tendency exists in matters of general theory of contracts, the same happens when dealing with associative relations. In this matter, much more than in exchange relations, the socially relevant element is the continuation of the relations. So relevant is it that corporate law talks about discipline of an activity, not of isolated acts. The acts are taken not as such, but rather as initial moment of the activity.[91] This is what happens, for instance, with the corporate by-laws. The chaining and inclination towards an end are fundamental in matters of associative relations. Not by chance, the associative relation is the natural space for recognition of the factual relations, the so-called de facto associations.

There is no reason why not to apply the theory of de facto contractual relations and the criteria for the identification of de facto associations to cartels formation. These may be regarded, in fact, as de facto associations because there is a conjunction of objectives and sharing of profit (although in indirect form, as a consequence of the joint and common price changes) as long as there is continuation and habitude of the conduct.

Consequently, and this is a really relevant legal result, the habitual conduct of identical market moves accompanied by the existence of structural conditions for the market dominance allows, indeed, the assumption of the existence of cartels. As always, in matters of typical social behaviors, it is not relevant to be sure that the only rationality for such behaviors is cooperation. It is not about logical judgement on the certainty nor even probability of the behavior. Other explanations for the behavior may exist in de facto associations.

Therefore, the parallelism of behaviors and the structural data are key for the identification of de facto contractual relations relevant for the identification of cartel behavior. We shall analyze them individually.

CONFIGURATION OF PARALLELISM   Not all practices of similar prices are aimed at reducing competition. They can be, on the contrary, especially in monopolistic structures, a symptom of intense competition between the parties.[92]

---

[91]   See P. Ferro, Luzzi, *I contratti associativi*, 1976, p. 215.

[92]   For a similar reason, the Brazilian Competition Tribunal ('CADE') has been consistently dismissing lawsuits in which there is accusation and price agreement if the evidence is proximity – or equality – of prices in the market. The reason is the impossibility – legally and economically – of inferring anything from mere price proximity. On this matter, there is an important CADE decision, from June 18, 1997, on the ruling of the Processo Administrativo 3/91, involving the Departamento de Abastecimento e Preços do Ministério da Economia, Fazenda e Planejamento and the companies Goodyear do Brasil – Produtos de Borracha Ltda., Pirelli Pneus S/A, Indústria de Pneumáticos Firestone Ltda. and Companhia de Pneumáticos Michelin Indústria e Comércio. The amendment to the ruling states: 'Conduta uniforme – Prática concertada de preços – Setor oligopolizado – Pneumáticos – Insuficiência ao reconhecimento da

Parallel price changes, regular stocking and also the continuation of relative participation in the market are all clear examples of parallel behavior between economic agents. They are, however, neither sufficient nor necessary for the characterization of intention. They only evidence the parallel behavior. It is impossible to know whether the behavior is intentional, with the aim of eliminating internal competition, or simply behavior determined by the circumstances at that moment or by the rationality of the agents who act as true competitors. Being the competitors in the same market, the cost pressure is often identical on both, which forces the simultaneous upwards shift in prices.

The ordinary price shift can only be considered a sufficient indicator to characterize tacit agreement when it is done persistently in one direction only, that is, price rise, and when it is not justified by any significant change in costs by both participants. This situation is incompatible with the existence of competition, since situations in which agents change their pricing policies, and shift from price increases to price reductions in the market (that is, use price reduction as a means of gaining market share, being immediately followed by their competitors), are in fact a common sign of intense competition between market agents.

On the other hand, the persistent and unjustified parallel rise in price by competitors who together possess market power, using the reasoning of game theory, indicates that the players are adopting behavior that aims at a collective rather than an individual goal. It is, therefore, cooperative behavior.

Well, the key element in determining the existence or not of cooperative gaming characteristic is the duration – determined or undetermined – stipulated by the economic agents.[93] The behavior of the agents who always raise prices and resist reducing them demonstrates the understanding by all that a price reduction can be profitable only in that same round, becoming immediately disadvantageous in the following, owing to the price reduction of the other player.

---

infração — Controle governamental de preços.' According to CADE's understanding, 'o simples fato de o setor de pneus ser oligopolizado (formado por três ou quatro empresas) não é suficiente para caracterizar conduta uniforme ou concertada entre os concorrentes. (...)' (José Inácio G. Franceschini, *Lei da Concorrência conforme Interpretada pelo CADE*, 1998, p. 313). Also in the judgment of the Processo Administrativo n° 0.8000.014677/94-18 and the Averiguação Preliminar n° 08000.004493/97-00, CADE has decided on dismissal owing to the understanding that the mere presence of similar prices is not sufficient evidence to prove tacit collusion by them, as well as the existence of cartel.

[93]   For the main conclusions regarding individual strategy games applied to oligopolies, see D. Baird, C. Gertner, & R. Picker, *Game Theory and the Law*, cit., p. 166 and ff..

In the event of the agents having very similar market and financial power, they may presume the infinite possibility of reaction by competitors and, consequently, extend the game indeterminately. In this hypothesis, the individual strategy is not the most favorable. The 'game' tends, therefore, to be cooperative.

In the absence of such constant, parallel and positive rise in prices by the oligopolists, it is necessary to add to the suspicious behavior other indicators that allow the assumption of intention.

A requirement for parallel behavior is the existence of an information system that allows each participant to promptly know what the behavior of the other will be. For this reason, commercial associations, at least the ones aiming at providing producers – and only them (with the exclusion of consumers) – with information on prices and revenue amount by the others, are regarded as ways of facilitating parallel behavior between competitors.[94]

The reason for that is simple and once again is reached through the coherent application of the theory of games. In the absence of an institutional system of information exchange, a cartel is absolutely unstable.

Imagine, for example, that, owing to lack of information, competitor A misinterprets a price reduction by competitor B, motivated by an immediate problem, as a defection of the tacit agreement. Its counterstrike may be interpreted as a defection and generate a reaction by competitor B and so on. One single mistake, in the absence of adequate information, may lead to non-cooperative *behavior ad infinitum*.[95] This sort of cooperation is, therefore, eminently unstable. No collusion can derive from parallel price increase.[96]

---

[94]   In two famous and already very distant cases, the Supreme Court dealt with the matter. In the first, *American Column and Lumber Co v. United States* 257 U.S. 377 (1921), it was investigated whether the American Hardwood Manufacturers Association, a business association that congregated over 400 manufacturers, infringed antitrust legislation by collecting and disseminating to its members detailed information on prices and quantities produced by its members, inspecting the associates' plants and publishing – for the use of its members – a detailed report on the market conditions. The Court ruled that this behavior violated antitrust rules, that such could not be the behavior of real competitors, but the one of economic agents united in an express or tacit agreement. Four years later, in *Flooring Manufacturers Association v. United States* 268 US 563 (1925), the Court expressed diametrically opposite opinion, by stating that mere exchange of information did not suffice to characterize price agreement. Currently, the doctrine tends to consider this sort of exchange of information, especially when not extended to the consumers, indication of the existence of agreement. For definite evidence, the presence of structural elements, which shall be analyzed below, is necessary – see D. Baird, C. Gertner, & R. Pickner, *Game Theory and the Law*, cit., p. 177.

[95]   D. Baird, C. Gertner, & R. Pickner, *Game Theory and the Law*, cit., p. 174.

[96]   It is interesting to notice that similar idea is expressed in German doctrine

Another element that may act as a qualifier of parallel behavior is the immediate reaction of economic agents to their peers' moves. The speed of the price change in the market is also a good indicator of the existence of such behaviors because it demonstrates that the price increases do not derive from demand pressures, but from a well-structured system of institutional exchange of information[97] (the word institutional is used in order to avoid confusion with the express agreements already mentioned). Here, thus, the immediate reaction is only an indicator of the initial element, the repeated exchange of information.

These remarks are far from exhausting the matter from the logical standpoint. Once one has analyzed the sufficient requirements for the characterization of the intention, one must question whether they are always necessary. Especially, it is vital to question whether the collusive behavior must always be repeated; otherwise the collusive behavior is disqualified by the existence of occasional price wars.

Traditionally, especially in the environments more influenced by the Chicago School, these episodes were considered evidence of the difficulty in carrying on price cartels in such markets.[98] These ideas have currently been abandoned. Relevant economic studies demonstrate that such episodes, very common in times of great economic depression or great increase in economic activity, are compatible with cooperation.[99]

---

through the concept of *Geheimwettbewerb* (hidden competition). It states that hidden competition, i.e. the possibility of the economic agent being in the competition without the other having previous knowledge, must be protected. This concept is of little use as a general means of transfer of the collusion prohibition to the concept of competition, since it suffices to understand that the freedom of definition of behavior in the market is fundamental to the notion of competition. Perhaps for this reason, it has fallen out of use in the German doctrine – see U. Immenga & E. Mestmäcker, *GWB Kommentar*, ci.t, sub paragraph 1, Rdn. 213–215, p. 117. Perhaps it is more interesting to observe that the concept of hidden competition is useful in those situations where there is coercion to collusion, the hypotheses in which collusion is involuntary. The practice is exclusionary since the economic agent has its means of competing hindered by the competitor. The situation is simple. Imagine that a certain competitor A wishes to increase its prices but knows that if this is done it will lose market share, since B will increase production. A may opt for forcing B to collude. In order to do so, it must know all the competition strategies of B. If B is dependent on the distribution, it may impede its access to it, forcing it to collusion – see J. Baker, 'Developments in Antitrust Economics', in *Journal of Economic Perspectives*, 13, 1999, p. 181 (186). In such hypotheses, the more ways, unknown to A, in which B has to compete, the less effective the strategy will be. The *Geheimwettbewerb* is, then, useful.

[97] See D. Baird, C. Gertner, & R. Pickner, *Game Theory and the Law*, cit., p. 176.

[98] See J. Baker, *Recent Developments*, cit., pp. 649–50.

[99] See on the periods of economic expansion and price war, respectively, J. Rotemberg & G. Saloner, 'A Supergame-theoretic Model of Price Wars', in *American*

What occurs is simply that, in such periods, the immediate gain by economic agents is so vast with an individual strategy, even if the losses after the reaction are considered, that competitors tend to act in a non-cooperative manner. In other words, the economic agent transforms the super-game (game with infinite or non-determined rounds, or game repeated indefinitely) in a sub-game of definite duration when comparing profits and losses.

Despite knowing that they will not be able to repeat the behavior (price reduction, for instance) and that competitors will follow them, the economic agents reduce their prices in the expectation of extraordinary temporary profits that surpass the future losses.

It is clear, then, that the requirement for parallel behavior does not exclude the existence of brief episodes of price war. In the presence of the other elements herein described, such episodes, so long as quickly leading to a return to the parallel behavior, reinforce the idea of collusion rather than disqualifying it.

Having said that, it is necessary to question: why are the elements heretofore listed able to demonstrate the existence of intention? The answer may be very simple, especially if we accept an objective definition of intention in economic matters.

If it is possible to infer from recurrent parallel behaviors that the company has learned which way of acting is more lucrative and that it is collusion, the existence of business planning in that direction is undeniable. Note that, in this case, it is not even necessary for the administrators to know and/or have the subjective intention to collude. What matters, in fact, is that the company has learned and included in its plan the notion of collusion. Its business plan is a representation of its 'rational' economic intention to collude.

Structural requirements   Before analyzing the structural requirements, it is necessary to understand their function. They are ways of demonstrating the possibility of production of effects. Hence, they are particularly important in demonstrating the presence of a rational objective intention of pursuing those feasible goals. They are particularly important in the case of parallel behavior, where intention cannot be demonstrated through any express agreement.

In such cases, there not being express agreement, it is only possible to assume the possibility of producing any effect from the analysis of the structural elements. No intention can be characterized without the presence of such requirements.

Economic Review, 76, 1986, p. 390; J. Baker, 'Identifying Cartel Policy under Uncertainty: The U.S. Steel Industry, 1933–1939', in *Journal of Law and Economics*, 32, 1989, p. 47.

The reason for that lies in the fact that no company, acting rationally, would define its price practice according to the policies of the competitors if it did not assume the latter might affect it.

Structural requirements can also be relevant in case of express agreement, as long as the agreement itself is not able to guarantee stability and possibility of expression to the deal between competitors.

We shall analyze two basic requirements. Firstly, the effective existence of oligopoly. It is within it, and only within it, that the intentional parallel behavior might characterize itself. Next, the effective existence of market power or threat of dominance by the structure created. The study of the barriers to entry is particularly important in this specific item.

EXISTENCE OF INTERDEPENDENCE As seen above (Chapter 2), the existence of interdependence cannot be completely demonstrated from simply structural elements. The search, typical of behavioral theory, of the possibility of producing effects is necessary.

From this realization derives an important consequence. Since the market structure does not have the imagined strength, that is, not being able to have sole responsibility for the behavior of the agents, it is not possible, as defended by some scholars (and not exclusively the ones with institutionalist inspiration), to develop structural sanctions for this type of conduct. It is argued that, there being parallel behavior and being possible to demonstrate that the economic agent 'learned' the most profitable way of acting, cooperating with the competitor (hence, cooperative game), no way of behavioral control would be effective. Constant price control would be necessary.[100] To others, structural control over the oligopolies behaving in such way would be convenient.[101] These statements cannot be admitted without criticism. The very theory of the games evoked to demonstrate intentional parallel behavior and its risks, may be here used to demonstrate the effectiveness of the intervention of the antitrust authority.

In fact, there being a behavioral sanction once the indicators described above are present, the economic agents would understand that there is another 'player' in the market, the regulator or antitrust authority, who reacts to their behavior. Therefore, actions tending to avoid parallel behavior, after it is initiated, may be

---

[100] This is the argument of P. Areeda, *Antitrust Law*, vol. VI, cit., pp. 174 and 175, who, very differently from his Harvard structuralist predecessors, defends, based on this argument, the theory that there should not be any sanction – behavioral or structural – to the conduct.

[101] See K. Kuhn, *Abgestimmtes und sogennantes bewußtes Parallelverhalten auf Oligopolmärkten*, cit., p. 195. See also the Harvard structuralist school position discussed in Chapter 2.

extremely efficient because, more than just avoiding oligopolistic behavior in that specific situation, it disincentives future parallel behavior. Also, in future 'games', the oligopolists will resist much more to the idea of following any action by their competitor. Using the terminology of game theory, the game will shift from an indeterminately or infinitely long game to a finite, discrete game (and the last round might be exactly intervention by the antitrust authority). There will be, then, incentive to independent behavior (individual strategy) by the oligopolists in the future.

MARKET SHARE VS MARKET POWER   As is known, market power and market share absolutely cannot be mixed. In order to be sure of the existence of power from high participation in the market, or even from the prospect of achieving such power, it is necessary to be sure that the participants in the market are protected by high barriers to entry by other competitors; that is, the economic possibility of other competitors entering the market as a consequence of price increase by the group accused of cartelization is non-existent. Only under those circumstances can any cartelization strategy, express or tacit, succeed.

Such importance of the barriers to entry, fairly settled in the field of antitrust law, leads to a deeper view of market structures. These structures cease to be merely static, becoming dynamic. The markets are not taken as they are, in order to determine the degree of power in the market, but rather as how they can be owing to the existent potential competition. The market is 'contestable' because a series of companies exist that may enter it and contest the prevalence of the ones already present.[102] This possibility determines the behavior of the companies that are in the market and, on a final analysis, also its structure.

In order for the market to work according to competition rules, its adherence to the unreal model of perfect competition is not, therefore, necessary. What suffices, in fact, is to ensure contestability.

A perfectly contestable market is defined as being one in which entry is absolutely free and exit does not imply relevant costs to the producer. The expression 'absolutely free entry' does not mean it is easy; it does not imply costs, but that the new company does not have any disadvantage regarding productive technique or perceived product quality when entering the market.[103] Besides, the entry is also considered free because the exit does not

---

[102]   The theory of contestable markets is discussed in the following works: W. J. Baumol, J. Panzar, & R. D. Willig, *Contestable Markets and the Theory of Industry Structure*, 1982 and W. J. Baumol, 'Contestable Markets: An Uprising in the Theory of Industry Structure', in *American Economic Review*, 72, 1982, cit., pp. 1–15.

[103]   See W. J. Baumol, 'Contestable Markets: An Uprising in the Theory of Industry Structure', cit., pp. 3–4.

imply sunk costs. These are the most important barriers to the entrance of competitors in the market.

Although it has long been acknowledged in legal antitrust theory, especially the one inspired by ordo-liberalism,[104] consideration of the importance of the barriers to entry in economic theory is much more recent. Relegated to the background in neoclassical thought,[105] it was only with the post-Chicago School reasoning that its relevance was rediscovered.

With it, scale gained importance as a barrier to entry. The need to compete on a large scale has always been abnegated by the emphasis on a very strict concept of sunk costs, that is, exclusively those that cannot be recovered at the moment of exit from the market.

The attitude shift takes place when it is verified that the scale itself can indirectly consist of sunk cost. In industries where large scale is necessary to compete (that is, it is indispensable to make marginal costs competitive), which frequently occur in oligopolies (precisely for being oligopolies), the very entry suffices to reduce the prices to values probably inferior to the marginal costs.[106]

This means that the investment will not be recovered by subsequent profits. The concept of sunk costs must, therefore, also encompass the costs including the non-recoverable profit reductions during the lifespan of the company.

Well, a company operating in a rational manner will not enter a market where its expected post-entry prices are not superior to the marginal costs. This reasoning is extended to constitute the basis of the theory of strategic entry deterrence.[107] If companies may convince their competitors that the entry will lead to price decrease, they will not enter. This can be done by means of costly but effective strategies, such as the maintenance of low-cost installed capacity, intense advertising, etc.

Undoubtedly, this theory emphatically demonstrates the risk of market dominance represented by the oligopolistic structures in all those industries where scale is a relevant competitive element. It reinforces, therefore, the presence of

---

104   See M. Streit, 'Economic Order, Private Law and Public Policy: The Freiburg School of Law and Economics in Perspective', in *Journal of Institutional and Theoretical Economics*, 148, 1992, p. 677 (681).

105   R. Bork states that companies are unable to erect entry barriers without the help of the government and that, if they do so, it is only through anti-competitive conducts. If these have not yet been penalized, it is because the barriers are efficient – *The Antitrust Paradox*, cit., p. 329.

106   See S. Salop, 'Measuring Ease of Entry', in *Antitrust Bulletin*, 31, 1986, p. 551 (563) and also J. Baker, *Recent Developments*, cit., p. 651.

107   See Salop, 'Strategic Entry Deterrence', in *American Economic Review*, 69, 1979, p. 335.

the structural element necessary for the qualification of the intentional parallel behavior in cases of oligopoly and, in the cases involving express agreements carried out in a sector that has scale of production, a substantial factor of price reduction.

Note that, admitted that the theory above defended that market power is not wielded by the domination of a single company (or companies) but often by the dominance of a technological pattern that spreads through various markets horizontally, vertically or even without correlation, then the appearance of entry barriers also depends heavily on the self-protection capability of these technological assets. The existence of recurrent hypotheses of technological predation is an indicator of this self-protection capability and, therefore, of the existence of technological entry barriers. The risk of production of effects in parallel behavior of such structures is thus much higher.

THE EXTENSION OF COLLUSION: SINGLE MARKETS AND MULTI-MARKET COLLUSION
Something important to be understood regarding collusion is the fact that, be it by agreement or intentional parallel behavior, it must not necessarily take place in a single market.

It can occur through multi-market contact. In this case, it can even be much more difficult to be discovered than the single-market collusion.

Known as 'multi-market contact that facilitates collusive forbearance',[108] this kind of collusion is based on the extreme reactivity of the companies to the foreseen behavior by the others. Unlike what used to be assumed, the fact that certain companies compete in different markets (for instance, companies that sell toothpaste, shampoo and detergent) may have a direct effect on their cooperative behavior in each market.

The same can and must be said regarding structures in markets with unique technological power abovementioned. In such hypotheses, there is a unique element and pattern to allow collusive behavior, which is precisely the standard technology.

POSSIBLE JUSTIFICATIONS FOR COLLUSION   The agreements or behaviors dealt with in this item are exclusively those that do not imply any structural change in the relation between the companies involved.

Consequently, our aim is to examine the agreements or behaviors that affect the competition variables directly. If this is the case, the scope of the justifications for the referred agreements or conducts is dramatically reduced.

---

[108]   See regarding this J. D. Baker, *Recent Developments in Economics*, cit., pp. 650–51.

Actually, all justifications have the same roots. It must be proven that the agreement is not directed at building market power positions but rather at producing a public good that can be appropriated by both competitors and consumers (users) of the products.

We shall deal with three basic ones (although there might be others that fulfill the same requirements stated above). First, the agreement on prices, quantities to be produced or market division, when necessary to protect the sector from cyclical crises. It is necessary to understand that, in such hypotheses, the agreement will only be pro-competitive if it is really instrumental for the companies to overcome the crisis.[109]

Very effective in such cases is the need for specialization of production that allows each of the agents to have cost reduction and leads, at the same time, to a decrease in excessive offer in the market.

If these conditions are fulfilled, the deal may not be considered illicit. The objective is simple survival, not market dominance. The effect will not be dominance either, being market power created only in sufficient degree to compensate the power from the demand side derived from the overproduction crisis.

The second hypothesis of pro-competitive agreement is the one that aims at avoiding price dispersion. Very common in industries where there is a vast consumer base with relevant diffusion, price dispersion can cause expressive losses to the consumer and the competition. It suffices to note that prominent overproduction crises or, conversely, supra-competitive prices may be created by price dispersion.

Price dispersion is characterized by the existence of disperse sales, sometimes in really isolated areas. This means that different retailers may sell the same product at very diverse prices and that communication among consumers does not exist. This situation is more common than one might suppose. The consequence is that the producer or service provider and the distributors begin to have information that is completely incongruous regarding the demand for their product. The demand curve, already difficult to be formed, is thus completely distorted.

Hence the reason why the resulting price is often excessive or the supply over-dimensioned. The problem with price dispersion as a justification for agreements is the fact that the premise does not necessarily lead to the conclusion. The objective of avoiding price dispersion is, undoubtedly, a desirable

---

[109] For these reasons, crisis cartels are systematically better treated within the study of antitrust structures. See regarding their structural treatment C. Salomão Filho, *Direito concorrencial – as estruturas*, cit., p. 184. As the fact that, within an emergency situation, companies resort to an immediate and simple price agreement should not be disregarded, debate over it within structure control is de rigueur.

competition aim. However, in order to achieve such objective, a rigid price agreement is not necessary. It is generally sufficient to indicate suggested prices, visible to the consumer.

Price should not thus be mandatory for the retailer or distributor, but only suggested.[110] This is enough to allow the accurate visualization of the demand while allowing competition flexibility. In order for the referred prices to become mandatory a relevant competition-related reason is necessary.

The price dispersion phenomenon allows a generalization regarding the exchange of information between competitors. As seen above, the information exchange is a potentially noxious element. It is generally used to facilitate the establishment and permanence of price cartels. It shall only be allowed when it can be individuated as a way of creating a market and not as a means of cartelization.

This happens when there is price dispersion. In such hypotheses, there is not a single market that respects the supply and demand rules, congregating all suppliers and buyers around the formation of a price that represents the relative scarcity of a product. There are, in fact, many markets for the same product that may behave in a monopolistic manner, precisely because they are isolated geographically or by difficulty of access to information by consumers.

In such case, the indication or price list, as long as shared with consumers, is pro-competitive. It allows the preferences of consumers from the entire country to influence the price of the product and not exclusively the preferences of the region where the retailer is located.

In such a hypothesis, therefore, the requirements for the characterization of the illicit are not present. The entrepreneurial plan is not to eliminate competition, but only to create a truly competitive market, reducing imperfections and avoiding crisis. There is no intention to dominate the market and so the production of such effect is not possible either.

A third hypothesis to be discussed is the one involving agreements for discount concession. The discussion basically emerges in German law, where this form of cartel was predicted by the laws (GWB, §3). According to the German rules, such cartels may be submitted to the approval of antitrust authorities. If certain conditions are fulfilled,[111] it is possible for them to be

---

[110]   Based on this justification, CADE has authorized Kibon to maintain indicative prices for their ice creams in bakeries. It was argued by the company and accepted by CADE that, without them, prices tended to rise. The economical justification was that, there being a great number of retailers and geographical dispersion among them, retailers would not be aware of the ideal equilibrium. There would therefore be price dispersion (Processo Administrativo n. 184/94).

[111]   The GWB foresees in its section 3 [*Rabattkartelle*]:

'(1) § 1 gilt nicht für Verträge und Beschlüsse über Rabatte bei der Lieferung von

approved. They are thus subjected to structural control. The basic reason alleged for the introduction of this rule was to avoid discrimination between consumers and price war, while providing the consumer with an advantage.[112]

This provision was heavily criticized in German doctrine,[113] resulting in substantial restriction by courts of the scope of its application.[114] It was argued, not without reason, that such an agreement leads to substantial reduction in price competition. It is, in fact, an invitation to an agreement between competitors. Restraining discounts, which are the competition element par excellence, ends any possibility of individual behavior, leaving no alternatives for competitors (especially in oligopolies) other than behavior coordination.

If this is the case, deals over discounts are only admissible in two very restrictive hypotheses. First, when they are indispensable for the survival of a crisis cartel. In this hypothesis, it is vital, as seen above, that they be accompanied by structural measures necessary for overcoming the crisis.

The second alternative is that such cartels serve the use of counterbalancing situations of great inequality between competitors, allowing rather than hindering competition. This is what happens when the cartel is of the type the Germans call *Gesamtumsatzkartell*. In such forms of agreement, the discount is offered according to the amount of product acquired from any of the components of the agreement.

Waren, soweit diese Rabatte ein echtes Leistungsentgelt darstellen und nicht zu einer ungerechtfertigt unterschiedlichen Behandlung von Wirtschaftsstufen führen, die gegenüber den Lieferanten bei der Annahme von Waren erbringen.'

Further on, the legislator elucidates the criteria established in section 1:

'(3) Verträge und Beschlüsse der in Absatz 1 bezeichneten Art werden nur wirksam, wenn die Kartellbehörde innerhalb einer Frist von drei Monaten seit Angang der Anmeldung nicht widerspricht. Die Kartellbehörde hat zu wiedersprechen, wenn: nicht nachgewiesen ist, daß die in Absatz 1 bezeichneten Voraussetzungen vorliegen und daß die Wirtchafsstufen gehört worden sind, für die die Rabattregelung gelten soll, oder der Vertrag oder Beschluß offensichtlich schädliche Wirkungen für den Ablauf von Erzeugung oder Handel oder für die angemessene Versorgung der Verbraucher hat, insbesondere die Aufnahme der gewerblichen Tätigkeit in einer Wirtschaftsstufe erschwert, oder Marktbeteiligte innerhalb eines Monats nach Bekanntmachung der Anmeldung (§10 Abs. 1) nachweisen, dass sie durch den Vertrag oder Beschluß ungerechtfertigt unterschiedlich behandelt werden.'

[112]   See U. Immenga & E Mestmäcker, *GWB Kommentar*, cit., section 3, Rdn.2, p. 223.

[113]   See E. Mestmäcker, *Der verwaltete Wettbewerb*, cit., p. 285.

[114]   Currently, the *Funktionsrabatte* and the *Gesamtumsatzrabatte* are only accepted in German and European jurisprudence. The first are those granted to distributors in relation to the sales (the so-called efficiency awards). The latter are granted to consumers for amount of purchase with any member of the agreement – see E. Mestmäcker, *Europäisches Wettbewerbsrecht*, cit., pp. 246–7.

Such form of agreement may allow small competitors to benefit from the other competitors' large scale supplying to consumers who, in order to obtain a discount, would normally only buy from big retailers. Evidently, in order for them not to be discriminatory, it is necessary that all producers from a certain market benefit from them.[115] They cannot be admitted in oligopolized markets either, unless there are substantial differences between products that are reduced by means of the agreement and that allow – at least in theory – for more effective competition between its members.[116]

The agreements for the concession of discount according to the quantity, including all producers and being carried out in an industry in which there are large differences in scale between producers or in the quality of the products, allow producers to become similar to each other, even if they are different in size, increasing price competition. They have not, therefore, the potential of generating market dominance.

Vertical collusion
Two hypotheses of vertical collusion shall be analyzed. First, the vertical agreement, tending to favor an economic agent in detriment of others. Then, the fixation of prices or resale conditions.

It is important to note that the framing of such practices, referred to by economic doctrine as vertical restrictions, is different from the traditionally proposed. The same neoclassic theory usually frames such wrongdoings among exclusionary practices.

Their classification here is different. When such practices are classified as collusive conducts, the intention is to give prominence to vertical restrictions owing to their relevance both for competition between producers and competition between distributors. Not considering vertical restrictions as behaviors tending to exclusion (of the competitor that exercises it), but rather as collusion (between producer and retailer or between retailers and imposed by the producer), means attributing higher importance to this sphere (vertical) of economic relations. This happens because the sole concern with the horizontal effects of the conducts is innate to the idea of exclusion. As will be demonstrated, the vertical effects exist, are capable of being demonstrated and are

---

[115]   German and community jurisprudence have long been oriented in that direction – see E. Mestmäcker, *Europäisches Wettbewerbsrecht*, cit., pp. 246–7.

[116]   This seems to be the case of civil aviation, where agreements on mileage between companies may or may not be anti-competitive. If, as frequently occurs, they are celebrated between companies who operate in different regions, they allow the consumer to obtain discount (or a new ticket) to more destinations. If, however, the agreement is made between companies operating in the same geographical region, it only serves the purpose of facilitating collusion of behaviors, thus being anti-competitive.

dangerous. Vertical restrictions have, as will be seen, structural consequences over economic power (in many spheres) that will provide it with individual antitrust relevance. This is what shall be demonstrated next.

Discriminatory practices   Vertical agreements are structured very differently from horizontal ones. The objective is not to eliminate competition, but to eliminate the conflict of interests between its members.

This definition makes it clear that the antitrust problem in discrimination lies, precisely, in the collusion. Only by understanding that the anti-competitive effect of discrimination is in collusion and the elimination of tension in the vertical line, is it possible to focus our attention on the relevant aspect of the matter.

Discrimination itself is not relevant to antitrust law. It is, as seen above, an indication of economic power, which can and should be dealt with differently. Discrimination is only unlawful when part of a cooperation agreement on the vertical line.[117]

The classification of price discrimination as collusive practice, and not exclusion, is essential. It avoids the (otherwise useless) demonstration of the possibility of elimination of the competitor. As will be seen, the potentially harmful element is much more likely to be an unreasonable benefit offered to one competitor than economic harm to another.

Any agreement establishing a stable relationship between market agents can, in theory, be harmful to other market participants, owing to the strategies that it enables. The difference is that unlawful vertical integration is unlawful exactly because of the collusive objective.

As will be seen, all vertical collusive procedures are aimed at eliminating competition. Whether it be through influencing the distribution structure, or by electing them as special partners, the essential and healthy (intra-brand) competition is eliminated, moving towards total market dominance (with elimination of inter-brand competition and total cartelization of the market). The requirements to identify that illegal conduct are analyzed below.

COLLUSIVE OBJECTIVE   It is possible to apply here the method of analysis of unlawfulness previously developed. First, we must ask what is necessary to be able to infer, from the action, a collusive objective.

As seen, in order to identify intention, a business plan is necessary. We must then analyze the content of the plan regarding discriminatory vertical agreements.

---

[117]   Cf. In this case E. Mestmäcker, *Europäisches Wettbewerbrecht*, cit., pp. 188–9.

Collusion has to relate to a competitive variable. Since the relationship is not between competitors, of little value is the agreement on price and quantity produced.

The object of the agreement should be, instead, discrimination between competitors, that is, the systematic unequal treatment between the parties to the agreement and their other competitors. In the systematic disadvantage of the other competitors is configured the strategic conduct of the parties to the collusion to dominate the market.

Thus, for example, agreements, whereby a single distributor is benefited by a producer, who systematically offers him lower prices for the same product. Here, collusion between producer and distributor for anti-competitive purpose is evident and undeniable.

The existence of this objective is easily observed through the discrimination among distributors, not justified by any market difference between them.

By market difference we shall understand not only the most obvious hypothesis of the existence of different costs or conditions of supply for each one (using the case of distributors as an example) but also the fact that both are located on different points of the demand curve, that is, the producer has different degrees of market power in relation to the various distributors or distributors have varying degrees of dependence on the producer (owing to different contract terms, for example).

In this last case, as mentioned above, discrimination is factual and is not worrying for antitrust law. It is just an indication that, with respect to one (or more) participant(s), the producer has market power (monopoly), which must be controlled by specific rules of conduct and structure (see above, Chapter 2).

POTENTIAL EFFECTS The intentional practice described above is not punishable if not accompanied by the potential effects. This practice must put the collusive company's other competitors in an unfavourable position, that is, without another supplier who can provide the same prices or conditions that the economic agent participant to the collusion can.

Without this, not only there will not be any adverse effect on the competitive system, but also intent cannot be inferred. Demonstrating once again the already discussed tendency of convergence between potential effects and intentions, an apparently discriminatory conduct that must not lead to any discrimination, surely, can have some extra-antitrust justification that eliminates the risk of harm to other competitors.

Two basic consequences of this process of vertical collusion raise antitrust concerns. First, if at least one of the collusion participants has market power, or comes to have market power, the collusive process will spread into the market and very few alternatives will be left for producers and/or independent distributors in terms of selling or buying products under competitive conditions.

The second consequence is as vicious as the first – or more. The potential competition is limited substantially. Discrimination affects both existing competitors and potential ones, who will need to collude with someone vertically if they wish to enter one of the markets or have their own presence in both markets. There is therefore an undeniable increase in barriers to entry of new competitors.

The basic question then is related to the conditions necessary for these effects to exist. Two issues are relevant: is only the collusion between players with market power dangerous to the competitive system; and, in competitive markets, is there a number of collusive processes that must exist in order to constitute a risk to competition?

The answers to both questions are quite simple, provided a structuralistic perspective is adopted. In the first case, the answer is clearly no. To accept such a statement would imply admitting the traditional Chicagoan argument that only power on the horizontal line is worrying for the competition law.

As seen, vertical collusion entails specific concerns (in particular the potential exclusion of competitors and the creation of entry barriers) and cannot be reduced to a problem of power formation in each one of the horizontal markets.

The second question must also be answered in the negative. It is not convenient or possible to wait for the market to be fully vertically integrated by collusion to start punishing the behavior. Especially because it implies explaining what the justification would be for doing nothing in relation to the former and punishing only the latter.

Once the antitrust concerns of incipience are applied, it is clear that any collusion should be punished, so long as it is the result of a plan to discriminate between economic agents.

Game theory teaches us that the process of vertical collusion is a game with a finite number of rounds. For each participant there is only one 'move' – to integrate with the competitor. Consequently, each economic agent adopts an individual strategy. Nash equilibrium occurs when everyone has adopted the best strategy based on the competitors' behavior. This can only be vertical collusion; otherwise it will negatively affect the non-colluding economic agent in the market compared to other competitors (just as the prisoner who does not confess, in the prisoner's dilemma). Therefore, one can assume that, if the initial vertical collusions are accepted, others will follow.

Thus, the anti-competitive effect here is a direct result of the type and extent of the agreement achieved. If it is durable and long enough to assume that there is real integration between the parties through a collusive agreement and that they will operate together to discriminate against other competitors, the potential risk of incipient market dominance can also be assumed.

Standardization of price or resale conditions   Among the major categories formulated here, the last one that requires specific analysis is called the standardization of price or resale conditions.

It consists of a series of uniform conditions imposed on or suggested by the producer for the sale of a particular product. They may standardize the maximum price or minimum resale price, divide territories or otherwise eliminate competition among distributors. These two features, elimination of competition and their orchestration within a market level other than that where it occurs, attribute individuality to such conduct. As a result of these features, its various forms will be called vertical restraints on competition. And that is how they will be referred to from now on.[118]

It is therefore necessary to accurately determine the meaning and function of such a clause so as to evaluate its illegality, that is, in what circumstances would this come to be illicit market dominance.

ECONOMIC CONCEPTIONS   Perhaps of all the anti-competitive practices, the concept now being addressed is the most heavily debated in the legal and economic worlds. Stands are most disparate, ranging from defending per se legality to defending per se illegality.

In the economic world, a rather lenient approach still prevails in terms of the vertical restraints, based, as always, on the efficiency defense. The most assiduous criticism to this concept seems to be legal, which has been gaining support in recent economic developments, and which demands a more consistent explanation for the genesis of such conduct.

In order to understand it, a clear grasp of the economic problems involved in vertical restraints is necessary.

Neoclassical theory   Neoclassical theory provides a simple and attractive explanation of vertical restraints.[119]

---

[118]   This is how it will be referred to from here on. It is important to make clear, however, that this should not be confused with the term vertical restraints sometimes used by the neoclassical economic theory. Often, economists who endorse the theory of transaction costs included in this expression also typically exclusionary conduct, such as the exclusivity clause – see accordingly O. Williamson, 'Assessing Market Restrictions: Antitrust Ramifications of the Transaction Cost Approach', in *University of Pennsylvania Law Review*, 127, 1978, p. 953 ff. The reason is obviously the conception of the phenomenon and its principles from the purely economic point of view. Where there are transaction costs, there are vertical restraints. Here, instead, the principles are elaborated through the legal perspective, making conduct, intent and effect important. Collusive practices differ from exclusionary conduct and collusive practices differ if they derive from a vertical relationship. Here we will address collusive practices exclusively.

[119]   Cf. R. Bork, *The Antitrust Paradox*, cit., pp. 290–1.

Imagine a producer with several distributors who compete on price. One of them (dealer A) assembles a sophisticated point of sale, where he keeps all of the products and trained salesmen, ready to give the widest range of explanations to potential buyers.

Dealer B behaves in the opposite way. He keeps a single store, does not have the complete line of products, and does not maintain staff. As a result, his costs are much lower than A's, so he can offer very attractive resale prices.

The consumer can go to store A, obtain all of the necessary information, choose the product that suits him best and then go to store B and acquire the product for a cheaper price.

This means that producer B is benefiting from additional services provided by A without having to absorb its costs, thus setting up a classic case of so-called free riding. The consequence is that the long-term loss of sales will eventually force A to leave the market and there will be a general disincentive to invest in sales promotion. The same can be said in relation to other possible investments from retailers such as those in advertising and after-sales services.

There are two consequences that neoclassical theory sees happening in such a situation. First, consumers will find themselves deprived of additional services (such as sales promotion and after-sales service) that for them (as will be seen, especially for the marginal consumer) proffer undeniable utility. There is thus a loss of efficiency (in the standard neoclassical, allocative sense).

On the other hand, the same theorists affirm that the competition itself is impaired. Indeed, intra-brand competition cools competition between brands. Because there is no additional investment in advertising and additional services, this fundamental competition channel is weakened.

As a result, the argument is for outright acceptance (per se) of all types of vertical restraints. They would serve the purpose of eliminating these evils. The imposition of uniform prices for resale, for example, prevents one from taking advantage of the other who invests in advertising. There would be an incentive for everyone to compete in this area. Territorial division of sales areas would have the same effect.

By encouraging such investment, both constraints lead to greater competition with products from competing manufacturers. Inter-brand competition would therefore be strengthened. According to neoclassical scholars, this is what really matters, since that is where consumer prices are formed, and the relationship between producer and retailer becomes a mere contest to determine who obtains the biggest share of profit. As we shall see, these conclusions are, for various reasons, absolutely equivocal.

<u>The refinement of the theory: Transaction costs</u>   The theory of transaction costs does not represent a break with the neoclassical paradigm. Its roots are

very close. The theory of transaction costs alone is considered the refinement of some neoclassical assumptions.

In the analysis of various forms of vertical integration, this proximity can be noted quite blatantly, and not by chance. It is specifically in vertical relationships that one identifies the biggest obstacle to the operation of an 'efficient' market.

Thus, with regard to vertical restraints, this theory does nothing more than add reasons for vertical restrictions to be defendable, owing to its 'efficiency'.

For this, all of the neoclassical explanation of vertical integration is reconstructed. It is argued that, in fact, the great importance of vertical restraints is to allow the treatment of situations that cannot be well regulated in the initial contract, because it could create insurmountable transaction costs.[120]

Vertical integration, then, helps to solve the big problem that the theory of transaction costs is designed to solve: the one related to uncertainties. There are basically two sources of these uncertainties: the tendency towards opportunism and bounded rationality. Actually, in antitrust economic theory, each of these concerns led to an independent theoretical line, respectively the theory of strategic behavior and the theory of limited rationality. Here, the influence of both hypotheses on the discipline of vertical restraints should be verified.

The first (tendency towards opportunism) adds very little to neoclassical design. Free riding is understood as the greatest manifestation of strategic behavior. Thus, vertical restraints are implemented in order to avoid it.

They will not be admitted if the same strategic tendency leads parties to adopt behavior aimed at excluding competitors. This could be facilitated by vertical restraints only in an oligopoly situation. That is why the very advocates of the theory of transaction costs argue that the only difference between their theory and neoclassical design is vertical restraints in the case of oligopolies.[121] It is said, in effect, that only in this case and, further, only in the presence of an exclusivity clause (not merely the imposition of price or conditions of resale) can one verify behavior that will lead to the elimination of the competition.[122] This is quite different from the hypothesis being discussed, and that just demonstrates how little development there has been on the theory of transaction costs and strategic behavior in relation to collusive behavior.

---

[120]   See O. Williamson, 'Assessing Market Restrictions: Antitrust Ramifications of the Transaction Cost Approach', cit., p. 954. An interesting development of these ideas is available in B. Klein & K. Murphy, 'Vertical Restraints as Contract Enforcement Mechanisms', in *Journal of Law and Economics*, 31, 1988, p. 265.

[121]   See. O. Williamson, 'Assessing Market Restrictions: Antitrust Ramifications of the Transaction Cost Approach', cit., p. 962.

[122]   See in this sense O. Williamson, 'Assessing Market Restrictions: Antitrust Ramifications of the Transaction Cost Approach', cit., p. 991.

On the other hand, uncertainties arising from limited rationality in relation to vertical restraints were more independently developed, perhaps because, unlike the theory of strategic behavior, its development has not been limited to situations of oligopoly.

Limited rationality derives from the inability to foresee all the variations that can occur in the relationship between producer and distributor or retailer. Comparing the vertical relationship to a work contract, one can assert that certain elements, such as employee performance and uncertainty with respect to the market, cannot be provided for in an employment contract.

The same is true for the relationship between producer and retailer. Investment in sales structure is evidence of the performance of the network, whose necessity and concrete merit should be evaluated in continued contractual relationship. Vertical restraints, such as imposition of resale price and territorial division are, for the reasons already explained, forms of reward and encouragement for the entire network to invest in product promotion. It is an important element in reducing transaction costs.

But that is not all; here is an important refinement brought on by the theory of transaction costs. Market uncertainties are a factor that generates cost. They are, perhaps the main concern of this theory. In the relationship between producer and retailer, there is a rather worrying uncertainty.

This is the amount of stock to be held in sectors of variable demand.[123] The interest of the producer is usually to keep inventories low. The dealer, on the other hand, is interested in a reasonable level of stock with the producer that enables it to cope with a sudden demand.

This shows that imposing a single price for resale, usually in such a case as compensation to a minimum guarantee of stock, is a way of preventing some dealers from reducing costs by maintaining little stock to the detriment of the producer and the consumers, who would be subject to increases in price in case of increased demand.

Therefore, vertical restraints appear here, also, as an important tool to allow the producer to deal 'efficiently' with temporary demand situations. Upon reducing uncertainty, prices tend to be lower for the final consumer (which, incidentally, for the advocates of this theory is the natural result of reduced transaction costs).

CRITICISM OF THE ECONOMIC THEORIES   For the development of a coherent legal theory on vertical restraints, we must first go through a critical analysis of the prevalent economic ideas. This criticism is part of the legal analysis

---

[123]   H. Marvel, 'The Resale Price Maintenance Controversy: Beyond the Conventional Wisdom', in *Antitrust Law Journal*, 63, 1994, p. 59 (73).

because it can be filtered through economic principles consistent with a structural understanding of competition. Upon finishing the analysis, we can try to formulate the basic principles of the legal concept of vertical restraints.

Two are the cornerstones of neoclassical design outlined above. First is the idea that vertical restraints are 'efficient', allowing for the elimination of free riding. Second is the belief that these restrictions are pro-competitive, as they stimulate inter-brand competition.

On the other hand, transaction cost theory rests on the idea that the main goal of antitrust law is to reduce transaction costs. Each requires separate analysis.

Efficiency: Marginal and inframarginal consumers   As for efficiency, we must first understand the assumption upon which it is based. The economic concept takes the marginal consumer as the rule of thumb in analysis, that is, the last consumer willing to purchase the product, the consumer for whom the marginal utility (presumably identical to the price) is exactly equal to the marginal cost.

For this consumer, neoclassical reasoning may make sense. For him, offering an extra service, for example, services to promote the sale or the post sale services (maintenance) represent a theoretically useful benefit. He is, by nature, the consumer in doubt; he is not sure of the best option or actual utility of the product.

Even in these cases, relevant doubt may arise. In the case of an uninformed consumer, or a product that requires explanations relevant to the decision to purchase, the dealer can easily induce the marginal consumer to purchase one that provides him with more profit, by definition, the one subject to the vertical restraint. The restriction may also represent a disutility, in that it could lead to the purchase of lower quality products for supra-competitive prices.[124]

What can be said, then, of the inframarginal consumer? Not every consumer is marginal. Something totally unspecified in the neoclassical models (among many other things) is exactly the number of marginal consumers and inframarginal consumers for each industry. For the inframarginal consumer, advertising campaigns or sales promotion services make almost no difference. This is the consumer who places a high value on the product (marginal utility of the product far exceeds its marginal cost) and is very well informed. Only the lowering of prices would be of real utility to this consumer.[125]

---

[124]   See W. Grimes, 'Brand Marketing, Intrabrand Competition and the Multibrand Retailer: The Antitrust Law of Vertical Restraints', cit., pp. 107–9.

[125]   The repeatedly cited, classic piece that develops this line of criticism is W. Comanor, 'Vertical Price-fixing, Vertical Market and the New Restrictions Antitrust

Thus, for this consumer, the vertical restraint that eliminates competition in price and stimulates competition in services (particularly sales) is useless. There is thus a loss, not a gain, in allocative efficiency.

This particular observation is tied, in fact, to a broader criticism of marginalist reasoning, as mentioned above. The economic results of vertical restraints are absolutely uncertain.[126] There can be neither gain nor loss of total utility (allocative efficiency). Everything depends on the number (absolutely uncertain) of marginal consumers and inframarginal consumers.

What has been said so far serves to demonstrate that, from the standpoint of the consumer, it is by no means a certainty that there is an increase in total utility. This reasoning can go back to the distributor. If there is no certainty of results, it is not safe for the distributor to invest in promotional spending. That is exactly what occurs when using the vertical restraint as a way to discourage free riding in relation to these expenditures.

The results of this uncertainty add to another criticism that can be made to vertical restraints as a protection against free riding. There are many other ways as effective as vertical restraints to achieve the same goal.

As seen, free riding can occur only in those situations where there are several conjugated services, always paid jointly by the consumer. There is no indication that they are viewed by consumers as a cluster, that is, as a single product. Evidence does exist, however, to the contrary. It would prove to be much more certain if they were to separate the various products offered and allow the distributor to get paid for each of them separately.[127]

Take the post-sale service, for example. The best way to prevent a distributor from taking advantage of it is to sell after-sales service separately and not

---

Policy', in *Harvard Law Review*, 98, 1985, p. 983 ff. Contrary argument is presented by H. Marvel, 'The Resale Price Maintenance Controversy: Beyond the Conventional Wisdom', cit., pp. 67–9. For this author the price increase owing to higher spending on promotion would lead to a fall in demand. That would force the producer to reduce its price to the dealer. So everything would be resolved in a redistribution of profits between producer and retailer, with no effect on the consumer. This argument is contrary, however, to the very logic of the imposition of vertical restraints. Of course, if this meant reducing their profit margin, producers would not use it. What actually occurs is thanks to the vertical restraints; demand becomes less elastic for the producer. The sales efforts tend (especially when it comes to multiproduct distributor or reseller) to capture the consumer. So it becomes possible to increase the price, losing proportionately less demand – see W. Grimes, 'Brand Marketing, Intrabrand Competition and the Multibrand Retailer: The Antitrust Law of Vertical Restraints', cit., pp. 111–3.

[126] See R. Pitofsky, 'The Sylvania Case: Antitrust Analysis of Non-price Vertical Restrictions', *Columbia Law Review*, 78(1), 1978, p. 33, affirming that the attempt to compare gains and losses is 'an effort to measure the unmeasurable'.

[127] See B. Ann White, 'Black and White Thinking in the Gray Areas of Antitrust: The Dismantling of Vertical Restraints Regulation', in *George Washington Law Review*, 60, 1991, p. 1.

in conjunction with the sale of the original product. This is the case with most post-sale services, which is why this kind of service, today, is not even mentioned as a source of free riding.

Slightly more complex is the situation when it comes to sales promotion and advertising. It is hard to imagine that the consumer can pay separately for such services, so great is its connection with the sale of the product itself. This does not mean, however, that the goods cannot be separated. Just as the producer pays fees or prizes to every distributor willing to perform this service; if it is really useful to the consumer, it may be included in the price. Thus, the producer will not proceed to redistribute benefits and maintain stimulus (allegedly) provided by the rules of vertical restraint.

These later observations seem to suggest that the traditional system of unbundling (separation on the vertical line), often used in the sectors of infrastructure as an (additional) instrument for protection of competition, may be more useful than vertical restraints to achieve that end. To determine the accuracy of this statement it is still necessary to analyze the neoclassical design of the pro-competitive effects of vertical restraints.

Intra-brand and inter-brand competition　　For logical consistency, to analyze the competitive effects of vertical restraints from the neoclassical perspective, some assumptions must be made.

Imagine, therefore, a sector formed only by uninformed consumers with little interest in the product, that is, a sector where it can be assumed that a significant part of consumers is marginal. Imagine, further, that this sector's products and services cannot be separated (unbundled), for whatever reason.

In such a situation (very imaginative and unlikely) it might be asked: is vertical restraint pro-competitive?

The neoclassical answer is yes, and for a simple reason: investment in sales promotion translates into an increase in inter-brand competition. The pattern of sales and service of a given distribution network, connected with a certain producer, will act as a catalyst for competition for other producers, who need to offer more attractive prices or heartier services.

Two consequences can be derived from this reasoning. First, inter-brand competition takes place only between producers and never between distributors or resellers. Second, intra-brand competition can successfully be replaced by inter-brand competition.

Both conclusions can be challenged. Analyze, for example, the hypothesis of multi-brand distribution. In multi-brand distribution, which occurs mainly with homogeneous products, the distributor or reseller distributes or sells competing products.

Take the case of supermarkets, for example. Their natural tendency is to cool the inter-brand competition. To maximize their outcome, they tend to raise prices of all similar products to whatever is closest to the most expensive product. This is a way to reverse part (the highest possible) of the sales results to the distribution or resale sector. If the dealer does not change prices, he would do nothing more than respect the numbers negotiated with producers. Increasing prices of products offered to him by producers for lower prices and selling, therefore, all similar products at similar prices, homogenizes the demand, and maximizes his total profits (revenue rises for products sold to him at cheaper prices). In such cases, they are doing nothing more than promoting a cartel (involuntary) among producers.

It is quite evident, in this case, that the relevant competition comes to be between the distributors, which is nothing more than intra-brand competition. More than that; the intra-brand competition itself will depend on inter-brand competition. And it will only be possible if the distributors themselves can compete with each other.[128]

Imagine what would happen if a uniform resale price were imposed. Eliminating the competition between distributors and reducing the competition between products by the action of the distributors themselves, consumer choice would vanish. The market as a whole would behave like a large tacit cartel, not punishable as such (since there is no horizontal agreement) but also clearly anti-competitive.

Transaction costs: Vertical restraints and vertical integration   Finally, we must examine the transaction cost theory and its assumptions. As we have already seen, it is composed of two branches. The first, of opportunistic behavior, is identified by the neoclassical idea of free riding, and has already been addressed above.

The second, limited rationality, presents a coherent explanation for certain types of restrictions. It so happens that it is applicable only to extremely exceptional cases, that is, only in those cases where there is variable demand and where there is no possibility of harm to the competitive system (which does not occur, as seen in multi-brand distribution). Thus, its usefulness remains limited.

---

[128]   This possibility is explored in an interesting piece (within the many that the author wrote criticizing the neoclassical explanation of vertical) of R. Steiner, 'Sylvania Economics: A Critique', in *Antitrust Law Journal*, 60, 1991, p. 41. The author describes the *Levi Strauss* case, where the company maintained retail prices impositions on their jeans throughout the 1970s. In 1976, under the action promoted by the FTC against such practice, Levi Strauss was stopped from imposing prices. The consequence was not only the reduction of prices of all competitors (Wranglers, and Sears own brands and Penney), but the gain in market share by Levi Strauss. The dismantling of the cartel (unintentional) in price between the producers (through the elimination of intra-brand competition). Moreover, according to estimates by Steiner, consumers 'saved' $261 million between 1977 and about 1978.

The greatest utility of the theory of transaction costs for the formulation of a coherent legal theory of vertical restraints is in one of its assumptions. It is the inclusion of vertical restrictions among the cases of vertical integration.

This allows the visualization of restraints and concentrations as species of the same gender, distinguishable on the basis of the degree of integration that each provides. The consequence is to make it possible to identify those cases in which a restriction is needed so a certain product can easily enter the market or compete, and where it is therefore necessary to avoid a potentially even greater concentration of power, as would occur in a vertical merger.

Take the franchise, for example. The franchise is a means by which the producer, or holder of a piece of technology, can reach the public without having to have his own distribution network. The essential requirement for the product to appear to the public under one common brand is the uniformity of prices of the franchisees.

This homogeneity here serves two perfectly competitive purposes. First, it enables the delivery of goods by the producer without having to reach this level of distribution via vertical concentration. Second, it allows franchisees to feel safe in making the necessary investments to ensure product quality.

In this case, we can apply the theory of free riding. No franchisee will be interested in making any sort of investment if they believe they will suffer competition from another franchisee. This would go against the very spirit of the franchise, as it would allow a retailer to reduce product quality to compete with another.

One can therefore conclude that, in the analysis of constraints on competition derived from vertical restraints, it is necessary to take into account the need for this constraint to avoid an integration of production to distribution and resale. In these cases there is no risk to competition on the horizontal line either, since the restriction is to ensure the entry of other competitors. The rationale of the restrictions ends up being preventing the creation of more market power in the vertical line. As will be seen below, this is actually a coherent application of the structural approach to market power and traditional antitrust law.

STRUCTURAL UNDERSTANDING OF VERTICAL RESTRAINTS   What has been said above demonstrates that the main problem behind neoclassical theory is its disregard of the intrinsic value of choice in each of the levels: inter- and intra-brand.

It is impossible to correctly measure benefits. There is complete uncertainty regarding the economic efficiencies of production, even if taken in an exclusively allocative sense. Furthermore, there is relevant economic evidence that vertical restraints are not necessary for the purposes indicated by neoclassical orthodoxy.

On the other hand, intra-brand competition has shown itself to be essential and this is a fundamental reason for recognizing the importance of studying vertical collusion. Its replacement by inter-brand competition is not only immeasurable; it is not feasible either. We found that, in many cases, intra-brand competition is the only way to give rise to inter-brand competition.

Finally, it was found that, following the same institutional principle, vertical restraints cannot be considered wrongful where it is necessary to allow the entry of new competitors in the market, which, without it, would either have to concentrate vertically or would not have access to the market. This applies to franchises, in which case the restriction is clearly pro-competitive, with no need to refer to the intra- and inter-brand dichotomy (because if there was a vertical merger, there would not be any intra-brand competition).

The structural design of competition appears, then, once again, as the only way to overcome this economical *non-liquet*. In order to understand its meaning, it is necessary to solve two major groups of problems that arise from it. First, we must differentiate between vertical restraints and the horizontal restraints that sometimes arise from them. It is then necessary to determine the relevance of the traditional distinction, based on economic constraint, between price and non-price competition. Finally, we will need to discuss the requirements for setting up the institutional harm to competition.

Vertical and horizontal restraints   A major problem to be overcome in the case of vertical restraints is how to differentiate them from the horizontal restraints that derive from them. One argument, indirectly derived from neoclassical reasoning, is that with oversight and strict punishment of horizontal restraints, it would be unnecessary to pursue the vertical ones.[129]

This statement contains a conceptual and logical error that is quite important. The horizontal cartel-like restriction, punishable in antitrust law, results from an agreement, express or implied between competitors, to eliminate competition between them. This agreement, in this case, does not exist. To accept punishment as a cartel would be to accept punishment merely on the basis of its effects, that is, the elimination of competition on the horizontal line.

This would not only identify all conduct that aimed at eliminating competition as cartel behavior, but would also disregard one of the basic pillars of the institutional structure of competition: the criterion of intent for the configuration of wrongdoing.

As was seen, in the cases of vertical restraint there may be involuntary cartels among producers, particularly when the distributors and resellers are

---

[129]   R. Bork, *The Antitrust Paradox*, cit., p. 292.

common to many brands. It is not, however, a cartel, but a mere effect of the occurrence that is worrisome, namely the elimination of the intra-brand competition that created it.

In the distributors' relationships, the search for the existence of horizontal restraint (cartel), in addition to vertical restraint, is more relevant. There, we are dealing with the configuration of one or the other offense, with different penalties: in the case of vertical restraint, the penalty goes to those who imposed the restriction. Imagine that the imposition of uniform price is the result of pressure from the distributors or dealers on the producer, by means of this artifice, so they can better organize, and better punish defections in a cartel. In that case, however, it is usually not difficult to identify horizontal agreement. First, this is because agreements between distributors, involving many participants, are not easy to control or conceal.[130] Moreover, if the imposition of resale prices is nothing but a cover for an agreement among distributors or retailers, the producer, once accused, will easily defend himself by showing what happened, and in this case showing that there was an agreement among retailers.

Price and non-price restraints   In antitrust traditional doctrine, there has been a long-standing doctrine on the differences between price vertical restraint and non-price vertical restraint.[131] This distinction does not hold, owing solely to historical circumstances of American jurisprudential evolution.[132]

There is no difference between price and non-price restraints. The non-price restraints, basically establishing sales quotas and exclusive territory, have the same effects as price restraints. Territorial exclusivity, on the other hand, has the same effects as territorial restraint. By eliminating competition between the distributors or dealers, one allows for the dreaded standardization of conditions both inter-brand and intra-brand.

---

[130]   See on this matter R. Bork, *The Antitrust Paradox*, cit., p. 292.

[131]   What the Supreme Court sought to do was soften the strict rule of per se prohibition of price restraints on dealers established in Dr Miles (*Dr Miles Co. v. John D. Park & Sons Co.*) in 220 U.S. 373 (1911). The opportunity came in 1977 in the *Sylvania* case (*Continental TV Inc. v. GTE Sylvania Inc.*) in 433 U.S. 36 (1911), a case of territorial restraints, which established a rule of reason in the neoclassical sense, stating that it was necessary to weigh the anti-competitive effects of the elimination of intra-brand competition with the pro-competitive effects of increased inter-brand competition.

[132]   Explicitly rejected by the Chicago school academics – R. Bork, *The Antitrust Paradox*, cit., p. 280; and simply disregarded by post Chicago antitrust doctrine – W. Comanor, 'Vertical Price-fixing, Vertical Market and the New Restrictions Antitrust Policy', cit., p. 983, which only refers to the distinction in its title, O. Williamson, 'Assessing Market Restrictions: Antitrust Ramifications of the Transaction Cost Approach', cit., p. 953, and R. Steiner, 'The Sylvania Economics: A Critique', cit., p. 41, among many others.

Brazilian law, for example, explicitly recognizes this irrelevance by mentioning, without distinction in Article 21, XI, non-price restraints and price restraints as examples of antitrust violation.

All the above applies, therefore, to both types of restraint.

INTENTION AND ANTI-COMPETITIVE EFFECT   We can now conclude by identifying the specific requirements for characterizing vertical restraints as illegal.

For this to occur, the imposition of resale prices or conditions should be characterized by an objective and real opportunity to dominate the market.

What has been said above suggests an initial differentiation between multi-brand and exclusive distributors and dealers. For the latter, the critique of neoclassical analysis has shown that vertical restraints have a high anti-competitive potential. Not only do they themselves impose a restriction on competition but they also invite more restrictions. Imagine the possibility of imposing a single resale price. There is a real call for standardization by the distributors of all competing products based on price or conditions for the product subject to restrictions.

Note that, here, the same reasoning used for horizontal restraints applies. This attractive potential of horizontal restraints, coupled with understanding of the restrictions on competition in the theory of incipience, leads us to conclude that vertical restraint on distribution always has as its objective market dominance.

In the case of exclusive distributors, the influence of intra-brand restrictions on inter-brand restrictions is lower; absent the ability of the distributor/dealer to standardize the prices of various products. That does not mean that there is no risk to competition. Every time the producer holds market power, separately or together with other producers, the risk is present. In the case of oligopoly, in addition to the direct restriction of choice, there is the invitation to identical behavior of other producers – as a means of obtaining competitive advantage, it tends to be seen as a strategy to be followed by other economic agents. Once widespread in the market and having eliminated intra-brand competition there will be a great incentive to eliminate inter-brand competition.

It is much easier to control a cartel between producers, where the internal defection (intra-brand competition) is not possible. Under these assumptions, we once again show the interdependence of intra-brand and inter-brand competition. Once the first is eliminated, there is great stimulus to eliminate the second.

Finally, also based on structural reasoning, we conclude that whenever the vertical restriction of competition is essential to ensure market access with no vertical merger, the restriction is lawful and pro-competitive. This occurs, for example, in the case of the franchise.

This last point is particularly important in economies where there is a great need for diversification, that is, where international technological drainage is felt.

The discipline of vertical restrictions therefore changes its character. In the structural conception, it is not seen any more as a system of allowing the production of efficiencies or preventing free riding, that is, as an instrument for the better functioning of a free market. Its main characteristic seems simply to be the prevention of the formation of complex structures with multi-draining capabilities. As well as the standard consumer and labor market drainage, preventing vertical collusion also implies restraining intersectoral drainage, by better protecting adjacent sectors from the effects of monopolies, since it protects the independence of dealers and distributors, an essential element of connection to consumers. It signifies, therefore, an important element in structural control of market power.

Collusion, market power and development

The relationship between collusion and macro social and economic problems is even more direct and easier to understand than that of exclusionary practices.

As a building instrument for market power, both in the horizontal and vertical lines, it is a powerful draining instrument, be it for consumers, workers or the development of different sectors of the economy (see Chapter 1, section 2).

It also highlights the dark side of cooperation, putting in the dark more substantive or positive forms of cooperation. Actually non-cartel cooperation is an extremely important element for economic development.[133]

3. LEGAL MONOPOLIES AND DYNAMIC ABUSE

Having studied market behavior, it is important to now study the conduct that stems from power structures established by law. As was stated in the introduction to this chapter (section 1) these structures can result from abuse of situations of power, or the structure of the relationship itself, both established or guaranteed by law. It is from such point of view that the legal structures will be studied hereafter.

---

[133] For further discussion on this issue, see C. Salomão Filho, 'Direito como instrumento de transformação social e econômica', in *Revista de Direito Público da Economia*, 2003, pp. 15–44.

Patents: Limits of Use and Compulsory Licensing

Patents are perhaps the most purely legal of power structures. As was seen in Chapter 2, section 4, this characteristic affects the manner by which the law is to address such power structures. Not only that; the behavior of patent holders also ought to be assessed.

In classic intellectual property law, sanctioning of patents and trademarks revolves around rules stemming eminently from private benefit, such as the invalidation of the registration and expiration of the patent on one hand, with rules on nullity sanctioning the non-compliance of rules and regulations of the registration process, and rules on the expiration of the patent on the other.

Both have a static perspective, precisely because they see a privilege in the patent, and in turn within the intrinsic and extrinsic factors for their concessions. The fact is that, since the patent is seen as a private asset, just formal errors in the granting itself can justify its disappearance.

The logic of privilege and monopoly tends to draw attention to the explicit and implicit conditions for obtaining the privilege, thus focusing on compliance with formal rules.

Structuralist understanding sees the patent from another perspective. It extends and makes the discipline public precisely because it focuses on the abuse of its rights. The patent is no longer seen as an unlimited privilege.

A patent, like any situation of market power, can lead to abuse, which must be curbed. Patent law, therefore, must include a specific discipline that deals with abuse of power.

This approach to patents has two distinct consequences. On the one hand, it is necessary for patents that effectively generate monopolistic power to be distinguished from others. There are various characteristics that can generate power. A relevant one, socially speaking, is the importance of the product to its user or consumer. The more essential the product is to the consumer, the more power it generates.

This generally happens to products of great value to consumers (as medication). In this hypothesis there is a clear social benefit, which is derived from its availability to a large number of users. There is, as a result, a duty to provide these products at a non-abusive price.

This point of view, which is an eminently structuralistic-competitive view of the question at hand, is consistent with different legal systems around the world (as the Brazilian or the South African ones, for example), which allows for compulsory licensing and effectively applies compulsory licensing strategies in cases of abuse of economic power, through abuse of prices or creation of scarcity in the market. Not surprisingly, the examples come exactly from countries that have huge poor populations and face serious health problems in providing medication for all of them.

Note that the consequence of non-compliance with this type of rule is the breaking of the monopoly through compulsory licensing. The competitive inspiration behind the rule is thus obvious. The justification for structural intervention is the abuse of patent rights, especially in sectors in which, owing to the essentiality of the product, competitive relations and consumption can be hindered owing to the abusive exercise of such rights (areas of biochemistry, electronics and information technology). Sensitivity to final consumer prices generates a serious unbalance within the market, making some products simply inaccessible to various groups within the population.

The access of less privileged segments of the population to essential drugs for the treatment of infectious diseases as well as endemics is only possible if abuses of price and creation of scarcity in the market are sanctioned. In the case of medicines, when patent protection has disappeared for certain patents, for various reasons (expiration, compulsory licensing, etc.) countries (especially in the developing world) have used strategies to promote the generic drug industry, which represents great potential for substituting previously patented drugs in the possession of large pharmaceutical companies.[134]

In the second half of the 1990s, for example, Brazil managed to use such a strategy, especially in connection to the reduction in purchase prices of essential drugs that were no longer exclusive to specific companies, but that were provided by a wide range of suppliers in developed and underdeveloped countries.[135]

It shall not be a surprise that the country that has been most capable of developing its generics pharmaceutical industry over the last decade, India (which in fact became the developing world main source of generics), was the country that took longer to admit patenting of medicines.

---

[134]   The WHO estimates that in most underdeveloped countries and developing countries less than 20% of essential medication is protected by patents. Many of them are public domain, but were never made generic, and are extremely expensive, because they are often imported directly from developed countries.

[135]   In Brazil, the definition of generic drug was determined by Law 9787, February 10, 1999 ('Generic Drug Law') to amend the provisions of Law No 6360 of September 23, 1976, which regulates health surveillance in the country. In article 3, paragraph XXI, which defines generic as 'a medicine similar to a reference product or innovative one, that is to be interchangeable, usually produced after the expiration or waiver of patent protection or other exclusive rights, with proven effectiveness, safety and quality'. According to estimates, in recent years 39 170 (2001), 75 650 (2002) and 79 161 (2003) units have been produced, with a significant increase of almost 482% between 2001 and 2002, being sold for almost 40% less than patented drugs. According to the Pro-Generic website (www.progenericos.org.br) there were 83 registrations of this type in 2001 and 1124 in 2004.

In fact, both facts demonstrate that the treatment of patents should be carried out with a structural perspective directed at full access and that such a perspective is actually an instrument for the construction of a new technology basis for production.

Drugs patents and compulsory license

Upon recognition of the importance and consistency of such a policy of full access to essential patented products, the question is to identify the most coherent instruments from the theoretical standpoint for the achievement of such goals.

The most effective, but least common, alternative is the implementation of compulsory license policies. This hypothesis is compatible with the principles of TRIPS, and is one of the most common expedients used for local production of essential medicine. In Brazil, Lei n. 9.279/1996, article 68, explicitly provides for the possibility of the granting of compulsory licenses in cases related to insufficient local production or abuse by the holder of the rights as conferred by the patent.[136]

It is easy to link such patent law provisions to the structural principles of market power regulation. In addition, the structuralist interpretation of patent law is still able to shed light on another important issue concerning the compulsory license, namely, the value of remuneration for the licensed patent.

The economic value of the patent that is compulsorily licensed must be well understood as being different from the value of a contractual license. It does not have a compensatory nature, but rather serves the aim of guaranteeing full access to the product (once again no compensation but organization of the different interest involved). This conclusion is not surprising. The remuneration provided for in TRIPS, its laws and regulations, should not and cannot be interpreted as compensatory.[137]

As a principle, the value is referred to its economic use by the acquirer (or the licensee). When it is a contractual and voluntary license, parties can freely discuss such value and calculate the amount of profits to be obtained by the licensee as a basis for the license price. When referring to compulsory licenses of essential products, the reasoning is different. If the license is basically

---

[136]   Subsequently promulgated in the Decree 3.201/1999, which regulated the compulsory license in Brazil in cases related to national emergency and public interest. More recently, this decree was modified by Decree 4830, from September 4, 2003, which incorporated in Brazil the principles of the Doha Declaration on TRIPS and Public Health 2001.

[137]   Art. 31 (h) of TRIPS provides that the holder be paid adequate remuneration within the circumstances of each case, taking into account the economic value of the authorization.

destined to supply the population of low income, the price charged for the sale of the medicine will be equal to the cost or something very close to it (which typically occurs in situations of perfect competition, especially in low-income markets).

We conclude, therefore, that, once the structural rationale of patents is accepted, the license value could/should be calculated as a fraction of the profits of the private producer (whether it be the beneficiary of the license or the outsourced producer), and that this profit should be kept to a minimum (or even equal to zero in cases of social relevance) so as to satisfy the social needs for the essential drugs involved.[138]

Legitimate parallel importing

A very important element for the effectiveness of compulsory licensing is to allow that while the country is getting ready for the production of the good (which generally takes time), the essential good is already available for the population. This is why most national legislations foresee the hypothesis of legitimate and authorized parallel imports, provided that the product has been marketed directly by the patentee or with his consent. There are innumerable legitimate international sources that supply these products at prices much lower than those offered by pharmaceutical companies.[139]

The requirement of consent of the patent holder should also be well understood. The consent can be either express or tacit. Consequently, consent should include: (i) donations of patented medication done by the pharmaceutical industries to charitable organizations; and (ii) sales of patented drugs in countries that do not recognize patented rights for drugs. This source is particularly important for the importation of patented and generic medication from countries like India that until recently did not recognize patents for drugs. Thus interpreted, parallel importation becomes an essential instrument to guarantee the immediate suspension of the effects of abusive monopolistic practices regarding essential medicines, that is, abusive prices and shortages.

---

[138] The reasonableness of this argument can also be viewed from another angle. Possible market value of the license, understood as severance, would mean in practice, the impossibility of access to essential medicines, as this would be passed on to the final price. Everything would be passed on to the licensee and end user, as if the compulsory license had never existed.

[139] For their description and enumeration, see F. Polido & P. Cesar, 'Fundamentos da interface entre direito à saúde e propriedade intelectual', in *Direitos de Propriedade Intelectual e Saúde Pública*, 2007, p. 5.

Neglected diseases: Structural legal mechanisms

From what has been described so far, the balance of the compulsory licensing instrument, both from a theoretical and practical standpoint, is quite clear. On the one hand, domestic markets, especially in developing countries, are facing increasing shortages for poor people of essential products, as a result of monopolistic prices.[140] Compulsory licensing, with the aid of parallel importing, by intervening in this reality, does nothing more than re-establish equilibrium.

Compulsory licensing and parallel imports, however, do not solve all issues related to access to essential drugs in the developing world. It is necessary to seek a structural answer to another burning issue of access to public health in developing and least relatively developed countries. That is the tropical diseases that affect local populations. There is no research in developed countries for such diseases, as they do not exist there. So, it would not be effective to implement some sort of policy on differentiated prices, even if based on compulsory licensing for these drugs aimed at treating and curing tropical diseases, simply because there would not be sufficient research and development (R&D) in the pharmaceutical industry located in developed countries.

The challenge is, therefore, to stimulate research and development in the absence of the perspective of differentiated returns that finance R&D. From a structuralistic perspective of patent law it is definitely possible to envision a system of cross-subsidies in matters of R&D.

In other words, the developing country concerned could acknowledge that certain categories of drugs (and possibly the consumer market where there are larger economic conditions to absorb price increases) are exempt from the policy of differential pricing (that is, exempt from compulsory licensing or parallel imports) as a compensation for the obligation undertaken by the pharmaceutical company to invest in R&D for the tropical diseases in question. The price increase could serve to subsidize R&D of drugs for the treatment of tropical diseases.

Three observations, more or less evident, should then be made. Firstly, such a measure can be introduced only after a coherent pursuit of a policy of differentiated prices in the country (compulsory licensing and parallel imports). Only then will there be a product that supports the cross-subsidization, that is, the 'subsidizing' product.

Second, it is evidently necessary that a coherent legal framework be established, which ensures that, in the absence of the promised investment in R&D for tropical disease medicine, the benefit of exemption of the differentiated

---

[140] Cf. relevant data found in F. Polido & P. Cesar, 'Fundamentos da interface entre direito à saúde e propriedade intelectual', cit., item 4.

price be immediately cancelled, and the difference paid to the pharmaceutical industry be returned to the consumers who paid more for their medicine.

Third, the legal framework to be established would most probably require the creation of a fund originating from the cross-subsidies and properly regulated to ensure investment in neglected diseases research and development.

The legislative elaboration of such a solution is entirely consistent with the principles abovementioned. From the structuralistic point of view, patents serve as a means of stimulating competition in R&D for its own and/or other product segments. This is what would be done through such a 'cross-subsidization of patents' scheme.

Regulated Sectors

It is in regulated sectors that the dynamic expression of power, embedded within the structure, is most felt. Economic agents, protected by regulatory safeguards, have the use of this power as the main guide of their economic behavior. Power, and not law, rules the relationships. More than that, power created by the law governs the relationships. Hence the difficulty and need for legal intervention.

Per se concept of antitrust violation

The rule of reason in antitrust matters is, undoubtedly, the most important and perhaps the only matter of consensus within the national doctrine. In different countries and different times rule of reason has represented a reaction to excessive, formal application of antitrust rules.

The rule of reason has two distinct parts and two specific justifications that cannot be disassociated from modern antitrust law, for one simple reason. They ensure the possibility of production of competitive effects and therefore only in their absence can one assume an anti-competitive purpose. The rule of reason is therefore a fundamental guarantee of the legality of administrative punishment.

The two components of the rule of reason are, respectively, the existence of market power and the justifications (antitrust or extra-antitrust) for the act.

The first is the existence and/or possibility of the creation of economic power. This requirement makes sense when dealing with illicit dominance and/or abuse of dominant position.

When lacking real or potential power, antitrust control is unnecessary and ineffective, precisely because the purpose/necessity of the conduct's legal discipline is to prevent the unlawful gathering/misuse of power. If power is non-existent, there is no reason for prosecuting the behavior. Thus, it is imperative that thorough research be done as to the existence or not of market power.

The second component of the rule of reason comes from logical imperative and economic policy. The logical imperative consists in the absence of pro-competitive justifications for the act. In its presence, the illicit act obviously does not exist.

However, not only antitrust justifications are traditionally accepted, but also those involving economic policy or outside the realm of competition. In an economic system that coexists with several imperatives of economic policy, this element is actually acceptable in antitrust.[141] Thus, it is always a justification that, even allowing for some competition harm, it is possible to demonstrate the existence of advantageous benefits to other objectives of economic policy.

It is not hard to understand that everything changes when dealing with regulated sectors. Firstly, as has been seen, in the sectors now dealt with, regulation is needed precisely because there is no minimum condition of existence/maintenance of competition without it. Thus, market power is a given, and need not be searched for. The first element of the rule of reason thus disappears.

The understanding of the general lack of necessity in regulated sectors for the second element of the rule of reason is not so obvious. What can be said is that no non-competitive justification is admissible in the case of regulated industries. This conclusion derives from the very prevalence of this structural reasoning in this form of regulation.

If inexistence or lack of strength of the competition within these sectors leads to, as has been seen, absolute dominance of power structures, then non-competitive justifications for antitrust restrictions should not be generally admissible. In other words, the pursuit per se of limitations to economic power positions is justified by the purpose of the regulation.

This is a general rule. We shall not exclude, especially in relation to endogenous objectives and goals explicitly stated in the antitrust system, joint implementation of certain economic policy objectives with the antitrust principles. Note that another difference is manifested here. What is proposed is the joint application of antitrust and extra-antitrust principles, not the replacement of one by another, as occurs frequently in antitrust matters. Economic policy justifications can and should be evaluated and accepted only when compatible with antimonopoly goals. The justification should be clear at this point.

If concentration of economic power is so central as a reason for underdevelopment, as is sustained in this book, then it must be a part of any legal policy in the economic realm. The effects of antimonopoly rules are not on the

---

[141] For its limitations, see C. Salomão Filho, *Direito Concorrencial – As Estruturas*, 3rd ed., cit., p. 201.

parties involved but have redistributive impact, preventing triple draining and allowing for more economic dynamism. Therefore, they should not be subject to other economic policy objectives. It is not for any other reason that, in most jurisdictions, antimonopoly principles are inscribed in the constitutions as fundamental goals that shall be any way pursued.

Conducts

There is no need to analyze anti-competitive practices one by one. It is interesting to note the general trend in adapting the antitrust rules in the regulatory realm.

The most illustrative case is undoubtedly that of refusal to deal. The change in the discipline of the so-called 'refusal to deal', typical of antitrust law, is the focus of the very development of the concept of regulation based on antitrust principles, to the point of constituting the basis for development of the principle of full access to monopolized networks.

The development of 'refusal to deal' is nothing more than a demonstration of the general movement of regulation, away from neoclassical microeconomic rationality and closer to a general requirement for access and competition. From an antitrust illicit to a regulatory principle, its movement reveals a move towards per se interpretation of antimonopoly rules. The same can be observed in the path followed by the three major groups of antitrust wrongdoings when applied to regulated sectors: *compulsory negotiation*, *predation* (among acts of exclusion) and *collusion*.

The regulation of compulsory negotiation Within the generic category of compulsory negotiation are various types of behavior: exclusivity, refusal to deal, tying, reciprocal dealing, etc. There is a common source to all of them: the dependence of an economic agent on another, with monopoly granted by the law, causing the first to lose its contractual freedom, being forced in several ways to contract with the seller in order to obtain a certain good (mutual negotiation), not to deal when dealing is necessary (refusal to deal), to contract solely with the agent on which it depends (exclusivity), or to buy another product from the same agent in order to get the product needed (tying). In all cases, economic dependence creates legal dependence and lack of contractual freedom.

It is for this reason that, in traditional antitrust law, all the attention is focused on whether or not there is dominance. Dominance existing, the first element of the rule of reason is automatically present. Only the second pillar is then left, that is, the existence of justifications for behavior that can be made compatible with antitrust goals. In the case of compulsory negotiation, the justification boils down to protection against so-called free riding.

Protection against free riding is, in certain cases of restriction of contractual freedom, the protection necessary for an investment that would be enjoyed at no charge if the practice was considered illegal. Thus, a prohibition per se of exclusivity could restrict investment in technology, infrastructure or sales as the economic agent would know that without, for example, the exclusivity clause, the economic benefit of that investment could be obtained without cost by its competitors.

This situation does not arise in the regulatory field for several reasons. First, in a sense, the networks and increasing returns to scale that are provided already constitute free riding. The mere fact that each new consumer serves as an increase of use for the next consumer is already a benefit to which the owner of the network made no investment. Thus, we should not think of recovery of investments through additional restrictions to the already limited contractual freedom of the competitors that depend on the network.

Without this justification, punishment becomes, in reality, exclusively related to the conduct, or punishment per se – unless, of course, there is some justification (not linked to general defense of free riding) for one specific situation.

Regulation of predation   By 'regulation of predation' one should understand rules implemented to avoid or prevent the predation of competitors. In the case of predatory behavior such rules are of absolute necessity, for two reasons.

Firstly, because of the rule of reason, the punishment for predation based on antitrust is quite rare. The criteria for recognition of the existence of predation, especially those used to determine if predation will effectively lead to a situation of domination, are extremely stringent.

On the other hand (and this is the second reason suggested above), predation is the most common practice in dominated sectors. There being a network, the most effective way to prevent any competition is to create barriers (especially technological ones) to prevent competitors from having access to it. So-called 'technological predation' is, in these markets, the general rule.

Moreover, in controlled sectors, the very limit to the expansion of the market and supply, in comparison to the inexistence of limit to the expansion of demand; makes competition tend to be destructive or predatory. The problem is so severe and predation is considered so endemic that regulatory mechanisms to prevent the increase in prices that follow predatory decreases have already been suggested.[142]

There are instead solutions that are much better and much more practical. And the solution is again a reinterpretation of the antitrust principles and rules

---

[142]   W. Baumol, 'Quasi-permanence of Price Reductions: A Policy for Prevention of Predatory Pricing', cit., p. 1.

applicable to regulated industries. Financial power and the possibility of eliminating competition, the traditional components of the rule of reason for predatory pricing, in the case of regulated industries, are derived directly from the
structural conditions described above. They must not be proven since they are
the very reasons for regulation. With this in mind, we must differentiate
between situations in which price reductions represent, or do not, actual
attempts to competition.

In order to do so, the economic doctrine has provided substantial assistance
so that today we can consider an accepted conclusion, the presumption that
prices below average variable cost cannot possibly have pro-competitive aims
(see Chapter 3, section 2).

Thus, in the case of regulated industries with the structural characteristics
described (Chapter 2, section 4), the anti-competitive practice of illegal predatory pricing can be determined directly from the prices. The same can be said
for technological predation. There is no need to demonstrate the possibility of
eliminating competitors; the domination of the net and the technological limitation created (or price reduction below the accepted levels) are sufficient for
the existence of illegal practice.

Regulation of collusion: Game theory and its limitations   The current legal
treatment of collusion rests primarily on game theory. In terms of oligopolies,
its primacy has been unchallenged since the award of the Nobel Prize to J.
Nash for the study of non-cooperative games and their application to oligopolies.

Paradoxically, the very centralization (guarded by Nash) of attention of
game theory and the theory of oligopolies exclusively around the idea of individual strategy game is one of the main reasons for its small explanatory
power, especially in regulated industries. Since von Neumann, in his famous
book *The Theory of Games and Economic Behavior*,[143] laid the cornerstone
for the study of economic relationships from game theoretic reasoning, two
possible ways of development were possible.

The first way is to focus on games of individual strategy that have a precise
mathematical result (at least regarding the definition of equilibrium point).
That has been the only line adopted by game theory since the famous article,
'The Bargaining Problem' by J. Nash.[144] The consequence has been, without
doubt, a more mathematically rigorous analysis of the behavior of oligopolies.
Its usefulness in prediction of behavior is, however, very limited.

---

[143]   J. von Neumann & O. Morgenstern, *The Theory of Games and Economic
Behaviour*, 1944.
[144]   J. Nash, 'The Bargaining Problem', *Econometrica* 18, 1950, p. 155, consulted
in K. Kuhn, *Classics in Game Theory*, p. 5.

The reason is simple. There was very little development of the opposite idea, the second line of possible development of game theory: an analysis of how, when and why economic agents cooperate. Nash's theory states that cooperation is rare, and only justifiable when in line with the individual agent's strategy.

What game theorists failed to see is that, in the real world, especially in regulated sectors, the legal framework makes collective strategy the only possible one.

On the other hand, the theory based on individual strategy contains questionable assumptions and is certainly inapplicable to regulated sectors, since it presupposes a single type of behavior in all individuals. It is the individual strategy, guided at pointing to the best decision *in light of the strategy to be adopted by the competitor.*

What can be seen is that this assumption is not in any way applicable to any hypothesis of economic interrelationship in an oligopoly, regulated environment. Looking at others' behavior, whether they are adversaries, or co-participants in any form of social interaction, is not only a way of finding desirable behavior, but of acquiring knowledge.

Upon understanding this obvious premise of economic behavior – that is, that one first acquires knowledge, and behavior is defined next – we can redirect the attention of game theory. If this is true, individual behavior determination is influenced not only by a single strategic objective. Its disposition and goals are greatly influenced by the conceptions that agents have of this reality. The individual must first understand how the market operates, so as to, in turn, define his/her individual modus operandi (individualistic or cooperative). The knowledge one has of reality – in fact – is determined by examining and comparing others' behavior.

Well, it is easy to understand that, in regulated markets, observing the behavior of others leads to a cooperative game, rather than to individual strategy. The basis for regulation (at least in its competitive aspect) in regulated markets is nothing more than the existence of structural conditions that allow predatory competition (variable demand, entry barriers etc.; see Chapter 2, section 2).

It so happens that the possibility of predation leads directly to the need for explicit cooperation and not to eventual collusion as a result of individual strategic behavior. The threat of predatory competition has a direct effect on the economic agent's understanding – he/she comes to understand that any non-cooperative behavior may lead to a predatory war, with extremely negative consequences. Explicit and formal cooperation, then, is necessary precisely because the perception of the existence of freedom to compete may return the agents to a situation of predatory competition, which is inconvenient for everyone.

Observation of past agent behavior, therefore, leads to the conclusion that there is a need for cooperation. It helps to understand reality. And it is from its understanding that the patterns of behavior emerge.

The consequence is, naturally, that behavior regulation should have two goals.

First, structural conditions must be put into place so as to prevent overproduction crisis and, consequently, predatory competition. Entry barriers and their elimination, if necessary, should be carefully regulated to prevent the worsening of supply crises (read here as both overproduction crisis and crisis of scarcity).[145]

---

[145] The Brazilian air transportation system is a clear example of the negative effects that regulation can have on the market. Started in 1992, the opening of the sector was marked primarily by decrease in tariffs and by exploitation of regular air transport by airlines. The effects of overproduction are directly related to the relaxation of oversight of airline operations. It is worth mentioning that, previously, Brazilian air transportation was divided into regional lines, special and national. The relaxation resulted from gradual changes introduced in each of these sectors. Among the major changes implemented were those experienced by regional lines, which had previously been subject to clear territorial restriction. The territory was divided into five areas of exclusive rights of exploitation, in which no other airline could operate. Likewise, the airlines that operated there could not explore other territory or national/special lines (Decree 76,590 of December 1975 regulated by Ordinance 22/GM5 of January 7, 1976, and thereafter by Ordinance 956/GM5 of December 19, 1989). At first the relaxations abolished restrictions thus allowing regional airlines to become national (MG5 Ordinance of May 17, 1990, repealed by Art. 6 of Ordinance 956 of December 19, 1989, which imposed these restrictions). Subsequently, the territorial restrictions were abolished allowing regional companies to operate throughout the national territory (687/GM5 Ordinance of December 15, 1992). The distinction between regional and national lines was maintained. The same Ordinance 687/GM5 introduced the definition of regional lines as those 'characterized by affluence or complementary' to national lines, or those that connected 'two or more locations not served by national lines' (formerly, regional transport was defined as 'air lines and services in one region [that are intended to cater] to the localities of high and low potential traffic' – 956/GM5 Order of December 19, 1989, art. 1). Years later, Ordinance 504/GC5 of August 12, 1999, eliminated the restriction, and expressly allowed that the regional domestic airlines connect 'two population and economic centers'. It was precisely these changes in regulations that allowed the regional companies to expand their activities in the country. Similarly, they enabled the entry of new companies to the regional market. This way, the number of participants in the regional market increased from 5 in 1991 to 18 in 1999 (IV Development Plan System of Civil Aviation, p. 31). The market for national airlines, regional and special was gradually increased with the greater flexibility. If, on the one hand, this phenomenon has led to intense competition in the airline industry, simultaneously, it has also led to the rise in the volume of supply. To the extent that this has not been accompanied by growth, in the same proportions, of demand, a result that followed was a crisis of overproduction, and the ensuing price war in early 1998. This was followed by the parallel behavior of competitors already considered in

Second, in the presence of parallel conduct, one must assume intent through economic data, and not the – often impossible to detect – demonstration of collusive intent.

In the presence of the structural factors mentioned above (that is, barriers to entry and the possibility of excess supply – variable demand), repeated parallel behavior is enough to characterize possible illegal conduct. Moreover, the only acceptable justification is the existence of structural crisis so great so as to make cooperation essential.[146]

Again, here, the ultimate justification for such a rigorous application of antimonopoly rules to regulated sectors lies in the social importance of the discipline and in the social sensitivity of the sectors.

Undoubtedly, triple draining effects in socially sensitive fields like electricity, telecommunications or financial services have a much bigger impact on the redistributive patterns of society and therefore on social and economic development.

4. EXPLOITATION OF NATURAL RESOURCES: THE ENVIRONMENTAL PROBLEM

Following the same sequence of the first chapter, after studying the behavior of market structures and dominant structures created by the law, it is now necessary to understand how the practices of structures with economic power may affect the common goods and scarce natural resources. Predatory conduct by economic agents with economic power related to natural resources shall

---

the previous chapter and the strong rise in prices for consumers. More recently, the economic power of companies operating in the loosely regulated market has led to the apparent capture of the regulatory agency (ANAC, created by Law 11,182 of September 27, 2005), unable to cope with the demand or to guarantee minimum quality and safety of the service.

[146] In the face of an acute crisis in any one sector of the economy, competition law allows for the formation of cartels of crisis, defined as an agreement between companies for control or maintenance of productive capacity. In particular the European Courts have accepted such cooperation between companies in specific cases (see *Re Synthetic Fibers* [1984] OJ L 207/17; BPCL / ICI [1985] 2CMLR 330). The approval of such conduct, at first, seems to be an exception to the antitrust law because it allows for an apparently anti-competitive merger. There are, however, competitive justifications for this apparent exception: if not allowed to cooperate, agents having to leave owing to the crisis would imply a greater concentration of power in that market. A crisis cartel is not, therefore, an exception to the principles of competition, but it is a real implementation of these. In this sense, see C. Salomão Filho, *Direto concorrencial –as estruturas*, 3rd ed., cit., pp. 214–15. It should also be noted that the possibility of cooperation of companies in case of structural crisis may be insufficient to solve the problem of the sector. As a result, in some cases the only solution to the crisis would be the business combination.

therefore be analyzed. The discussion proposed has its peculiarities in comparison with the previous one. The matter of abuse of power in such cases is related not only to common goods but also to private goods in connection with natural resources and, therefore, the analysis is, in a way, broader than the one carried out in Chapter 2 (section 5).

Productive Systems, Lack of Choice and Abuse of Power

The first observation to be made is related to the very mode of production and its economic use. Take the example of agriculture and farming land. The existence of a predominant mode of production (large farms, based on the intensive use of capital goods and the extensive exploitation of the land) generates consequences for industrial diversification, consumers and the labor market.

There are no incentives for the development of industry aimed at small rural properties that may be handled according to its productive and environmental specificities. The possibility, typical of small property farming, of use of energy sources that are adaptable to each region, for example, disappears. An entire alternative mode of production is drained by the power of the already established mode of production.

In the labor markets, the draining is also evident. Reduced utilization of the labor force in extensive farming, which on its own is a cause for unemployment and exclusion, is worsened by the fact that small farms allow for the fixation of rural workers to the fields, and, therefore, create a decrease in migration and urban poverty.

Both are typical components of underdevelopment, especially in the Southern Hemisphere. Large farms with extensive use of land and intensive use of capital goods, to the extent that they predate (that is, prevent the possibility of existence) alternative types of farming, stimulate migration and urban poverty, and thus underdevelopment.

Note that the 'competition' between the two systems of farming is absolutely asymmetric. On the one hand, extensive farming benefits from large profits derived from the productive scale. On the other, small family farms make smaller profits but have the possibility of eliminating many of the drainages produced by economic power in the farming industry.

The background is the increasing drama of land scarcity and abusive use of the environment and energy sources. The existence and absolute prevalence of a single mode of farming production in relation to a scarce good (such as the land) impedes the development of cheaper alternatives of energy use (such as wind or solar power, more adaptable to small properties).

Evidently, there is a paradox here. Because it is a form of economic power, often with historical roots, the exclusion of models takes place naturally as a by-product of the operation of the concentrated structure.

The social synergies created by small properties are not relevant in the economic realm, so they easily succumb in the face of the 'economic efficiency' (and social ineffectiveness) of the bigger structures. There is no market rationality or irrationality here to be disciplined by the law. Consequently, the structural remedy for such situations lies in public policies that are able to promote the survival of alternative structures, such as small and medium farming.

Power Abuse and Ownership of Natural Resources

When there is dominance of natural resources, dominance and abuse are closely related, much more than in market relations. In the latter, the relation between each other depends on the rationality or not of the behavior.

In connection with natural resources, there is nothing to intermediate dominance and abuse. This happens because dominating goods that contain socially useful resources is in itself an abuse. Artificial scarcity and the existing exclusivity are already abusive since the rule, deriving from collective needs, must be broad access.

Therefore, in relation to such goods, there is no regulation of the possible abuse that is not structural intervention. It is also necessary to resort to the idea of bundles of rights (see Chapter 2, section 5) contained within the concept of property and to imagine, in a creative manner, which of those may be removed in a way that allows the social interest use intrinsically necessary for natural resources.

The relevance of the problem regarding common pool resources and the enormous correlation between dominance and abuse make behavior responses to abuses simply not satisfactory. The problem must be understood in a behavioral sense (since there is clear predation of other structures and environmental predation). But the response here must be plainly structural.

4. Conclusion: From a general theory of economic power to a general theory of law?

The intention of building a general legal theory of economic power, expressed in this work, is justified.

As demonstrated, the fundamental traits of a common empiric phenomenon are present in many ways by which economic power manifests itself. There are at least three important common features identified in this book.

Be it deriving from market structure, legal structure, or social structure of dependence in relation to natural resources, economic power always ends up generating totalizing social and economical draining, able to subject social and political spheres to its intent. The many ways of social and economic draining, identified throughout this work, are nothing but an example of the broad effects of the structures of economic power.

More importantly still, economic power, in any of its manifestations, has as its feature and nature the ability to substitute law in the organization of the social relations. This is its most worrisome face (at least for the jurist). By substituting the law, it is able to eliminate any possibility of reaction and social transformation arising from the realm of values.

That is why the third common trait of the structures of economic power deserved special attention to the point of becoming the guideline of the work. It is the structural discipline to which economic power must be subjected. Even if they have different methods depending on the source of economic power (market, law or social relations) they have common traits that were revealed throughout the work.

It is important to emphasize that these common traits of the discipline do not lie only in the shift in focus from inter-individual compensations to the organic operation of society.

Stating that compensatory solutions do not suffice and that an organizational law, able to influence the internal and external operations of such structures in order to transform or even deconstruct them, is necessary, implies that there is another possible general theory of law; a general theory concerned with law as an organizing element of society and not just as an instrument of compensation between individuals or groups.

Therefore, the challenge offered by the present work is not mere debate over the coherence and possibility of a general theory of economic power. The question that may be proposed is whether or not, in the legal problems and solutions, elements may be identified for a general theory of law.

An innovative general theory, less conformist than the current and able to remove the law from the positivist stagnation in which it has been for over 200 years. This, however, must be the object of other reflections, perhaps another book, in appropriate time.

Bibliography

Ackerman, B. (1984), *Reconstructing American Law*, Cambridge, MA: Harvard University Press.

Akerloff, G. (1970), 'The Market for Lemons: Quality Uncertainty and the Market Mechanism', *Quarterly Journal of Economics*, 89.

Areeda, P., J. Solow and H. Hovenkamp (1980), *Antitrust Law*, v.IIA, Boston/Toronto: Little, Brown & Co.

Areeda, P. and D. Turner (1975), 'Predatory Pricing and Related Practices under Section 2 of the Sherman Act', *Harvard Law Review*, 88.

Arthur, B. (1989), 'Competing Technologies, Increasing Returns and Lock-in by Historical Events', *Economic Journal*, 99.

Axelrod, R. (1984), *The Evolution of Cooperation*, New York: Basic Books.

Axelrod, R. and D. Dion (1988), 'The Further Evolution of Cooperation', *Science*, 242.

Ayres, I. (1985), 'Rationalizing Antitrust Cluster Markets', *Yale Law Journal*, 95.

Baird, D., C. Gertner and R. Picker (1994), *Game Theory and the Law*, Cambridge, MA/London: Harvard University Press.

Baker, J.B. (1994), 'Predatory Pricing after Brooke Group: An Economic Perspective', *Antitrust Law Journal*, 62.

Baker, J.B. (1989), 'Identifying Cartel Policy under Uncertainty: The U.S. Steel Industry, 1933–1939', *Journal of Law and Economics*, 32.

Baker, J.B. (1999), 'Developments in Antitrust Economics', *Journal of Economic Perspectives*, 13.

Baker, J.B. and C. Shapiro (2008), 'Reinvigorating Horizontal Merger Enforcement', in R. Pitofsky (ed.), *How the Chicago School Overshot the Mark: The Effect of Conservative Economic Analysis on U.S. Antitrust*, Oxford: Oxford University Press.

Barthel, C. (2002), 'Predatory Pricing Policy under EC and US Law', Master's Thesis, Faculty of Law, University of Lund.

Baseman, K., F. Warren-Boulton and G. Woroch (1995), 'Microsoft Plays Hardball: The Use of Exclusionary Pricing and Technical Incompatibility to Maintain Monopoly Power in the Market for Operating System Software', *The Antitrust Bulletin*, 40.

Bauer, J.P. (1980), 'A Simplified Approach to Tying Arrangements: A Legal and Economic Analysis', *Vanderbilt Law Review*, 33.

Bauman, Z. (2000), *Liquid Modernity*, Oxford: Polity Press.

Baumol, W.J. (1996), 'Predation and the Logic of the Average Variable Cost Test', *Journal of Law and Economics*, 39.

Baumol, W.J. (1979), 'Quasi-permanence of Price Reductions: A Policy for Prevention of Predatory Pricing', *Yale Law Journal*, 89.

Baumol, W.J. (1982), 'Contestable Markets: An Uprising in the Theory of Industry Structure', *American Economic Review*, 72.

Baumol, W.J., J. Panzar and R.D. Willig (1982), *Contestable Markets and the Theory of Industry Structure*, New York: Harcourt Brace Jovanovich.

Beales, H., R. Craswell and C. Salop (1981), 'The Efficient Regulation of Consumer Information', *Journal of Law and Economics*, 24.

Becker, G. (1976), *The Economic Approach to Human Behavior*, Chicago: The University of Chicago Press.

Blair, R. and J. Harrison (1993), *Monopsony: Antitrust Law and Economics*, Princeton: Princeton University Press.

Borenstein, S. and J.K. Mackie-Mason (1995), 'Antitrust Policy in Aftermarkets', *Antitrust Law Journal*, 63.

Bork, R. (1993), *The Antitrust Paradox*, 2nd ed., New York: The Free Press.

Bork, R. (1998), 'The Most Misunderstood Antitrust Case', *The Wall Street Journal*, May 22.

Bos, P., J. Stuyck and P. Wyntick (1992), *Concentration Control in the European Economic Community*, London: Graham & Trotman.

Burns, M. R. (1986), 'Predatory Pricing and the Acquisition Cost of Competitors', *Journal of Political Economy*, 94(92).

Carlton, D., R. Gertner and A. Rosenfield (1997), 'Communication among Competitors: Game Theory and Antitrust', *George Mason Law Review*, 5.

Carlton, D. and J. Perloff (2000), *Modern Industrial Organization*, 3rd ed., Addison Wesley Series, London: Longman.

Christiansen, A. (2006), 'The Reform of EU Merger Control: Fundamental Reversal or Mere Refinement', available at http://ssrn.com/abstract= 898845.

Clover, C. (2006), *The End of the Line*, New York: The New Press.

Coate, M. and J. Fisher (2009), 'Daubert, Science, and Modern Game Theory: Implications for Merger Analysis', available at http://ssrn.com/abstract= 1268386.

Coing, H. (1989), *Europäisches Privatrecht*, vol. II., Munich: Beck.

Comanor, W. (1985), 'Vertical Price-fixing, Vertical Market and the New Restrictions Antitrust Policy', *Harvard Law Review*, 98.

Comparato, F.K. (1983), *O Poder de Controle na Sociedade Anônima*, São Paulo: Forense.

Denoon, D. (1983), *Settler Capitalism: The Dynamics of Dependent Development in the Southern Hemisphere*, Oxford: Clarendon Press.

Denozza, F. (1988), 'Chicago, l'efficienza e il diritto antitruste', *Giurisprudenza Commerciale, I.*

Dowding, K. (1996), *Power*, Buckingham: Open University Press.

Easterbrook, F. (1981), 'Predatory Strategies and Counterstrategies', *University of Chicago Law Review*, 48.

Edlin, A. (2010), 'Predatory Pricing', available at http://works.bepress.com/ aaronedlin /74.

Eggertsson, T. (1996), 'The Economics of Control and the Costs of Property Rights' in S. Hanna et al. (eds), *Rights to Nature: Ecological, Economic, Cultural and Political Principles of Institutions for the Environment*, Washington: Island Press.

Ehaulge, E. (2007), 'Harvard, Not Chicago: Which Antitrust School Drives Recent Supreme Court Decisions?', *Competition Policy International*, 3(2).

Elzinga, H. (1970), 'Predatory Pricing: The Case of the Gunpowder Trust', in *Journal of Law and Economics*, 13.

Ezrachi, A. (2007), 'Merger Control and Cross Border Transactions: A Pragmatic View on Cooperation, Convergence and What's in Between' in P. Marsden, *Handbook of Research in Trans-Atlantic Antitrust*, Cheltenham, UK: Edward Elgar Publishing.

Faraco, A. D. (2001), *Regulação e Direito Concorrencial – uma análise jurídica da disciplina da concorrência no setor de telecomunicações*, J.S.D. Dissertation, University of São Paulo.

Federal Trade Commission Release (2009), 'Federal Trade Commission and Department of Justice to Hold Workshop Concerning Horizontal Merger Guidelines', September 22, available at http://www.ftc.gov/opa/2009/09/ mgr.shtm.

Ferro Luzzi, P. (1976), *I contratti associativi*. Milan: Giuffrè.

Fiss, O. (1982), 'The Social and Political Foundations of Adjudication', in *Law and Human Behaviour*, 6.

Franceschini, J.I.G. (1998), *Lei da Concorrência conforme Interpretada pelo CADE*, São Paulo: Singular.

Gal, M. (2009), 'Regional Competition Law Agreements: An Important Step for Antitrust Enforcement', New York University School of Law, NYU Center for Law, Economics, and Organization. Law & Economics Research Paper Series, Working Paper No. 09-47.

Gavil, A., W. Kovacic and J. Baker (2008), 'Antitrust Law in Perspective: Cases, Concepts and Problems', *Competition Policy*.

Gibbs, D. (2002), *Local Economic Development and the Environment*, London: Routledge.

Gotthold, J. (1981), 'Neuere Entwicklungen der Wettbewerbstheorie – kritische Bemerkungen zur neo-liberalen Theorie der Wettbewerbspolitik', in *ZHR*, 145.

Goyder, D. C. (1988), *E.E.C. Competition Law*, Oxford: Clarendon Press.

Grimes, W. (1995), 'Brand Marketing, Intrabrand Competition and the Multibrand Retailer: The Antitrust Law of Vertical Restraints', *Antitrust Law Journal*, 64.

Habermas, J. (1998), *Faktizität und Geltung- Beiträge zur Diskurstheorie des Rechts und des demokratischen Rechtsstaats*, Frankfurt: Suhrkamp.

Hardin, G. (1968), 'The Tragedy of the Commons', *Science*, 162.

Hart, H. and A. Sacks (1958), *The Legal Process*, New Haven: Tentative Edition.

Hay, G. (1993), 'Is the Glass Half-empty or Half-full? Reflections on the "'Kodak case'"', *Antitrust Law Journal*, 62.

Hayek, F. A. (1937), 'Economics and Knowledge', *Economica – New Series*, 4(13).

Hayek, F. A. (1945), 'The Use of Knowledge in Society', *American Economic Review*, xxxv(4).

Hazlett, T. W. (1995), 'Predation in Local Cable TV Markets', *Antitrust Bulletin*, 40.

Hostiou, R. (2007), 'Vers un nouveau príncipe general du droit de l'énvironment – le principe protecteur-payeur', in *Pour un deoit commun de l'environment – melanges em honneur de Michel Prieur*, Paris: Dalloz.

Hovenkamp, H. (2005), 'Unreasonable Exercises of Market Power', in H. Hovenkamp, *The Antitrust Enterprise: Principle and Execution*, Cambridge, MA/London, Harvard University Press.

Hovenkamp, H. (2005), *Federal Antitrust Policy: The Law of Competition and Its Practice*, 3rd ed., Miami, FL: Thompson Reuters/West.

Hovenkamp, H. (2005), *The Antitrust Enterprise: Principle and Execution*, Cambridge, MA and London: Harvard University Press.

Hovenkamp, Erik N. and Herbert J. Hovenkamp (2010), 'Tying Arrangements and Antitrust Harm', *Arizona Law Review*, 52.

Immenga, U. and E.J. Mestmäcker, *GWB Kommentar* (1992), 2nd ed., Munich: Beck.

IPEA (2011), Comunicado no. 75, Comunicados do IPEA, available in Portuguese at www.ipea.gov.br.

Joskow, P. and A. Klevoric (1979), 'A Framework for Analyzing Predatory Pricing Policy', *Yale Law Journal*, 89.

Junqueira Azevedo, A. (1986), *Negócio Jurídico e Declaração Negocial*, São Paulo: S.N.

Kamerbeek, S. P. (2009), 'Merger Performance and Efficiencies in Horizontal Merger Policy in the US and the EU', Munich Personal RePEc Archive, MPRA Paper No. 18064, October, available at mpra.ub.uni-muenchen.de/18064/.

Kaplow, L. (1985), 'Extension of Monopoly Power through Leverage', in *Columbia Law Review*, 85.

Katz, A. W. and C. Shapiro (1994), 'Systems Competition and Network Effects', *Journal of Economic Perspectives*, 8.

Klein, B. and K. Murphy (1988), 'Vertical Restraints as Contract Enforcement Mechanisms', *Journal of Law and Economics*, 31.

Klevorick, Alvin K. (1993), 'The Current State of the Law and Economics of Predatory Pricing', *American Economic Review*, 83(2).

Koyama, S. M. and E.K. Toonoka (2002), *Relação entre Taxa de Juros e Participação de Mercado segundo a Modalidade de Crédito – Avaliação de Três Anos do Projeto Juros e 'Spread' Bancário*, Brasília: Banco Central do Brasil.

Krugman, P. and R. Wells (2009), *Microeconomics*, New York: W.H. Freeman & Co.

Kuhn, K. (1978), *Abgestimmtes und sogennantes bewußtes Parallelverhalten auf Oligopolmärkten – Bedeutung, Unterscheidungsproblematik und Konsequenzen für die Wettbewerbspolitik*, Zürich: Deutsch.

Lande, R. H. (2007), 'Market Power without a Large Market Share: The Role of Imperfect Information and Other "Consumer Protection" Market Failures', AAI Working Paper No. 07-06, 2007, available at http://www.antitrustinstitute.org/ Archives/wp07-06.ashx.

Landes, W. and R. Posner (1981), 'Market Power in Antitrust Cases', *Harvard Law Review*, 94.

Larenz, K. (1989), *Allgemeiner Teil des deutschen Bürgerlichen Rechts*, Munich: Beck.

Lerner, A. P. (1934), 'The Concept of Monopoly and the Measurement of Monopoly Power', *Economic Studies Review*.

Lopatka, J. and W. Page (1995), 'Microsoft, Monopolization and Network Externalities: Some Uses and Abuses of Economic Theory in Antitrust Decision Making', *Antitrust Bulletin*, 40.

Love, J. L. (1994), *Economic Ideas and Ideologies in Latin America since 1930*, in *Cambridge History of Latin America*, vol. VI, 1, Cambridge: Cambridge University Press.

Manzini, P. (1994), *L'esclusione della concorrenza nel diritto antitruste comunitário*, Milan: Giuffrè Editore.

Markert, K.K. (1992), in U. Immenga and E. J. Mestmäcker, *GWB Kommentar*, 2nd ed., Munich: Beck.

Marvel, H. (1994), 'The Resale Price Maintenance Controversy: Beyond the Conventional Wisdom', *Antitrust Law Journal*, 63.

McGavock, D.M. (1991), 'Licensing Practices, and Business Strategy: Factors Affecting Royalty Rates', *License Law and Business Report*, 205.

McGee, J. (1958), 'Predatory Price Cutting: The Standard Oil (NJ) Case', *Journal of Law and Economics*, 137.

McMahon, K. (2010), 'Developing Countries and International Competition

Law and Policy', in J. Faundez and C. Tan (eds), *International Law, Economic Globalization and Development*, Cheltenham, UK: Edward Elgar Publishing.

Meese, A. (1997), 'Tying Meets the New Institutional Economics: Farewell to the Chimera of Forcing', *University of Pennsylvania Law Review*, 146.

Mestmäcker, E. J. (1973), 'Markt, Recht, Wirtschaftsverfassung', *Zeitschrift für das gesamte Handelsrecht und Wirtschaftsrecht*, 137.

Mestmäcker, E.J. (1958), *Das marketbeherrschende Unternehmen im Recht der Wettbewerbsbeschränkungen*, W. Eucken Institut-Vorträge und Aufsätze, Tübingen: Möhr.

Motta, Massimo (2007), *Competition Policy: Theory and Practice*, 8th ed., Cambridge: Cambridge University Press.

Nash, J. (1950), 'Equilibrium Points in N-Person Games', *Proceedings of the National Academy of Sciences*, 36(1).

Nash, J. (1950), 'The Bargaining Problem', *Econometrica*.

Nery Junior, N. (1999), *Código Brasileiro de Defesa do Consumidor – Comentado*, São Paulo: Forense Universitária.

Ordover, J. and R. Willig (1981), 'An Economic Definition of Predation: Pricing and Product Innovation', *Yale Law Journal*, 91.

Ostrom, E. (1990), *Governing the Commons: The Evolution of Institutions for Collective Action*, Cambridge: Cambridge University Press.

Ostrom, V. and E. Ostrom (1977), 'Public Goods and Public Choices', in E.E. Savas (ed.), *Alternatives for Delivering Public Services: Towards Improved Performance*, Boulder: Westview Press.

Panzar, J. (1992), 'Regulation, Deregulation and Economic Efficiency: The Case of the CAB', in G. Burgess Jr, *Antitrust and Regulation*, Cambridge: Cambridge University Press.

Pereira Neto, C.M.S. (2005), 'Universal Access to Telecommunications in Developing Countries: The Brazilian Case', J.S.D. Dissertation, Yale Law School, New Haven, CT (on file with the author).

Perloff, J.M. (2008), *Microeconomics: Theory & Applications with Calculus*, University of California, Berkeley, Prentice Hall.

Pitofsky, R. (ed.) (2008), *How the Chicago School Overshot the Mark: The Effect of Conservative Economic Analysis on U.S. Antitrust*, Oxford: Oxford University Press.

Pitofsky, R. (1990), 'New Definitions of the Relevant Market and the Assault on Antitrust', *Columbia Law Review*, 90.

Pitofsky, R. (1978), 'The Sylvania Case: Antitrust Analysis of Non-price Vertical Restrictions', *Columbia Law Review*, 78(1).

Polanyi, K. (1957), *The Great Transformation*, Boston: Beacon Press.

Polido, F.B.P. and P.M.D.G. César (2007), *Fundamentos da interface entre direito à saúde e propriedade intelectual, em Direitos de Propriedade Intelectual e Saúde Pública*, São Paulo: IDCID.

Pontes de Miranda, F.C. (1968), *Comentários à Constituição de 1967*, São Paulo: Ed. RT.

Popper, K. (1957), *Die offene Gesellschaft und ihre Feinde*, v. I ('Der Zauber Platons'), Bern.

Posner, R. and F. Easterbrook (1981), *Antitrust: Cases, Economic Notes and Other Materials*, 2nd ed., St. Paul, MN: West Publishing Co.

Posner, R. (1976), *The Law and Economics of Antitrust*, Chicago/London: University of Chicago Press.

Posner, R. (1974), 'Theories of Economic Regulation', *Bell Journal of Economics and Management Science*, 5(2).

Poteete, A., M. Janssen and E. Ostrom (2010), *Working Together: Collective Action, the Commons and Multiple Methods in Practice*, Princeton: Princeton University Press.

Priest, G. (1998), 'A Case Built on Wild Speculation, Dubious Theories', *The Wall Street Journal*, May 19.

Rist, G. (2007), *Le development – histoire d'une croyance occidentalle*, Paris: Presses de Sciences Po.

Rivero, J. (1989), *Les libertés públiques*, v.2, Paris: PUF.

Rotemberg, J. and G. Saloner (1986), 'A Supergame-theoretic Model of Price Wars', *American Economic Review*, 76.

Russell, B. (1938), *Power: A New Social Analysis*, London: George Allen & Unwin.

Sahrkey, W. (1982), *The Theory of Natural Monopoly*, Cambridge: Cambridge University Press.

Salomão Filho, C. (2003), *Direito Concorrencial: As Condutas*, 1st ed., São Paulo: Malheiros Editores.

Salomão Filho, C. (2007), *Direito Concorrencial: As Estruturas*, 3rd ed., São Paulo: Malheiros Editores.

Salomão Filho, C. (2010), *Histoire critique des monopoles – une perpective juridique et economique*, Paris: L.G.D.J.

Salomão Filho, C. (2008), *Regulação da Atividade Econômica: Princípios e Fundamentos Jurídicos*, 2nd edn, São Paulo: Malheiros Editores.

Salomão Filho, C., B. Ferrão and I. Ribeiro (2009), *Concentração, estruturas e desigualdade – as origens coloniais da pobreza e da má distribuição de renda*. Grupo Direito e Pobreza.

Salomão Filho, C. and M.S. Richter Júnior (1993), 'Interesse Social e Poderes dos Administradores na alienação de controle', in *Revista de Direito Mercantil*, 89, January–March.

Salomão Filho, C. (2003) 'Direito como instrumento de transformação social e econômica', *Revista de Direito Público da Economia*, Belo Horizonte, 1, January–March.

Salop, S. (1986), 'Measuring Ease of Entry', *Antitrust Bulletin*, 31.

Salop, S. (1979), 'Strategic Entry Deterrence', *American Economic Review*, 69.

Samtleben, J. and C. Salomão Filho (1995), 'O mercado comum sul-americano – Uma análise jurídica do Mercosul', in J. Grandino Rodas, *Contratos Internacionais*, 2nd edn, São Paulo: Ed. RT.

Samuelson, P. (1954), 'The Pure Theory of Public Expenditure', *Review of Economics and Statistics*, 36.

Sasswell, H. and M. McDougal (1943), 'Legal Education and Public Policy: Professional Training in the Public Interest', *Yale Law Journal*, 52.

Scherer, F. (1976), 'Predatory Pricing and the Sherman Act: A Comment', *Harvard Law Review*, 89.

Sen, A. (1997), 'Rational Fools: A Critique of the Behavioral Foundations of Economic Theory', in A. Sen, *Choice, Welfare and Measurement*, Cambridge, MA/London: Harvard University Press.

Sen. A. (1982), *Poverty and Famines: An Essay on Entitlement and Deprivation*, Oxford: Oxford University Press.

Sen, A. (2009), *The Idea of Justice*, Cambridge, MA: Belknap Press.

Serdarevic, G. and P. Teply, 'Efficiency of EU Merger Control in the 1990–2008 Period', IES Working Paper, No. 28/2009.

Shapiro, C. (1995), 'Aftermarkets and Consumer Welfare: Making Sense of Kodak', *Antitrust Law Journal*, 63.

Sharkey, W. (1982), *The Theory of Natural Monopoly*, Cambridge: Cambridge University Press.

Slawson, W. D. (1980), 'A Stronger, Simpler Tie in Doctrine', *Antitrust Bulletin*, 25.

Spence, M. (2001), 'Signaling in Retrospect and the Informational Structure of Markets', Nobel Prize Lecture, December 8.

Spivack, G. and C. Ellis (1993), 'Kodak: Enlightened Antitrust Analysis and Traditional Tying Law', *Antitrust Law Journal*, 62.

Steiner, R. (1991), 'Sylvania Economics: A Critique', *Antitrust Law Journal*, 60.

Stigler, G. (1971), 'The Theory of Economic Regulation', *The Bell Journal of Economics and Management Science*, 2.

Streit, M. (1992), 'Economic Order, Private Law and Public Policy: The Freiburg School of Law and Economics in Perspective', *Journal of Institutional and Theoretical Economics*, 148.

Stürmer, S. (1997), *Netzzugang und Eigentumsrechte in der Telekommunikation*. Baden-Baden: Nomos-Verlagsgesellschaft.

Terhechte, J. (2009), *International Competition Enforcement Law Between Cooperation and Convergence: Mapping a New Field for Global Administrative Law*, The University of Oxford, Centre for Competition Law and Policy, Working Paper CCLP (L) 26.

Thomas, Victor Bulmer (1994), *The Economic History of Latin America since Independence*, Cambridge: Cambridge University Press.

Tom, W. (1997), 'Game Theory in the Everyday Life of the Antitrust Practitioner', *George Mason Law Review*, 5.

Troster, R. L. (1999), 'Regulamentação bancária brasileira: situação atual e perspectivas', *Anais do Seminário Internacional sobre Regulação e Defesa da Concorrência no Setor Bancário*, Brasília, CADE/ASBACE, March 30–31.

Turner, D. (1962), 'The Definition of Agreement under the Sherman Act: Conscious Parallelism and Refusals to Deal', *Harvard Law Review*, 75.

Turner, D. (1958), 'The Validity of Tying Arrangements under the Antitrust Laws', in *Harvard Law Review*, 72.

von Neumann, J. and O. Morgenstern (1944), *The Theory of Games and Economic Behaviour*, Princeton: Princeton University Press.

Waller, S. (2007), 'The Story of Alcoa: The Enduring Questions of Market Power, Conduct, and Remedy in Monopolization Cases', in Eleanor M. Fox and Daniel A. Crane (eds), *Antitrust Stories*, New York: Foundation Press.

White, B. Ann (1991), 'Black and White Thinking in the Gray Areas of Antitrust: The Dismantling of Vertical Restraints Regulation', *George Washington Law Review*, 60.

Williamson, J. (2002), 'Land, Labor and Globalization in the Third World, 1870–1940', *Journal of Economic History*, 62(1).

Williamson, J. (1996), 'Globalization, Convergence and History', *Journal of Economic History*, 56(2).

Williamson, O. (1977), 'Predatory Pricing: A Strategic and Welfare Analysis', *Yale Law Journal*, 87.

Williamson, O. (1979), 'Assessing Market Restrictions: Antitrust Ramifications of the Transaction Cost Approach', *University of Pennsylvania Law Review*, 127.

Ziebarth, J.A.B.M. (2010), 'Essential Facilities in Brazilian Telecommunications Sector', presented to the Latin American Competition Forum, OECD and IADB, September 8, San Jose, Costa Rica, available at http://www.oecd.org.

Index